The Parihaka Album

The Parihaka Album: Lest We Forget

Rachel Buchanan

First published in 2009 by Huia Publishers
Reprinted in 2024

39 Pipitea Street, PO Box 12280
Wellington, Aotearoa New Zealand
www.huia.co.nz

ISBN 978-1-86969-399-2
Copyright © Rachel Buchanan 2009
Cover image: Jacob Wilkins-Hodges
Cover design: Huia Publishers

This book is copyright. Apart from fair dealing for the purpose of private study, research, criticism or review, as permitted under the Copyright Act, no part may be reproduced by any process without the prior permission of the publisher.

A catalogue record for this book is available from the National Library of New Zealand.

Reprinted with the support of Te Takarangi, Te Rōpū Whakahau and New Zealand Libraries Partnership.

Published with the support of La Trobe University.

For Mike, Lily, Antonietta and Frances

Contents

List of Illustrations	ix
Foreword	xiii
Acknowledgements	xx
Heirloom	1
1 Back to Parihaka	3
2 The story so far	23
3 Illuminations	57
4 Road, telegraph, lighthouse	73
5 After the invasion	95
6 Pictures	111
7 The wrong that was done	145
8 Hearings	167
9 Dementia wing	203
10 Pioneers	235
Select Bibliography	269
Index	285

List of Illustrations

Figure	Illustration	Page
1	Te Whiti's monument and gas lamp, Parihaka, 18 June 2002. Source: Rachel Buchanan.	5
2	Seraphine Pick, *Riki and Ruru*, 2000, oil on canvas, 1805 x 1010 mm. Gifted by the artist to Parihaka Pā. Image reproduced courtesy of Seraphine Pick.	10
3	Jane Sawinson, training camp for colonial volunteers, ca. 1880, black and white original photographic print, Alexander Turnbull Library, reference number PA1-q-707-41.	43
4	Laurence Aberhart, The Prisoner's Dream (one panel from a sequence of five) *Taranaki from Oeo Road, under moonlight, 27–28 September 1999*, 190 x 245 mm. Five silver gelatin prints, gifted by the artist to Parihaka Pā. Image courtesy of Laurence Aberhart.	47
5	Laurence Aberhart, The Prisoner's Dream (two panels from a sequence of five) *View #3 Ripapa Island, Lyttelton Harbour 14 March 2000'*, 165 x 245 mm and *'View #4 Ripapa Island, Lyttelton Harbour, 12 March 2000*, 185 x 245 mm. Five silver gelatin prints, gifted by the artist to Parihaka Pā.	47
6	William Andrews Collis, armed constabulary awaiting orders to advance on Parihaka Pā, November 1881, ATL, reference number PA1-q-183-19.	49
7	Cape Egmont Lighthouse, Cape Egmont, December 2007. Source: Rachel Buchanan.	59

8	Benjamin Buchanan, *Untitled*, vinyl adhesive on paper, 305mm x 200mm, 2009. Image courtesy of the artist.	106
9	Arthur Schaef, stereoscopic photograph of a family sitting in an open car, parked at Parihaka, ca 1890, black and white original photographic print, ATL, reference number PA4-0553.	112
10	Arthur Schaef, stereoscopic photograph of a parked car at Te Whiti's Monument, Parihaka, 1909, black and white photographic print, ATL, reference number PA4-1053.	113
11	Unknown photographer, view of a comet in the sky above Mt Taranaki (Egmont) and Parihaka, 4 October 1882, black and white original negative, ATL, reference number 1/2-003184-F.	117
12	William Andrews Collis, view of Parihaka, Taranaki, ca November 1881, albumen print, 16.7 x 24.1 cm, ATL, reference number PA1-q-183-18.	118
13	William Andrews Collis, volunteer camp, Rahotu, black and white original photographic print, ca 1881, ATL, reference number PA1-q-183-01.	121
14	William Andrews Collis, view of Bells Falls, Mt Egmont, Taranaki, ca 1878, black and white original photographic print, albumen print 21.6 x 26 cm, ATL, reference number PA1-q-183-03.	122
15	William Andrews Collis, view of a mother and infant sitting outside a raupō house in Taranaki, 1875–1885, black and white original photographic print, albumen print 13.6 x 20.2 cm, ATL, reference number PA1-q-183-25-2.	124
16	William Andrews Collis (probably), view of a dining room of a large house, probably in New Plymouth, photographed in the period 1880–1895, albumen print 13.6 x 20.3 cm, ATL, reference number PA1-q-183-42-2.	125

List of Illustrations

17	William Andrews Collis, meeting at Parihaka Pā, with Te Whetu Moeahu, 17 March 1896, black and white original negative, glass negative, ATL, reference number G-12103-1/1.	130
18	Unknown photographer, Pākehā men and women in front of a whare at Parihaka with Māori children, ca 1895–1900, gelatin silver print, ATL, reference number PA1-0-405-13.	133
19	John Feaver, man with taiaha doing a haka, Parihaka, ca 1896, Feaver collection, Puke Ariki, New Plymouth, ARC2003-558.	135
20	John Feaver, Parihaka, view towards the south, showing Rangi Kapuia, ca 1898, Feaver collection, Puke Ariki, ARC2003-559.	138
21	Unknown photographer, opening of the house Rangi Kapuia, Parihaka Pā, 1927, black and white negative, part of John Reginald Wall photographs, ATL, reference number 1/2 -017411-F.	149
22	(a). Anne Noble, *Parihaka ... From the Record*. 2000. Reflections on the caption of a photograph by William Collis. Children of Parihaka with Taare Waitara, Parihaka, rephotographed with the permission of the National Library of New Zealand and the people of Parihaka ref.1/1-006430-G. (b). Anne Noble, *Parihaka ... seen and not heard*. 2000. Reflections on a photograph by William Collis. Children of Parihaka with Taare Waitara, Parihaka, rephotographed with the permission of the National Library of New Zealand and the people of Parihaka ref. 1/1-006430-G. (c). Anne Noble, *Parihaka, Tents of the Constabulary*. 2000. Reflections on a photograph by William Collis. Tents of the Constabulary surrounding Parihaka. Egmont Co. 1881. Re-photographed with the permission of the National Library of New Zealand and the people of Parihaka.	178 179

23	E S Richards, carte de visite of Hemi Parai, chief of Ngati Haumia, taken 1862–1872, black and white original photographic print, albumen print 92 x 52 mm, ATL, reference number PA2-2940.	205
24	P J E Shotter (Wellington City Sexton), Wallace family grave, plot 2209, Bolton Street Cemetery, taken 1965–1969, black and white original negative, cellulose triacetate negative, Shotter Collection, ATL, reference number 25510-21A-F.	238
25	Unidentified *Evening Post* staff photographer, aerial view of Wellington motorway under construction, 26 August 1969, black and white original negative, ATL, reference number EP/1969/3580/33-F.	242
26	John Wallace, view of Wellington Harbour from Thorndon Beach, 12 July 1845, watercolour and pencil, 253 x 422 mm, drawings and prints collection, ATL, reference number B-079-007.	245
27	Liz Mellish, the author at the Te Aro Pā site, Taranaki Street, October 2008.	261

Foreword

Like a flower deemed extinct that pushes to the surface and blooms, like a river that flows under a road or a mountain that moves, whakapapa makes the unimaginable real. No matter where I live or what I do, whakapapa is a pilot light that powers my writing and sustains my essence as a person.

This book is my first, and I was sure it would be my last. In my naivety, I saw *The Parihaka Album: Lest We Forget* as an end point, the conclusion of almost a decade of effort. First, there was the writing of a PhD on the historiography of the 1881 invasion and ransacking of Parihaka, then there was the rewriting of the thesis into a manuscript that met the requirements of HUIA, the publisher that my mentor, Parihaka historian Te Miringa Hohaia, had advised me to go with. I also gave birth to three children – and mourned a fourth pregnancy that ended in miscarriage – during this period. I don't know how I did it. With my partner, Mike, I was raising the children in our home in Naarm/Melbourne, but I was also raising myself, as a mother and as a Māori person, and my historical research was as much a part of the process as learning to breastfeed.

The various streams of my life converged one afternoon in 2009 in a room in the Media Studies Department at La Trobe University in Melbourne's northern suburbs. I was working on the final text for this book, responding to queries from the editor, Anne Else, but I was also caring for my three little girls because it was a 'bring your kids to work' day. A battle cry went out: 'Let's destroy Mum's office!' Little hands grabbed the chapters I had printed out and threw them into the air. Snow! Then the girls snatched papers off the floor and sprinted down the corridor towards philosophy, chortling and shouting, yelling at me to follow.

My darling pōtiki, Frances, has just turned eighteen, and I still haven't caught up with her yet – or her wonderful older sisters. I'm still chasing children down corridors, children like Taare and Turia, Charles and Julia, a brother and sister born at Te Aro Pā in 1848 and 1853 on whenua that would soon be whitewashed as Wellington. Their mum was a refugee from Taranaki; their dad was a boat person from Birmingham. What were their lives like? Their mother, Arapera, was an uri of Taranaki, a beautiful woman who would eventually wear the raukura that signalled she was a follower of Te Whiti o Rongomai of Parihaka. Their koro, Hemi, was a rangatira of Taranaki iwi, and I recall Te Miringa telling me that Matua was known to be handy with a mere and a patu. Their uncles, Mohi and Te Awhi, would become ploughmen and fencers during the first spell of non-violent resistance at Parihaka (1879–1880).

Those little children, Taare and Turia, ran down different paths as they grew up in a new nation that crushed their mothertongue – te reo Māori – destroyed their papakāinga (including Te Aro Pā) and derided their knowledge and skills. Taare stayed in Pōneke; Turia returned to Taranaki. All evidence of their place of birth was erased, or so it seemed. The resting places of their Māori grandparents, Hemi Parai and Tawhirikura Karopihia, became unknown, or so it seemed.

As I document in 'Pioneers', the final chapter of this book, in 2005 Te Aro Pā emerged from its hiding place under old buildings on Taranaki Street. In 2017, an uri of Te Aro Pā, Debbie Broughton, displayed her poetry in light boxes at Te Aro (a Wellington City Council initiative, the light boxes are on Courtenay Place, close to the intersection with Taranaki Street). Debbie's 'Magical Māori Mystery Tour' excavated Māori Wellington from beneath the rubble. I was glad to be asked to write a poem for one of the light boxes along with another uri of Taranaki,

Foreword

Professsor Alice Te Punga Somerville. Debbie's light-box poems grew into *The Ani Waaka Room* (2022), a brilliant and oh-so-funny collection about 'the re-Taranaki-fication of Te Aro Pā'.

Since 2021, Debbie has performed as part of Te Aro Pā poets, a collective that also includes my sister, Hana Buchanan, and me. In February 2024, Te Aro Pā poets were a headline act on the opening night of The Performance Arcade festival in Wellington, and the stage was literally at Te Aro, between Te Papa Tongarewa and Waitangi Park. I was not able to be there in person, so our youngest brother, Joe, agreed to be a kairīwhi and read a few pieces in my place. We held a zui to plan the performance, and our various children popped in and out of the online meeting. The youngest child, aged five, had just started in te reo Māori immersion strand at kura. As our kōrero unfolded, I realised that every single person on the call, except for me, was a Māori speaker – children included. I stopped the zui to give a speech about how wonderful it was to be the odd one out and to invite them all to ignore me and kōrero Māori! They refused. All of them are very modest about this taonga and don't even like to be described as fluent speakers of te reo Māori, but I just feel absolute awe at what they have achieved as uri of Te Aro Pā where the paepae has been bitumen for a long time. Iti noa ana, he pito mata.

Te Aro Pā has re-emerged in other ways too. In 'Pioneers', I describe our quest to find the resting place of Hemi Parai, a Te Aro Pā rangatira (of Taranaki iwi) who passed away in 1877. For many years, Dad, Tākuta Leo Buchanan (a paediatrician), had been obsessed with locating our tupuna. In about 2007 or so, Leo and I met Nick Perrin, a member of the Friends of Bolton Street Cemetery. As I write in this book, we had no luck that day, and my own archival research, in the Wellington City Council Archives, offered hints but nothing more. In 2022, Nick got in touch with my sister, Hana, to say that Hemi Parai had been found. In cemetery records, he was listed as 'Hari Pry' because the sexton had recorded the information given orally 'and misheard enough to get the spelling wrong'. Nick Perrin advised that our tupuna was the first burial in a row of three grave plots, 'which were in a very prominent location on the main path through the cemetery (but removed for the motorway between 1968 and 1971)'. We mihi to Matua and his other close relatives whose places of rest were so cruelly disturbed by the construction of the motorway. The final resting place of Hemi's first wife, Tawhirikura Karopihia, remains unknown, for now, as does the resting place of their daughter, Arapera Rongouaroa.

The re-publication of *The Parihaka Album* – as a physical object made from paper and as an e-book – is a further example of Te Aro and Taranaki determination to remain in view as a challenge to the bureaucratic, cultural, spiritual, historical and political norms in the nation's capital.

Even though it has been out of print for over a decade, this book has continued to find its way into the hands of influential readers, including Tui Ātua Tupua Tamasese Tupuola Tufunga Efi, the Sāmoan Head of State from 2007 until 2017, and Pākehā academics such as political scientist Professor Richard Shaw and Dr Patty O'Brien, an Australian historian. In 2017, Tui Ātua invited me to Sāmoa to help launch Patty's book *Tautai*, a biography of independence leader Ta'isi O.F. Nelson. It was a tremendous honour to speak in Apia about the direct connections between the non-violent resistance to colonisation enacted at Parihaka (1879–1881 and ongoing) and the non-violent resistance to colonisation of the Samoan Mau (which came to prominence in the 1920s in protests against the New Zealand government).

Like me, Richard Shaw grew up in Taranaki, and our paths first crossed in the early 1980s when we were both in the New Plymouth Operatic Society's production of *The Wizard of Oz*. I played Dorothy, and Richard played the Tin Man. Richard's history-memoir *The Forgotten Coast* (Massey University Press, 2021) is a forensic examination of how his family directly benefitted from te pahuatanga, the invasion and ransacking of Parihaka. One of his ancestors was a member of the armed constabulary who invaded the pā, and Richard traces how 'grants' of confiscated land made his poor Irish ancestors rich. While it is normal for Māori historians to relate our work to our whakapapa, it is rare for a Pākēhā scholar to do so, and I am glad that *The Parihaka Album* encouraged Richard to take this journey.

As will be clear by now, *The Parihaka Album* was not a conclusion; it was a prelude. The book led me to establish – or strenghten – relationships with whānaunga such as Te Miringa Hohaia, Honiana Love, Neville Gilmour, Lindsay McLeod, Tony Ruakere, Matua John Te Wharematangi Baxter, Alice Te Punga Somerville and her whānau, Debbie Broughton and others, creating a pathway inside myself that has enabled two more books on Taranaki to come forth. Te Miringa, Neville, Lindsay and Tony have all passed now, as has Tākuta Leo Buchanan, and *The Parihaka Album* may also be viewed as a memorial to their fire, their skill and their manaakitanga.

Finally, *The Parihaka Album* is special because it introduced me to Hon. Mahara Okeroa, a whānaunga who was raised at Parihaka. At the last minute, Matua Mahara was asked to launch *The Parihaka Album*. His initial response to this request would surely be summed up in one word: hōhā! Yet the work got under his skin. I recall the way Matua's kōrero magnified parts of the book that I had seen as asides. I had made a joke of the fact that my grandmother, Rawinia Queenie Agnes Buchanan, had refused to use her Māori name. Instead, she was Ra, Mrs B or simply Flossy. But Matua recognised this refusal for what it was, a survival mechanism, a defence against racism, a mask. I recall looking around the room and seeing tears on the faces of some of Dad's cousins – the release that can come when someone sees a deeper truth behind a well-established norm.

Matua's guidance has helped me stay safe and strong as I worked on *Ko Taranaki Te Maunga* (Bridget Williams Books, 2018) and *Te Motunui Epa* (Bridget Williams Books, 2022). He is the co-author of Te Motunui Epa in all but name.

In May 2023, Matua and I joined Richard Shaw, historian

Vincent O'Malley and former Attorney-General and Minister for Treaty Settlements Chris Finlayson for 'Invasion and Resistance: Facing up to Parihaka', a panel at Featherston Booktown. To prepare for the event, I re-read *The Parihaka Album* for the first time in years. I was expecting something a bit heavy and dull, an academic work bogged down with footnotes, but I was surprised by the intimate urgency of the writing and the unorthodox blend of personal anecdote and anti-colonial theory. The ideas still felt relevant and alive, and I began to hope that *The Parihaka Album* might re-emerge as an e-book. I was sitting in a cafe in Auckland discussing this wish with fellow Māori historian Paul Diamond when Eboni Waitere, the publisher at HUIA, walked in, and we had a bit of a kōrero about the idea. No promises were made.

Six months later, out of the blue, Eboni wrote to say HUIA would be reprinting the book at the request of legal scholar Professor Jacinta Ruru (Raukawa, Ngāti Ranginui) and historian Professor Angela Wanhalla (Ngāi Tahu).

The republication was being funded by Te Takarangi ki Te Ao, an initiative supported by the Royal Society Te Apārangi, the University of Otago and the New Zealand Libraries Partnership project. The project supports Māori scholarship, mātauranga and academic excellence by republishing important works of non-fiction by Māori authors. I am grateful to Professor Ruru and Professor Wanhalla for their patronage. I also mihi to Huia Publishers for excavating the original electronic manuscript of this book from redundant software and hardware. That day when my kids trashed my office at La Trobe seems so long ago, and the original Word file that I sent back to editor Anne Else and publishers Robyn and Brian Bargh is long gone, as is my career in academia.

I resigned my job at La Trobe the year after this book came out, and I have never worked as an academic again. I found it hard to belong in the university system, and I have felt sorry about this over the years, less so now. However, I continue to cherish the intellectual and spiritual training I received as a PhD student and afterwards as I wrote this book. Knowledge heals, just like medicine. 'Here come the tākuta tangata,' Matua Mahara said one day as Dad and I approached.

1 March 2024
Naarm/Melbourne

The Parihaka Album

Acknowledgements

I have been working on this book for a while, and a lot of people have helped me out along the way. It is good to be able to thank them here.

On a formal level, the research for this book began with my PhD at Monash University (2001–2005). But the research really started in 1987, when my dad, Leo, and I were two of the lucky students on a six-week total-immersion Māori language course at Kuratini, an offshoot of Wellington Polytechnic. Te Huirangi Waikerepuru ran the course, and he was also the kaumātua for the Parihaka exhibition at City Gallery Wellington in 2001. Te Huirangi and Te Miringa Hohaia met with me before I started on the doctorate, and their incredible work – as kaumātua, historians, mentors, supervisors, claimants and activists – has made this book possible. My book, one small perspective, is just a fraction of a much greater whole.

There are many other people to thank. Of course, many of you belong to more than one list!

Kai, care, whānau support: my awesome partner, Mike Gentile, and our three kids; my parents Mary and Leo Buchanan; my sisters and brothers and brothers-in-law, Felicity, Adrian, Hana, Lisale, Ben, Matt, Emma, JJ, Ruth and Joe; Aunty Leah Crompton; Raumahora Broughton and Aunty Agnes 'Bubs' Broughton; Honiana Love; Paul Walker and other Wallace whānau; my Australian family, especially Aunty Ann-Maree and Grandma and Pop; and the extended English family.

Acknowledgements

Cheer squad: Dianne McDonald; Aunty Ann Seabrooke; Frank Buchanan; Leanne Reinke; Ceridwen Sparke; Pania Ruakere; Philippa Larkin; Mary Roberts and Matt Ryan; Frances Atkinson and Emma Walker; my journalism colleagues at La Trobe University (Wendy Bowler, Lawrie Zion and Chris Scanlon); Joanna Sassoon; Paul Ashton; Maria Tumarkin; and Bridget Williams. You've all spurred me on in different ways. Thank you.

Brains' trust: Andrew Markus; Maria Nugent; Bain Attwood; Dick Scott; Dipesh Chakrabarty; Greg Dening (RIP to a generous, inspirational teacher); Donna Merwick; Graeme Davison; Alan Ward; Ngatata Love; Neville Gilmour; Liz Mellish; Holden Hohaia; Debbie Bird-Rose; Paul Hamer; Chris Healy; Michael Belgrave; Ann Curthoys; Anne Noble; Laurence Aberhart; and Seraphine Pick.

Readers: Klaus Neumann read the PhD and the first draft of the manuscript. Christina Thompson assessed the second version of the manuscript. Thank you both for your time and suggestions. Brian and Robyn Bargh at Huia Publishers have seen a few different versions, as has Anne Else, my editor, whose eye for the big and the little picture has made this a much better book.

Support crew: Many, many people in archives, libraries and museums. Special thanks to Nick Perrin of Friends of Bolton Street Cemetery; Joan Brookes at Taranaki Newspapers; Walter Cook and John Sullivan in the photography collection at the Alexander Turnbull Library; Dean Cowie at the Office of Treaty Settlements; Huia Kopua at the New Zealand Film Archive; and Aroha Bradley and staff at the Port Nicholson Block claimants office. Thank you to staff at Puke Ariki; the Alexander Turnbull Library; City Gallery Wellington; Dunedin Public Art Gallery; the National Archives; Te Papa Tongarewa; the Waitangi Tribunal; the Wellington City Council Archives; and the State Library of Victoria.

I would also like to thank La Trobe University for supporting the research and writing required to finish this book and my brother, Benjamin, for the cover artwork.

An earlier version of chapter 10 was published as 'The Dementia wing of History' in *Cultural Studies Review* (2007). Parts of chapter 9 were included in 'Decolonizing the Archives: The Work of New Zealand's Waitangi Tribunal', published in *Public History Review* (2007).

Heirloom

Hold the object in your hand. It is heavy and old. The cover is black, the cover is red, the cover has a picture of a mountain on it or a picture of a man who looks like Jesus. Contemplate this object. Is it a relic? A sacred text? A museum piece? An heirloom? A taonga? Turn this object over. Feel the dust rub off on you, the little scraps and specks and grit of the past. Feel the imprint of the other hands that have held this object too. Feel the contents ready to jump out and bite you. Open it!

This is The Parihaka Album. Look at it! Consider some of the snapshots torn from its frayed pages. There's the white glare of the over-exposed images and the gloom of under-exposed places and people. There's the wide angle and the tracking shot, the bird's eye and the zoom, the landscape and the close up, the picture postcard and the family portrait.

Parihaka is taonga, heirloom, trouble-spot, muse. It is war zone, peace zone, pop song, poem. Parihaka is a story told around a kitchen table, a sermon in a church, a sell-out art show, a hippy's wet dream. Parihaka is a story about my relatives, and it is a story about me. It is a sad story.

But this story is not over yet. The album still has many blank pages left and these pages are waiting for us to find other pictures to put in there, pictures that can tell a different story.

CHAPTER 1

Back to Parihaka

I first visited Parihaka in 1980. I was 12, a Form 2 student at Sacred Heart Girls' College in New Plymouth, where I had lived since I was four years years old. Our teacher was Sister Celine, a woman who wore the same veil and blue dress each day; but once a month or so, the colour of the fringe that poked out from the rim of her veil would change: red, brown, light brown (but never blonde).

Our class spent two or three nights at the pā. We went down the coast road in a bus, and we had to wait at the gate for ages to be called on. I remember that I and my friends, Paula, Pania and Elizabeth, had a huge giggling fit about something or other. Eventually we went in. We stayed in one of the meeting houses there. The kuia from Parihaka taught us stick games, poi and waiata. Time went very slowly. None of us liked the food. In the afternoons, we clambered around the paddocks behind the meeting house. There were small, ruined buildings up the back, shrunken, rotting, gabled versions of the enormous Victorian house I lived in back in town. I was lucky to have that time there; but I did not appreciate or understand the gift we had received.

My parents had a copy of Dick Scott's Parihaka book, *Ask That Mountain*, at home. I hadn't read it, but I liked the picture on the cover: the small, symmetrical black mountain shadow and the three wispy and gigantic white feathers floating above it, suspended, magically, in a soft pink and blue sky. I felt a connection with the picture because I knew the artist, Michael Smither, and I'd been to primary school with his son. I felt no connection with the story it illustrated.

At the time, it was unclear who had suggested the pā visit. Was it Sister Celine? The school? The pā? Now I think it was probably the parents of some of my school friends: maybe Pania Ruakere's parents, or Kim MacLeod's father, Lindsay, who would give the opening evidence in the Waitangi Tribunal's 1991 hearing at Parihaka. I now know that our stay would have been part of the many commemorative events held then to mark 100 years since Parihaka was invaded and ransacked by colonial soldiers and police. The Parihaka aunties, including Ngahina Okeroa, Matarena Rau-Kupa and Parekaitu Tito, sparked the rejuvenation of Parihaka in the 1970s and 1980s by teaching young people, such as me and my classmates, Parihaka songs, games and stories.

In 1981, there was also a big centenary fundraising exhibition at the contemporary art gallery, the Govett-Brewster, in New Plymouth, as well as some media coverage, including a television documentary made by director Merata Mita. Again, I don't remember being aware of this at the time. My ignorance was profound. Twenty-two years later, in 2002, when I went back to Parihaka with my sister, Hana, and my eight-month-old daughter, Lily Arapera, this had not changed much.

I was there to start my doctoral research. It was the middle of winter. We had been instructed to drive up to the top part of the marae and wait by Te Whiti's monument. Behind the marble pillar was a white van with an enormous black, red and white flag fluttering from its top. A short, solid man stood in front of it. He had tattoos on his face and neck. I didn't know what the flag meant. 'Tino Rangatiratanga,' my sister said.

Figure 1. Te Whiti's monument and gas lamp, Parihaka, 18 June 2002. Image: Rachel Buchanan.

Before too long, a coach pulled up. Dozens of people got out. Most were dressed in black. Many of them carried photographs. Again, I had a feeling of not knowing, of being swept along on an unfamiliar current. Instead of admitting to my fear, I hid it, desperate to look as if I, too, was quite prepared to go with the flow. I hunted for something familiar, anything, but really I was quite lost. Even my limited Māori language skills, rusty from decades of disuse, had evaporated. What was I doing here?

Our visit coincided with the annual celebration of Māori New Year, Matariki, a time when visitors to Parihaka bring photographs of their mate (deceased loved ones) to be blessed. Te Pae Pae, the meeting house where we slept, was pretty Wrun down. It was wet and cold with a dampness I remembered well from playing netball as a schoolgirl at tournaments in Stratford, Hawera and Inglewood.

The baby cried most of the night. When we woke in the morning, there was a lot of empty floor space around our mattresses. We were too noisy even for the boisterous schoolchildren staying there.

Although I had met with Taranaki kaumātua Te Huirangi Waikerepuru and Parihaka historian and leader Te Miringa Hohaia before I began my doctorate and made the trip to Parihaka, I was still totally unprepared. I had a tape-recorder, cassettes and spare batteries in my bag, and a pile of consent forms in a folder, pieces of paper that were supposed to reassure all parties concerned that my work was ethical. After all, I had filled out a twenty-five-page form, and my project had received approval from Monash University's ethics committee.

I planned to collect oral histories from Parihaka residents, histories that would enrich, contradict or unsettle the largely Pākehā-created written record about the place. I planned to do this in two or three days (in between breastfeeding a sick baby) and then drive back to Wellington and, from there, fly back to Melbourne.

I loved Michel Foucault from the moment I first encountered him as an undergraduate. Since those exciting days, I had read a lot more theory – on subaltern histories, history from below, postcolonial history. I had just finished Dipesh Chakrabarty's groundbreaking new book, *Provincializing Europe,* and I had read (twice) Linda Tuhiwai Smith's important book, *Decolonizing Methodologies: Research and Indigenous Communities*.[1] I believed I was ready to put all these exciting ideas into practice and start making a new kind of history. But the thing about theory is that it is really wonderful … in theory!

Linda Smith advises researchers to be patient and take time to build relationships with iwi, hapū and whānau; but it was as if I had erased all of that wisdom once I got going on my project. I was too busy for all that! So intent was I on getting those interviews, and so great was my desire to do the right thing (for the people of Parihaka, I told myself, when actually I was most concerned with doing the right thing for myself), that I wasn't even able to hear all the songs that the schoolchildren were performing at Toroaanui on the second day of our stay.

These songs had been composed in the nineteenth century. Here, right in front of me, was the longed-for insider story, a Parihaka history from a Parihaka perspective, a primary source archived within the families of eyewitnesses to the plunder. Some of the songs were ones that I, an ignorant uri (descendant) from Taranaki, had been taught as a schoolgirl at Parihaka.

Why was I so deaf and dumb? It seemed that despite the cumbersome ethics process and my supposed fervour to right historical wrongs and do things differently, I was, in fact, intent on replicating all of the worst things about journalism, a world I had studied so hard to escape from as a mature student at an Australian university. I'd trained as a journalist in New Zealand in 1986 and had written for many newspapers, including *The Dominion*, *The Evening Post*, *The Southland Times* and *The Waikato Times*. In Melbourne, I worked for *The Age*. Journalism can be satisfying, but it is also, necessarily, so often concerned with speed and surfaces. There is little time to seek depth or pursue relationships.

Even though I was now in a different world, it was as if I was programmed by my first career: I would find the talent quickly; I would get the talent to sign my forms quickly; I would interview the talent (with as much sensitivity that a quick encounter would allow); and then I would leave with my treasure trove of stories, words that were now mine, all mine, to be read and decoded and played with and edited and written up in whatever way I wished.

The first time we sat down to eat at Parihaka, I got a sense that my plans might, perhaps, be unrealistic. I started to tell the man opposite me that I had been to Parihaka once before as a schoolgirl. 'We stayed in a different meeting house to Te Pae Pae,' I said. 'We stayed in the meeting house with all the carvings.' He just stared at me. 'There are no carved meeting houses at Parihaka,' he said.

The dining room tilted. Was my memory so flawed that I had imagined that earlier stay at Parihaka? Was there another marae around here, somewhere with a lot of carvings, that I had actually stayed at? If so, where was it? My remaining time at the pā – a short stay that was cut even shorter by Lily's illness and my own stuttering efforts inside a place with complicated dynamics and a history of being done over by outsiders – was shadowed by doubt. Was I going mad?

Parihaka. You just never know what will happen there. It's never a simple story. In 2004, when I was back in New Plymouth to visit Puke Ariki, the city's new museum and library, and to make another trip to Parihaka, I had dinner with Pania, one of my old school friends. She remembered the trip to Parihaka much better than I did, especially the catastrophic giggling at the start of it. We stayed, she said, at Te Niho, and the walls there are covered not in carvings but in photos of ancestors and of the 1881 invasion.

It was photos and paintings that drew me back to Parihaka. At the end of 2000, I had just finished my honours year in history at Monash. I'd written a thesis on Melbourne Olympic hostesses in 1956 and was working on a doctoral proposal on Melbourne places and modernity. In November 2000, on a visit with my family in

Wellington, I went to see an exhibition at the City Gallery, a large art deco building that had once housed Wellington's central library. Its title was 'Parihaka: The Art of Passive Resistance'.

The exhibition blew me away. Each room was more beautiful than the last. Artist Tony Fomison's messiah-like *Te Whiti* gazed from one wall (and from the cover of the gorgeous award-winning catalogue). Colin McCahon's black and white *Parihaka Triptych* loomed from another. Around the corner skipped Ralph Hotere's *Te Whiti*, a dandy in a natty suit. Nearby Hotere's salmon-pink comet streaked across a black Taranaki sky.

Most of these Parihaka images had been painted in the early 1970s, but across the gallery foyer, new Parihaka pictures awaited. These included Anne Noble's magnifications of nineteenth-century Parihaka photographs, Shane Cotton's Parihaka patch, my relative John Baxter's curious black birds perched on the foothills of a miniature mountain, John Pule's steamer in the corner of a sea of black and red stripes, *The Prophets: Showing Us How Far We Must Go to Achieve Human Freedom*, Seraphine Pick's vivid *Riki and Ruru* mural and Laurence Aberhart's stunning long exposure photographs of Mount Taranaki and the scenes inside the caves at Ripapa Island, Lyttelton, where Parihaka ploughmen had been imprisoned in the nineteenth century.

Upstairs there was more. A plough said to have been used by Parihaka ploughmen was the centrepiece to a long gallery filled with Parihaka photographs and art. Mountains, white feathers, albatrosses and owls were dominant motifs. Inside a case, brightly-coloured kete tāniko (bags) were displayed. In yet another room, there were nineteenth-century photographs and news clippings. A side room was set up as a research space; Parihaka books and documents were waiting to be browsed. Snippets of just-commissioned Parihaka poems adorned other walls. Down the stairs and back to the foyer, the sounds of Tim Finn's Parihaka song blared through speakers: 'Come to Parihaka. Weep for my lost brother. The spirit of non-violence/Has come to fill the silence/Come to Parihaka.'

Figure 2. Seraphine Pick, Riki and Ruru, *2000, oil on canvas, 1805 x 1010 mm. Gifted by the artist to Parihaka Pā. Image reproduced courtesy of Seraphine Pick.*

Back to Parihaka

I stood in the foyer, listened to Finn sing and looked at the banner for this millennium exhibition, a partnership between the Parihaka Pā Trustees and City Gallery, Wellington. I was filled with pride. Didn't my family have some sort of connection with Parihaka? Hadn't I stayed there as a kid?

I bought the catalogue and pored over it. I bought a poster and got it framed. I downloaded the Parihaka chapter from the Waitangi Tribunal's 1996 report. What a polemic! I felt outraged, just as the authors intended. I changed my topic. I would leave Melbourne behind for a while and journey back, through research, to where I came from.

My idea was to examine how the Parihaka story had been represented between 1881 and the early twenty-first century. I wanted to trace a history of storytelling about the place, so as to figure out why Parihaka had become such an iconic site.

A few questions sparked the work off. I thought about Tim Finn's lyrics and about how Parihaka had come to fill a 'silence'. The scope of the exhibition seemed to suggest that whatever silence might once have surrounded Parihaka had long gone, surely. How did this happen? How did we – the nation, Taranaki, Māori – get here? How did this tiny settlement become so important that it was chosen as the subject for a millennium exhibition at the biggest and most adventurous gallery in the national capital? Why this invasion, this village? Why these Māori leaders?

As my work progressed, new questions arose. The exhibition welcomed the new millennium with an isolated, local and hardly representative moment in New Zealand's (and Taranaki's) past, a past that has as many moments of cataclysmic intra-racial and inter-racial violence as it does of cooperation. Why the art of passive resistance? Why not the art of armed resistance or the art of guerrilla warfare? Why not the art of ambiguous loyalties?

The answers to these questions can be found in the kinds of things Māori and Pākehā said about Parihaka in the nineteenth century, the stories, ideas and arguments that have been reused and recycled into the present. Parihaka is an appealing and appalling story because it illustrates many of the contradictory themes in contemporary Māori and Pākehā understandings of the past, present and future.

The Parihaka story is simultaneously a story of war and a story of peace, a narrative of Māori destruction and a narrative of Māori survival. It is a story loved by artists and writers. It lends itself to the poetic, the metaphorical and the symbolic.

The most iconic things in the Parihaka archive are the pictures – the chilling nineteenth century invasion photographs; the jollier images of the post-1886 restoration; the ghostly, depressing images of twentieth-century decline; and all those gorgeous paintings. All these images help make Parihaka into a filmic foundational moment, a pan-tribal site through which the many disparate invasions that have formed New Zealand can be condensed into a single visually, emotionally and spiritually compelling episode that can be replayed, over and over, yielding plenty of diverse but fundamentally feel-good lessons for the present and future.

Peace is a worthy thing, no doubt, but what other stories does this focus on the historic village of peace obscure?

The Parihaka Album is my attempt to understand the 'Parihaka story' – a story that always centres on the invasion – and its powerful, complicated legacy. It does not seek to provide a comprehensive, definitive history of the nineteenth century community and what happened there, but rather uses Parihaka as a starting point to explore the relationship between past and present in the places I come from – my family, my home towns of New Plymouth (the capital of Taranaki) and Wellington (the national capital) and my nation, New Zealand. The book is about what we, Māori and Pākehā, say about the past. It is about the places and the people and the buildings that we decide to cherish and remember, and the ones we decide to discard and forget.

Back to Parihaka

The title of this book was inspired by the real-life Parihaka Album, an intriguing collection of nineteenth-century photographs held at the Alexander Turnbull Library in Wellington. An album is a keepsake or a memento, a reminder of times past, a place to protect snapshots, autographs, stamps, clippings. Each photograph in an album presents a different view: there's the close-up and the wider-angle shot, the panorama and the zoom, the pictures where the focus was never quite right and the ones where everything appears to be just perfect. Similarly, this book is a series of personal, historical and political snapshots, encounters with places and memories of places, all linking back to Parihaka.

The Parihaka that is recalled in a photograph album compiled in the late nineteenth century by an anonymous white settler in New Plymouth is quite different from the Parihaka recalled at Parihaka itself, either today or in the past. The Parihaka captured by the young communist writer Dick Scott in a 1954 booklet is quite different from the Parihaka portrayed in his 1973 best-selling book, *Ask That Mountain*. The Parihaka of artist Ralph Hotere or filmmaker John O'Shea is different from the Parihaka of historian Hazel Riseborough or photographer Anne Noble.

Every Parihaka narrator, including myself, has their own frame, their own reasons for telling the story, their own spin on the voluminous evidence available in so many different kinds of archives. Parihaka is special, in part, because it is so well documented, yet it is still so often described as hidden or forgotten or little understood. This paradox – the persistently hidden nature of an over-exposed story – means that Parihaka is a historic site that can tell us a great deal about how history is constructed in a settler nation such as New Zealand, about what is remembered and what is forgotten, what is hidden and what is exposed, and why.

Studying how Māori and Pākehā have made histories about Parihaka between the 1880s and now suggests that different histories are possible at different times. For instance, in the twentieth century, most of the best-known Parihaka histories – such as the one contained in the Waitangi Tribunal's Taranaki Report – highlight the invasion, but give little attention to the reconstruction funded by Māori that followed. In the nineteenth century, it was the reconstruction, not the aftermath of invasion, that attracted visitors to Parihaka. As historiographer Marnie Hughes-Warrington has argued: 'History is not solely about events; it is also about the relationships between events, the order in which they are presented and the selection of emphases.'[2]

To understand why there are still so many 'blind-spots' in the Parihaka story and in New Zealand history more generally, it is necessary to first understand the relationship between Parihaka and other sites of Māori protest. Parihaka is exceptional; but it is important to recall the ways it is unexceptional too, to slot Parihaka back into the messy nineteenth century. Parihaka is part of a much bigger picture of Māori resistance, and the struggles, past and present, of Parihaka residents have been echoed around New Zealand and overseas.

Chapter 2 of this book, 'The story so far', puts Parihaka into this bigger picture and explains some of the contexts for the community's actions. It begins with translations of some Parihaka waiata (songs) and whaikōrero (speeches), snippets of some of the sung histories I had 'seen but not heard' on my first research trip to Parihaka.[3] These powerful documents, brought into the public domain by the work of Te Miringa Hohaia and others and by the testimonies of various Taranaki iwi before Waitangi Tribunal hearings, demonstrate the self-conscious way Parihaka's two leaders used their words as weapons.[4] The songs and speeches also reveal how Parihaka people understood their place as a radical, non-violent community protected by a sort of divine sanction.

The chapter then pans back to take a wider angle on Parihaka within the bigger story of nineteenth-century colonisation of New Zealand, a history in which war and peace, riki and rura, are intertwined. It gives an overview of the numerous Māori prophetic movements that sprang up after the arrival of Christian missionaries in 1814, the conflicting understandings behind the signing of the Treaty of Waitangi in 1840, the beginnings of mass white migration through the activities of the New Zealand Company and, finally, that century's many wars, from the inter-tribal 'Musket Wars' of the early 1800s to the equally cataclysmic wars of foundation fought, overwhelmingly, between imperial or colonial troops and different iwi across the North Island from about 1845 until the late 1880s.

Parihaka was set up in 1866 as a result of the government's decision, in 1865, to confiscate most of Taranaki in punishment for Māori 'rebellion'. Patricia Limerick, a historian of the American West, has argued that from a distance, colonisation is quite clear: 'Sometimes by negotiation and sometimes by warfare, the natives lost ground and the invaders gained it.'[5] But if you zoom in on the tricky realities of how each particular group was actually dispossessed, then, Limerick argues, all 'clarity dissolves'. This chapter concludes by 'zooming in' on Parihaka and the events that led to the 1881 invasion. It is one answer to the question: What happened?

Chapter 3, 'Illuminations', moves forward to the twenty-first century. It provides a different kind of close up, a story about my own recent encounter with one of history's many 'hiding places' – the Cape Egmont Lighthouse, just down the road from Parihaka. It explains how a story as iconic and seemingly over-exposed as Parihaka can still be silenced or hidden by what is said (or not said) in many different places – from the foot of a lighthouse to the streets of Wellington to a playground to our movie screens. This chapter argues that personal stories can help us get beyond historical blind-spots and allow us to see how the past and the present connect and overlap in unexpected places.

The next three chapters move back again to focus on the nineteenth century: how Māori and Pākehā used words, songs, pictures and buildings to make histories about Parihaka, and these histories laid the tracks on which each community planned to move forward into their imagined futures.

Chapter 4, 'Road, telegraph, lighthouse', examines the colonial archive to reveal why the lighthouse is one of three utilities that can help us understand the ideological battle that Māori and Pākehā fought through Parihaka. One of the many fascinating things about the Parihaka story is the way that both Māori and Pākehā were very aware of themselves as historical actors. They were sensitive about the way history – meaning accounts of their actions to be told in the future – would judge them. Both sides wanted to be 'kings of peace', to claim the title of non-violent peacemaker in one of New Zealand's bloodiest areas, Taranaki. Māori used non-violent protest or passive resistance, but settlers used the utilities – the road, the telegraph and the lighthouse. The forceful completion of public works would be a show of European might against Māori; but it would also maintain a veneer of peace and reason, two things that were important elements in the just colonisation that New Zealand settlers were so eager to enact in their new home. The utilities, three 'gifts' of modernity, would hide more ugly, violent intentions. Beyond these utilities, this chapter also reveals how the government's retribution was not confined to Parihaka: after the November 1881 invasion of that community, soldiers also ransacked the homes of 'loyal' or 'friendly' Māori who had never been involved with Parihaka. It finishes by arguing that this excessive, frenzied response to any kind of Māori presence in Taranaki revealed just how unsettling the community at Parihaka had become for the colonial government and its settlers.

Chapter 5, 'After the invasion', looks at the time immediately following the invasion. What kinds of stories did Māori tell about the ransacking of Parihaka? What kinds of things did Pākehā say? This chapter demonstrates the multiple, highly contested and shifting perspectives on Parihaka by looking at various aftermaths, most notably an 1886 libel trial in which John Bryce, the man who led the campaign on Parihaka as Native Minister, sued retired Victorian public servant and historian George Rusden over a couple of lines in Rusden's three-volume *History of New Zealand*, published in 1883.

The Supreme Court in London heard the case, and the evidence of many witnesses reveals the different interpretative strategies at work when white settlers and Māori described colonisation. What one side saw as civilising and civilised, the other saw as murderous and barbaric. What Māori and their supporters at Parihaka called 'absolute submission', settlers choose to see as 'absolute defiance'. The problem, this chapter reveals, was one of definition. Who was violent? Who was peace-loving? What sort of resistance, if any, might be legitimate?

Pictures of all kinds – photographs, postcards, stereographs, paintings, films, portraits, sketches, watercolours – are an important part of the Parihaka story. The richness and depth of this pictorial archive has helped Parihaka become an iconic site. Too often, photographs are read as portraying simple truths, truths that are beyond words; but as journalist Philip Gourevitch has argued in connection with photographs of American soldiers abusing Iraqi prisoners at Abu Ghraib, a photograph 'can best be understood not as an answer or an end to inquiry, but as an invitation to look more closely, and to ask questions'.[6] Chapter 6, 'Pictures', looks more closely at nineteenth century Parihaka photographs, including the ones pasted into 'The Parihaka Album', to consider what they might tell us about how white settlers understood the world they were claiming for themselves at Māori expense. The album tells a story in which the installation of the 'white house' of settler New Zealand quickly followed the installation of the lighthouse. While white settlers were making themselves at home, Māori were rebuilding and modernising Parihaka. By 1900, the village had its own reservoir and was generating its own electricity. It had an abbatoir, a butchery and a bank. Parihaka was one of the first places in New Zealand to have street lights. The chapter considers what kinds of stories Māori were telling through the self-consciously modern, European-style buildings and roads they made at Parihaka, and it explores the divisions that developed between followers of Tohu and followers of Te Whiti right at the time when photographs showed the place at its most crowded and prosperous. Parihaka was torn and its leaders bore an enormous strain because the community was both a source of innovation and a keeper of tradition.

Chapters 7 and 8 move forward to look at history-making about Parihaka in the twentieth century, specifically the stories generated by two major commissions of inquiry: the 1927 Sim Commission and the Waitangi Tribunal's Taranaki Report in 1996. Chapter 7, 'The wrong that was done', opens with the deaths of the prophets in 1907 and focuses on Maui Pomare, who was one of the orators at Te Whiti's tangi. Pomare and fellow doctor Peter Buck, both Māori from Taranaki, wanted to 'modernise' Māori people as a whole. They believed that two factors were holding Taranaki Māori back. The first was 'Te Whitism'. The second was ongoing grievances against Pākehā.

At its peak, Parihaka was a permanent home to about 2000 people. By 1920, only 200 permanent residents were left. The remaining residents were divided internally, but they were united in their support for the 1927 Royal Commission into Confiscated Lands (known as the Sim Commission). Te Whiti still spoke to his followers. Many Māori believed that the establishment of the commission was a fulfilment of one of the Te Whiti's prophecies. At the hearings, survivors of the 1881 plunder gave wrenching eyewitness testimony relating to the crimes committed at that time. The commission acknowledged the wrong that was done at Parihaka and elsewhere in Taranaki, but the problem of confiscated land was not fixed. Rather, a complicated series of trust boards created new problems that persist to this day. The chapter ends by looking at two kinds of history-making fifty years after the invasion – the handwritten stories told by Parihaka children at Pungarehu School and the jolly celebrations enjoyed by Pākehā Parihaka veterans at gatherings around the country.

Chapter 8, 'Hearings', traces the many different ways Māori and Pākehā have made Parihaka histories from the 1950s until the end of the twentieth century. These tellings include young communist

Dick Scott's self-published 1954 book, *The Parihaka Story,* and his rewritten best-selling 1975 version of the story, *Ask That Mountain*. They include the non-violent strategies used by Māori protestors and their supporters at Bastion Point, Auckland, in 1981, and the testimonies of Māori claimants before Waitangi Tribunal hearings in the Taranaki claims, as well as the Parihaka story constructed by the tribunal itself in the Taranaki Report. The pinnacle of Parihaka history-making was, of course, the Parihaka exhibition at the City Gallery in Wellington in 2000. Strangely, the greater the production of Parihaka stories, the stronger the claims that the story remains hidden. This chapter analyses the black and white Parihaka story exposed in the published tribunal report and the rather more complicated Parihaka story hidden in the claimant testimonies stored in tribunal archives. It suggests that these more hidden, complicated stories are, perhaps, a better starting point for 'hearing' Parihaka.

The Parihaka story is a gift. It is a priceless, potent heirloom. Working on Parihaka has led me to new pasts. The most significant of these, for me, is the Māori past (and present) of Wellington. This is the focus of the final two chapters of this book. The Parihaka story reaches beyond Taranaki and into the capital. The recent histories of Taranaki and Wellington are enmeshed in the Māori world, and this entangled story is the one that has been waiting for me. Parihaka is the gateway that got me there. My Parihaka story is not quite as dramatic as the one presented in the Waitangi Tribunal report or the one recounted at Parihaka itself; but it is still a story, I think, that deserves a hearing. These last two chapters are Parihaka stories inspired by my own whakapapa (genealogy). They are an experiment in storytelling. They are my efforts to safeguard against forgetting, my work to see and hear and feel the present past.

Chapter 9, 'Dementia wing', is about two memorial sites in Wellington – the Rawinia Buchanan Dementia wing in the retirement home built on the grounds of Athletic Park and the Tomb of the Unknown Warrior at the National War Memorial. It explores the histories that are remembered and the histories that are forgotten at each of these places and argues that while the Dementia wing named after my grandmother represents an end to our family's 'amnesia' about its Māoriness, the Tomb of the Unknown Warrior signals yet another erasure of New Zealand's wars of foundation. These wars remain in the background – hidden, difficult, hushed up. This site, like so many others, throws up literal evidence of this neglect. At the back of the grounds, far from the magnificent new tomb, is a small, bowed statue commemorating the Parihaka men who were imprisoned at Mt Cook on their way to the South Island.

Chapter 10, 'Pioneers', opens in the bony archive of the Bolton Street Cemetery with my search for the burial place of our tupuna, Te Aro Pā rangatira Hemi Parai. As with 'Dementia wing', this chapter uses family stories to challenge broader assumptions about heritage, early settlers, pioneers and historic sites. Thousands of bodies were disinterred in the 1960s to make way for the new motorway through Thorndon, and protestors were angry about the desecration of the graves of early settlers and the destruction of a place that was sacred to the memory of these pioneers, 'our Westminster Abbey'. Many Māori graves were also disrupted at this time, including the resting places of those involved with the Parihaka community; but these people were not seen as pioneers or early settlers. Why not? The work of one of my Pākehā forebears, historian John Howard Wallace, gives some clues. Even though Wallace had many Māori relatives (through his brother William's marriages), he was determined to commemorate the lives of only one group of people, white 'pioneer settlers', and to ignore totally the lives of another, including the lives of his Māori nieces and nephews. The recent unearthing of whare from Te Aro Pā restores Taranaki Māori to the centre of Wellington city.

A photo album doesn't tell the whole story of a family, and this book doesn't tell the whole story of Parihaka. Rather, it prompts you to look at Parihaka and see if you can find something new there; and then to look again at Parihaka and see what its fate might tell you about other places in Aotearoa New Zealand.

[1] Linda Tuhiwai Smith, *Declononizing Methodologies: Research and Indigenous Peoples,* London, New York and Dunedin: Zed Books and University of Otago Press, 1999.

[2] Marnie Hughes-Warrington, *History Goes To The Movies: Studying History on Film,* London and New York: Routledge, 2007, 9.

[3] This phrase refers to the photographs of Anne Noble made for Te Miringa Hohaia, G. O'Brien and L. Strongman, eds, *Parihaka: The Art of Passive Resistance,* Wellington: City Gallery/Victoria University Press, 2002, 103. Noble worked with the nineteenth century Parihaka archive to make a series called 'From the Record'. One work was called 'Parihaka … seen and not heard'. See, also, Justin Paton, ed., *Anne Noble States of Grace,* Otago and Wellington: Dunedin Public Art Gallery and Victoria University Press, 2001.

[4] See Te Miringa Hohaia, 'Ngaa Puutaketanga Koorero Moo Parihaka', in *Art of Passive Resistance,* 42-65. Many of these writings are transcriptions and translations of the work of Te Kaahui Kararehe, the nineteenth-century Parihaka scribe. Other songs and sayings from the time of the invasion of Parihaka can be found in Ngāti Mutunga and Her Majesty the Queen in right of New Zealand, 'Deed of Settlement of the Historical Claims of Ngāti Mutunga: Initialled Deed of Settlement for Presentation to Ngāti Mutunga', 14 December 2004, Wellington: Office of Treaty Settlements, 2004, available online at: www.ots.govt.nz

[5] Patricia Limerick, 'Haunted America', in Limerick, *Something in the Soil: Legacies and Reckonings in the New West,* New York and London: W.W.Norton & Company, 2000, 33.

[6] Philip Gourevitch and Errol Morris, *Standard Operating Procedure: A War Story,* London: Picador, 2008, 148.

CHAPTER 2

The story so far

Parihaka is a small Māori settlement on the west coast of the North Island, about seven kilometres back from the Tasman Sea, a place built in the hollows of the green hillocks under the shadow of the magnificent mountain, Taranaki. Parihaka sits in the centre of a province, also called Taranaki, that was at war, on and off, for most of the nineteenth century.

Parihaka was established in 1866 by tribal, political and spiritual leaders Te Whiti o Rongomai and Tohu Kakahi. The men were related. They were from Te Āti Awa and Taranaki, and their names signalled their futures. Tohu refers to instruction; he was the adviser and teacher, the quieter of the two. Te Whiti refers to light; he was the dynamic orator who Pākehā often mistakenly thought was Parihaka's leader. His full name, Te Whiti o Rongomai, means flight path of the shining comet.[1]

The two men used the knowledge they had gained in traditional Māori schools of learning and in their learning about Christianity – first, through contact with freed Ngā Puhi slave turned Anglican minister Minarapa Rangihatuake, and then at the Lutheran mission set up at Warea in 1846 in middle Taranaki – to found a non-violent community that offered a refuge to war-ravaged Taranaki people. The community grew in size and mana and used non-violent methods, including ploughing land that had been occupied by white settlers, to protest the continuing alienation of tribal lands. As the 1870s progressed, Māori from as far off as the Chatham Islands, Wairarapa, the King Country, Wellington, Auckland and the deep south moved to Parihaka or sought counsel from its charismatic leaders.

Then in 1881, in an episode that has been replayed many times in New Zealand books, paintings, plays, films, poetry, songs, hearings and documentaries, 1589 heavily-armed soldiers invaded Parihaka. About 2000 people, all dressed in their best clothes, sat on the marae waiting for them. Singing children greeted the soldiers. Behind the children, women carried loaves of warm bread, gifts for the visitors.

Under the watch of an Armstrong canon mounted on Purepo (Mt Rolleston), the soldiers arrested and exiled Parihaka leaders, they raped women and stole taonga, they evicted most of the 2000 residents and ransacked buildings and crops.

Part of the problem posed by Parihaka, and one of the reasons why the histories of this place are so compelling, is that Māori – a supposedly primitive race, an indigenous people in need of civilising – had claimed for themselves one of the central tenets of modern civilisation, the state of non-violence. In his study of the partition of India, Gyanendra Pandey notes that modern nationhood is characterised by 'this state of non-violence', where 'mature, adult human beings negotiate with one another to determine their rights and duties through national agreement'.[2]

People at Parihaka believed in a righteous non-violence backed by divine authority and protected by a sacred emblem, the raukura or albatross feather. The albatross feather had at least two meanings. According to one account, Tohu had a vision in which Melchizedec, the biblical prince of peace, appeared before him, anointing him as leader. In other stories, many Parihaka people saw a great albatross descend on the village and when it took off, it left a feather behind. In her biography, Ailsa Smith writes: 'Tohu's descendants tell how this movement was given divine sanction by the Holy Spirit in the form of a great albatross (Toroanui – the name of Tohu's marae.)'[3] Other accounts say the vision was in the sky, a celestial 'trail of light in the shape of a feather'.[4]

This feeling of being part of a sacred community, one that would transcend the present hardships and petty laws imposed by the new, foreign government, is made even more explicit in songs from this time. In Takiri te Raukura (Let the Raukura Dance), a waiata poi performed since the time Parihaka was invaded, Ngāti Mutunga sang:

Takiri te raukura
Let the raukura dance, go forth the raukura
Haere koe i runga
Fluttering above and arise upwards
Huri haere rā i te motu e
Throughout the land
Takiri te raukura
Let the raukura dance
Haere koe i runga
Fluttering above while
Waiho te ture kia rere i raro e
The laws are fluttering down below …[5]

The song goes on to describe Parihaka as a raft that people could cling to, saving themselves from the flood of colonisation and from the unjust laws, such as the Māori Prisoners Act, that had been introduced to imprison them without trial:

Ko te tongi a Noa
The symbol of Noah is the ark
He aka te oranga

> *A means for survival*
> *Ko te tongi a Te Whiti*
> *Likewise the symbol of Te Whiti*
> *He raukura e*
> *It is the raukura ...*

Te Whiti himself reportedly advised his followers to 'put both your hands and your feet on the new land and stand in the ark of patience'. He preached that there were two roads, 'one to life and one to death. God said, in the days of Noah, the earth will be destroyed; build an ark, or all will perish. Noah did as he was commanded and this was an example for us to follow.' Waiata counselled Parihaka people to cling to 'the ark of stout-heartedness'. On such a vessel they could withstand anything: 'What matter to us what happens; we have our ark, as Noah of old. I now say come into the ark.'[6]

It is said that Te Whiti's favourite part of the Bible was the Book of Revelations. Te Whiti sometimes described himself as the 'King of Peace', a reference to Melchizedec, King of Salem. Like many other millennial prophets, Te Whiti and Tohu considered the plight of Māori to be similar to that of the Israelites. Indeed, Māori were sometimes considered to be descendents of the Israelites.[7]

In a voice that was described as mesmerising, deep, lyrical, spellbinding, sweet and seething, Te Whiti drew from both Māori and Christian traditions to construct a foundation for a peaceful Māori promised land. The Bible was a book that affirmed and challenged Māori understandings of the world. Although it was a written text, the Bible was based on the spoken word, on 'genealogies, songs, moral stories and an opaque lyrical mode of telling'.[8] It offered a point of contact between the traditions of Māori and non-Māori but it also embodied the biggest struggles of nineteenth-century history-making in New Zealand: namely what historian Danny Keenan has described as the 'vigorous contest' between oral processes and the written word.[9]

The past was of deep concern to Te Whiti and Tohu, but so was the future. In their teachings, both men looked beyond the present to a future that would be radically different and better, a new time in which a divine rupture had swept away the injustices that had come with white settlement. Translations of their speeches published in newspapers and government reports are peppered with predictions of resurrections, plagues, earthquakes and giant waves that would sweep Pākehā into the sea. According to the *Taranaki Herald*, Te Whiti predicted that New Plymouth would be destroyed by an earthquake, that Europeans would be carted off their lands and that Taranaki would be visited by plagues like those that struck Egypt.[10]

Settlers, in turn, reportedly believed that Parihaka residents had buried dynamite in secret mines around the township and this dynamite 'was spoken of as the miraculous means by which Te Whiti was prepared to disperse like smoke the 2500 armed men around his abode'.[11] The prophets reportedly promised that, if Parihaka residents were virtuous, they would be able to raise from the dead all those who had been killed in the Taranaki wars.[12]

Although settlers feared that Parihaka was a hiding place for a stash of guns, dynamite and swords, the leaders had different kinds of ammunition in mind. Both men made countless references to their words as weapons, their tongues as swords. In a translation of an 1879 speech, surveyor and road-making engineer Charles Hursthouse reported that Te Whiti said: 'In the olden days laws were given to the prophets but I have only my tongue which is sharp on both edges.'[13]

Historian Hazel Riseborough has persuasively argued that historians need to beware of the biases, misunderstandings and racism embedded in Pākehā reports of Māori activities, especially at Parihaka.[14] But Māori primary sources, such as waiata handed down orally and whaikōrero recorded by tribal scribe Te Kaahui Kararehe, mirror the undoubtedly clumsy Pākehā translations. Like Te Whiti, Tohu used his tongue as a metaphor.

Kei te pakanga kee te matamata o taku aarero hei taaonga moo ngaa whakatupuranga/
The very extremity of my tongue is at battle as a treasure for the generations/
E haere ake nei i mua i a taatou/
Which continue on after us
Ko raatou hei kainoho i te rangatiratanga/
They will establish the self-determination
Moo ake tonu atu.
Forever.[15]

In another speech, Tohu reinforces his message.

Ka haere ko taku aaero
My tongue is in motion
E pakanga nei au ki te motu nei ki te aao
I battle this land and the world
Ka tuu au hei tangata whakakake
I stand as one who transcends
Hei tangata whakahii ki te motu nei
As one who inspires the country
Puta noa i te aao
And reaching into the entire world
Kei te pakanga ai au ki te motu nei
I do battle with this country
Kit e aao moo te maungaarongo.
And the world for the foundation of Peace.[16]

The story so far

Like 'Takiri Te Raukura', a song sung by the ploughmen reveals that followers believed the non-violent teachings of Parihaka leaders elevated their community to a divine level, which transcended the unjust laws and events (especially the confiscation of their land) that oppressed residents. The ploughmen sang:

I te raa o maehe ka iri kei te torona
On a day in March I was suspended by the throne of God
Ka mau taku ringa ki te parau
With my hand to the plough
E hau nei te whenua
Swept across the land.
Ka toro taku ringa ki te atua
My hand is extended to God
E tuu nei ko whakatohe
Standing resolute
Ka puta te hae a te kaawana
The ill-feeling of the Government emerges
E tango nei whenua
In the taking away of the land
E kore au e taaea
It will not deter me
He uri noo Hoohepa
A descendant of Joseph
Noo ngaa tuupuna
By way of my ancestors ...[17]

Parihaka was not the first Māori community to try non-violence as a way to hold onto Māori land, nor was it the only Māori community to use a white feather (the raukura, from the albatross) as an emblem of peace. Many iwi in both the North and the South Island used passive resistance to try to keep hold of their land and power. They pulled up survey pegs and took down theodolites, they dismantled fences and staged sit-ins and they went on protest marches.

Parihaka was not the first prophetic Māori community to use the Bible as a sacred text and as an inspiration, either. Anglican chaplain Samuel Marsden left Australia to open the first mission in New Zealand at Rangihoua, Bay of Islands, in 1814, and the Wesleyans opened their first mission at Whangaroa the same year.

Māori latched on quickly. It didn't take them long to see that perhaps this new Christian God could be some kind of ally or guide. By the 1820s, Christian-inspired dieties were being added to tribal knowledge. Between 1830 and 1860, as historian Bronwyn Elsmore notes, twenty different new Māori religious movements (especially healing movements, a pragmatic response to the introduction of foreign diseases such as venereal disease and influenza) came into existence. By the 1860s, Māori prophets proliferated.

The place that had not long been New Zealand was saturated in the divine. In Taranaki, Parihaka's lineage included two other significant, post-contact prophetic movements. In 1862, in response to a visitation from the angel Gabriel, Taranaki man Te Ua Haumene founded Pai Mārire (the 'good and peaceful'). Haumene and his mother had been prisoners of Waikato people, and he was introduced to Christianity at the Wesleyan mission at Kawhia. Pai Mārire followers worshipped around a niu pole, rather like a maypole or a ship's mast. The pole was bedecked with colourful streamers and topped with carvings of Riki and Rura, the Māori gods of war and peace.

Elsmore writes that the purpose of the niu was to help followers acquire 'the languages of all races upon earth'. Te Ua preached peace, but many of his followers acted violently, killing missionaries and attacking British soldiers. It has been suggested that Te Whiti and possibly Tohu were involved in the ill-fated 1864 Pai Mārire attack on a British redoubt at Sentry Hill in north Taranaki, but neither carried a gun. Instead, they were reportedly armed with a tokotoko (a carved stick used by orators on marae) and shielded by Pai Mārire incantations.[18]

Settlers feared Pai Mārire, calling them Hauhaus. Historians still struggle to understand the connection between this group and the community that would develop at Parihaka. The movement was mysterious. Its adherents' words and actions were contradictory, to say the least. In 1867, a former Pai Mārire believer, Ngā Ruahine chief Titokowaru, prophesised the 'year of the lamb', a time of peace. Two years of war followed.[19]

Like Māori and Pākehā, riki and rura, war and peace are intertwined in recent New Zealand history. One does not exist without the other. No place or event embodies this paradox more powerfully than Parihaka – a village of peace formed as a result of war.

For every example that can be used as part of a narrative of New Zealand as a place of humane, civilised, peaceful colonisation, there are many others that suggest just the opposite. At Parihaka, and elsewhere, the facts of New Zealand history will not settle themselves into neat rows. They keep jumping around, distracted and fidgety, resisting any sort of discipline, historical or otherwise.

Often these contradictions exist in the same event. Take the signing of the Treaty of Waitangi, for example. On 6 February 1840, almost 200 years after Abel Tasman sighted the place his cartographer named Nieuw Zeeland, and less than seventy years since Cook's *Endeavour* made its first journey around our islands, representatives of the Māori people and of the British Crown signed a treaty at Waitangi. Over the next eight months, 500 Māori chiefs signed one of the seven copies in Māori. Europeans signed the English version.

The signing of the Treaty was, perhaps, a moment of hope; but each side hoped for something different. The meaning of the two versions of the Treaty is still strongly debated. The archive produced by the Waitangi Tribunal, the permanent commission of inquiry set up in 1975 to examine breaches of the Treaty, gives a feeling for the misunderstanding, bewilderment and anger generated – on all sides of a complicated picture – by the different versions.

Broadly, Māori believed the Crown had acknowledged their ongoing rangatiratanga (chieftainship) over the land, but the Crown believed Māori had ceded sovereignty over it. Māori believed they would keep hold of their lands and forests and fisheries, as well as their sacred places (such as burial grounds), but the Crown believed that the Treaty would give it more access to land to cope with 'the rapid extension of Emigration from both Europe and Australia which is still in progress'.

The New Zealand Company, founded by former convict Edward Gibbon Wakefield, was behind this rapid settlement. The company planned the colonisation of New Zealand before the British Crown had even declared sovereignty over the place. In doing so, it angered almost everyone: Māori; the British Crown and the English settlers who arrived on New Zealand Company ships expecting to take up choice little pockets of cheap land and were surprised to find that the company had not, in fact, acquired 'very extensive tracts of land in the North Island' as promised.[20]

In 1839, the company's first ship, the land-buying *Tory*, sailed into what would become Wellington Harbour. It was followed by the *Cuba*, a storeship. The first settler ship, the Aurora, left Gravesend, Essex, in September 1839 and arrived in Wellington in January 1840. About 200 women, men and children were aboard the 'gallant old tub'.[21]

The company and its offshoots provided the immigrants to establish the cities of Wellington, New Plymouth, Nelson and Whanganui (set up to house the overflow of settlers from Wellington) in places already occupied by Māori. Dunedin and

Christchurch (1848 and 1850) were set up using the New Zealand Company schemes as a model.

Wellington grew especially fast. Historian Michael King notes that, in 1841, Wellington had 2500 European settlers, but by 1843, there were 4000. The other 'new towns' also gained thousands of residents within a few years of 'first settlement'. Overall, the company brought 15,500 settlers to New Zealand from Britain. Only Auckland had no formal immigration programme. Instead, historian James Belich argues, it grew from the efforts of local Māori, Sydney merchants and the new colonial government.

Marriage and commerce brought some Māori and Pākehā together. In the Waikato and Hauraki, Māori were active traders in the domestic and export markets. Tainui, for instance, were exporting produce to Australia. In the 1850s, Māori built 60 flour mills and Māori traders accounted for half of Auckland's custom duties.

Even so, it would not be truthful to say that Māori and Pākehā lived side by side. The Māori world and the European one were divided by geography, beliefs and language. By 1859, most Māori lived in the North Island and most lived outside the cities, in the far north or the forests of the central North Island or along the east and west coasts. Most Pākehā (about 75,000 of them) lived in Auckland, Wellington and the South Island, but these places were home to only a sixth of the nation's estimated 60,000 Māori.

In the South, Ngāi Tahu were inundated by settlers in search of gold. By 1860, the Crown believed it had 'bought' most of the South Island from them. But in the North Island the picture was different. There, Māori retained control of three quarters of the land and they had the people, the guns and the fortifications required to defend it.

Northland Māori got muskets in 1805. The arrival of guns sparked the brutal inter-tribal wars that began about 1806 and ended around thirty-five years later. The wars were fought in the North and the South Island and on the Chatham Islands. The fall-out from these little-understood battles was immense. Taranaki, for example, was almost emptied out as iwi fled south to Waikanae, then to Te Whanganui-a-Tara, to escape marauding Ngāti Maniapoto and Ngāti Toa war parties led by the warrior Te Rauparaha. The young Te Whiti and Tohu were likely to have been among the Taranaki people who fled to Waikanae to escape Waikato vengeance for losses sustained during the 1832 siege on Otaka Pā (at Ngamotu where New Plymouth is now) in 1832.[22]

Belich describes these wars as 'the largest ever fought on New Zealand soil. They killed more New Zealanders than World War One – perhaps about 20,000.'[23] In Taranaki, the devastation caused by these wars is recalled in the language and the land. In 1831, at Pukerangiora, above the Waitara River, in one of the musket raids, Te Āti Awa people were forced to their deaths over the 100-metre high cliffs as they fled the Waikato marauders. As many as 1500 people were killed or captured in this siege. High above the river, Waikato and Te Āti Awa trenches can still be seen. Many Taranaki children, including myself, have been given early lessons in the brutal side of life on visits to this site. How afraid the people must have been if they decided to leap over these massive white cliffs rather than risk capture.

Taranaki people suffered, and inflicted, years of violence before white settlement even began. In the 1820s, members of different Taranaki hapū had retreated to Te Maru, a pocket of pā sites hidden in the bush about 1500 metres up the western side of the mountain. They were found by Waikato and 'All the pā either fell when assaulted or were abandoned. Widespread pursuit of the survivors took place over a long period, and hundreds were killed or enslaved.'[24] A proverb, recalled by Taranaki historian Te Miringa Hohaia, recalls this devastation:

Te Maru Paa, ko toona whakataukii teenei:
Ko te maruutanga o te whenua
Ko te maruutanga o te tangata
i raro i toona waewae
i roto anoo i te kapuu o toona ringaringa

Maru Paa, this is its proverb:
It was the death of the land.
It was the death of the people
Under its feet
And in the hollow of its cupped hand.[25]

The damage and dislocation caused by these wars further complicated the wars with white settlers that would follow. Like the Musket Wars, the New Zealand Wars resist easy explanation. Writing about the conquest of the American West, Patricia Limerick has observed that from a distance, colonisation is quite clear. The big picture is the expansion of Europe into America, Australia, New Zealand, South America and Asia: 'Sometimes by negotiation and sometimes by warfare, the natives lost ground and the invaders gained it.'[26]

But if you zoom in on the tricky realities of how each particular group was actually dispossessed, then, Limerick argues, all 'clarity dissolves'. None of these wars of colonisation were ever as simple as white settlers against indigenous people. In America, as New Zealand, both sides were divided. Indians often fought with whites, and in New Zealand it was the same. Colonial forces relied on their Māori allies, the so-called kūpapa or 'neutral' troops.

Meanwhile, many Māori chose to remain apart from any fighting, and at least some white settlers were appalled by what the government was doing. Historians such as Lyndsay Head have argued that most Māori either supported or 'did not actively oppose' the colonial government; but she worries that Māori who did not fight or who fought as government allies 'are occasionally demonized but more frequently ignored'.[27] Even if it was only a minority of Māori who took up arms (either for or against the government), the nineteenth century wars affected everyone on the frontiers and at home, and Māori motives, strategies and positions – like those of their opponents – were rarely clear cut.

Parihaka was invaded towards the end of a century of inter-tribal and inter-racial violence. A brief chronology gives a feel for how many different wars there were. *The Penguin Field Guide to New Zealand Archaeology* (2007) describes the wars as:

> *the inter-tribal Musket Wars from 1810-1845, in North Island, South Island and the Chathams;*
>
> *the northern phase of the New Zealand wars from 1845-46 in the Bay of Islands;*
>
> *the Wellington/Cook Strait phase of the New Zealand Wars in 1846;*
>
> *the Wanganui phase in 1847;*
>
> *the first and second phase of the New Zealand Wars in Taranaki, 1860-61 and 1863-66;*
>
> *the New Zealand Wars in the Waikato and Tauranga, 1863-64;*
>
> *Titokowaru's War in South Taranaki and Wanganui in 1868-69;*
>
> *the New Zealand Wars Pai Mārire phase from 1864-76 in Taranaki, Bay of Plenty and the East Coast;*
>
> *the New Zealand Wars Te Kooti Arikirangi's War from 1868-72 in the East Coast, Taupo, Tongariro and Te Urewera ranges;*
>
> *New Zealand Armed Constabulary and police actions from 1868 until 1891 in Taranaki, Bay of Plenty, Waikato, East Coast, Taupo/Tongariro and Te Urewera ranges.*

Every war in this exhausting list is its own particular universe of suffering, and many battles intersected with each other. The causes of each outbreak of violence were different in each place; but broadly, it is possible to say that every encounter turned on disputes over either land or mana or both. Māori used many strategies to retain these two things, and the government used many strategies to acquire them. These strategies included mounting violent and non-violent resistance, forming alliances or seeking separation, finding God, rejecting God, fighting against the government and fighting with the government against other Māori.

The Northern War in 1844 began when Te Haratua, who was the lieutenant of Hone Heke (the first chief to sign the Treaty), cut down the Union Jack from the flagstaff at Kororareka. Fighting began in March 1845 and ended later that year with Māori victory – about 60 Māori were killed, compared with 300 imperial troops (which included so-called loyalist Māori troops).

The main phase of the New Zealand Wars began in Waitara, Taranaki, in 1860, after Governor Thomas Browne despatched imperial troops to force through a disputed government claim to Te Āti Awa land there. In the 1860s, wars blazed across the central North Island as Māori defended their land. Between 1860 and 1863, imperial troops fought Māori in Taranaki. In 1863, imperial and colonial soldiers and sailors, northern militia and some Māori allies invaded the Waikato, the seat of the newly crowned Māori King, Potatau Te Wherowhero. The battle, which eventually spread east to the Bay of Plenty, was a lopsided one. The governor, Sir George Grey, had up to 20,000 soldiers, the Kīngitanga never had more than 5000. About a third of the government's troops were military settlers from Australia.

By the time this phase of the fighting had finished, in 1864, more than 1000 Māori and 700 Europeans had died. The wars cost Britain dearly. Belich notes that: 'By 1864, there were more imperial troops in New Zealand than in Britain, and New Zealand was costing London 500,000 pounds a year'. In punishment for Māori 'rebellion', the government confiscated 1.3 million acres of Waikato land and 1.19 million acres of Taranaki land.

In 1864, some followers of the Pai Mārire prophet, Te Ua, killed and decapitated some army leaders. To quell this rebellion, soldiers fighting in the Waikato were redeployed to Taranaki. Further retribution followed against Taranaki Māori, including many in South Taranaki who had declared their allegiance to the Crown. In 1866, first Major-General Trevor Chute and then Thomas McDonnell led colonial, imperial and kūpapa soldiers on 'scorched earth' campaigns through south Taranaki. Soldiers demolished buildings and uprooted crops.

Fighting also started in the Bay of Plenty between Māori followers of Pai Mārire and kūpapa. Out of this mess arose Te Kooti, the founder of the Ringatū religion, a maverick prophet who waged guerrilla warfare across the central North Island until 1872, when he withdrew to the sanctuary of the King Country. Further battles were waged in 1868 when Ngā Ruahine leader Titokowaru attacked colonial troops at Patea, and his brilliant military campaign expelled almost all the interloping soldiers from South Taranaki.

Throughout these years of violence, Parihaka continued to grow. In 1870, Titokowaru visited. That year, Hazel Riseborough notes, Te Whiti and Tohu declared their independence from almost everyone and everything – from warriors, from kings and queens and from governments. A few years after that, Titokowaru and his people had joined the community, which was now a permanent home to at least 1500 people, but often hosted up to 3000 more at its monthly hui.

Parihaka was different from the non-violent movements that preceded it and from the other pacifist communities that sprung up in its wake – such as the one at Omarama in north Otago or another at Te Kumi near Te Kuiti – because it was so big and so well organised. The village was powerful, and a large part of this power, both then and now, stemmed from the refusal of its leaders or residents, no matter how great the provocation, to act with violence.

And the provocation was intense. In a drawn-out kind of retaliation for the wars of the 1860s, Māori in central Taranaki were needled by a combination of settler disdain, arrogance, fear and awe.

The 1863 New Zealand Settlements Act allowed the government to confiscate the land of iwi it deemed to be in rebellion. In 1865, the government declared it would punish rebellious Taranaki Māori by confiscating a great knuckle of land in the middle of Taranaki, a dart-shaped portion of the province that stretched from Parininihi in the north right down past Waitotara to Whanganui in the south.

The confiscated land was the choicest part of the province. It included the entire coastline, the mountain and parts of all the significant rivers, the Waitara, the Patea and the Waitotara.[28] It encompassed the land of iwi and individuals, such as Parihaka's leaders Te Whiti and Tohu, who had never borne arms against the government in the wars of the 1860s.

The government promised that it would return land in this area to friendly Māori, who would be allowed to live on reserves marked out for them. The rest of the land would be granted to white settlers. The problem was that both the confiscation and the reserves existed only on paper. The government did not occupy all of middle Taranaki, and reserves were never granted, as promised, to non-rebellious Māori. To Māori, then, the confiscation was a fraud. Their land was still theirs.

It is surely no mistake that Tohu and Te Whiti set up Parihaka at a site half-way between the mountain and the sea, right in the middle of the confiscated zone, and Parihaka became the centre of a stronghold of Māori autonomy. Māori controlled access to this part of Taranaki. They erected tollgates on the old beach road along the coast.[29] They held the contracts to deliver post. They stopped the colonial government from doing some of the things it wanted to do, such as erecting a lighthouse at the treacherous point known as 'Cape Egmont', extending the telegraph line and fixing the road.

Parihaka Māori got food from the sea and the land. Crops and livestock were tended on dozens of acres of fenced paddocks. They were industrious, appearing to follow closely the counsel of former Native Minister Donald McLean in 1873: 'Let your future fighting be with the soil ... Return to the land not as strangers but as children of the soil.'[30]

Pronouncements such as these led Māori to believe that the government would not act on the confiscation. Riseborough argues, 'it was well understood that the land between the Waingongoro and the Hangataua rivers, apart from 1400 acres at Opunake, was unavailable for settlement until sufficient reserves had been made for the local people.'[31] This understanding, though, was fragile.

By 1878, Sir George Grey's faltering government was burdened with debt. It needed more money, and it claimed to need more land for the white settlers who continued to arrive. But contemporary scholars, such as Belich and Riseborough, have questioned whether there really was a shortage of land. More important, they suggest, was the government's need to assert power and authority over Taranaki. Riseborough argues that the government could not accept the isolation and autonomy of Parihaka: 'It was a question of mana. Te Whiti and Tohu represented an alternative authority and were thus a reproach to Victorian notions of racial and cultural superiority.'[32]

Parihaka was an alternative centre of power, a challenge to the legitimacy of the settler government. Te Whiti reportedly said: 'I do not care for the parliament that meets in Wellington, my Parliament is at Parihaka.'[33] Te Whiti reportedly saw Parihaka as a third nation within New Zealand, an alternative to the European nation (embodied by the English Queen) and the Māori nation (embodied by the Māori King Tawhiao in the Waikato).[34]

The government would crush this rogue nation and ensure that 'the Queen's law' was paramount there too. Without consulting the leaders at Parihaka, it decided to start surveying all the land north of the Waingongoro River – the fertile Waimate Plains – for sale.

In July 1878, the first surveyors crossed the river into Titokowaru's land. It was almost 10 years since Titokowaru had routed colonial troops in Taranaki before he inexplicably fled inland. Eventually, he had returned to his tribal territory on confiscated land that had never been occupied by white settlers.

Titokowaru, like the Parihaka leaders, saw the confiscation as invalid. The land was theirs and the survey, therefore, was an act of aggression. 'I told Brown, the Commissioner, to take his guns away,' Te Whiti reportedly said to McKay, a government representative who visited him at Parihaka in 1878. 'He said he had none there. He misunderstood me. He thought I meant firearms. The surveyors themselves are the guns; that is, they will cause the guns to be used.'[35]

Surveyors began tentatively enough. Initially, the four sizeable parties did nothing more than cutting traverse lines in the soil. Māori did not hinder the work; but in September, an individual, Hiroki, enacted his own violent revenge against surveyors who reportedly stole his pigs. Hiroki allegedly murdered John McLean, a cook with one of the parties, then fled north to Parihaka where he sought the protection of Te Whiti.

In December 1878, Ngā Ruahine people turned back surveyors when they reached Titokowaru's cultivations at Taikatu Pā. Surveyors continued to cut lines through cultivations, burial grounds and grass-seed crops (for sale to Pākehā), and Ngā Ruahine people disrupted this work by pulling up survey pegs and chopping them up for kindling. Titokowaru suggested the government go to Parihaka to talk about the surveys. When they did not, Titokowaru went himself.

In March 1879, after a hui which Native Minister John Sheehan did not attend, Te Whiti ordered that the surveyors be removed from the plains. Māori quietly packed up every survey camp and used horses and drays to haul the contents back across the Waingongoro River.

Months passed. By late May 1879, when the government was still ignoring Māori requests to be informed about reserves, Te Whiti ordered an unarmed party of twenty men to plough land at Oakura that was being farmed by a William Courteney. The farm was the place where, in 1863, the second Taranaki war had begun.

The surveyors made their marks on the land, and Māori did too. They cut up settler soil with a plough, an action that Te Whiti described as 'ploughing the belly of the government'.[36] Within a few weeks, unarmed Parihaka residents had ploughed settler-occupied confiscated land along the coast between Pukearuhu and Hawera.[37] Māori had made their ploughshares, Riseborough notes, from their swords. Māori ploughed fields but they also 'did violence' to settler lawns – a crime that was perhaps even more serious.

By June 1879, the first ploughmen had been arrested. They were charged at the New Plymouth Resident Magistrate's Court with 'malicious injury, forcible entry and riot'. As the small teams of perhaps a dozen ploughmen were arrested and imprisoned, new teams took their place. By the end of August, the ploughing had stopped. Within three months, 200 men had been arrested.

Settlers were outraged and angry. Many offered to volunteer in any war against Parihaka natives. When the ploughing began, one of the local newspapers, the *Taranaki Herald,* wrote: 'If it should come to fighting then we have very little hesitation in saying the struggle will be a short one, and afterwards this district will never more receive a check to its progress from the same cause.'

Māori, in turn, were resolute, strengthened by their membership of a community that had divine sanction. The jails overflowed. About twenty-five ploughmen were sentenced to two months' hard labour in Dunedin. The rest were sent south to Wellington and imprisoned at Mt Cook, a military barracks that had been hastily reinforced with guards, platforms and palisades.

The men imprisoned in Wellington were never tried. In August, the government rushed through the Māori Prisoners' Trials Act that suspended 'the ordinary course of the law' and allowed that the trial of the prisoners could be postponed indefinitely. This was done, the government said, to ensure the peace and safety of the colony.[38]

In December 1879, the new government, headed by Canterbury farmer John Hall, introduced a double-barrelled bit of legislation to deal with the trouble at Parihaka. The Confiscated Lands Enquiry and the Māori Prisoners' Trials Act promised that a three-person commission (two Pākehā, one Māori) would investigate Māori grievances over confiscated west coast land. Meanwhile, the 'ordinary course of law' would be suspended and the trial of Māori prisoners would be delayed for up to sixty days.[39] A further Prisoners Act, passed in July 1880, allowed for Māori prisoners to be detained 'indefinitely' without trial.

Figure 3. Training camp for colonial volunteers, ca. 1880, black and white original photographic print, photograph by Jane Sawinson, Alexander Turnbull Library, reference number PA1-q-707-41.

In a speech to parliament opposing this Bill, as a document as slippery and slimey as an eel, Māori MP Henare Tomoana said: 'Te Whiti has always said he cares not to fight. His only weapon is his tongue … He has no firearms, no gunpowder. His tongue and his voice are all he uses.'[40] Other MPs also protested about the deep injustice of the Bill, but to no avail. In April 1880, at dawn, Māori prisoners were 'quietly transferred from Mt Cook prison and shipped to gaols in Dunedin and Hokitika'.[41] In the bitter, foreign, southern cold, the men built sea walls and roads and public gardens.

While the government's West coast Commission appeared to be pursuing justice by hearing Māori submissions over confiscated land, the new Native Minister, John Bryce, was increasing the pressure on Parihaka. In January 1880, Bryce ordered the first of several large detachments of armed constabulary to cross the Waingongoro River once again. Ostensibly, the soldiers had come to repair the old beach road. The repairs involved rather more than digging ditches and smoothing gravel. At Manaia, soldiers dug trenches, built blockhouses and erected a thirty-five-foot watch-tower.

'The blockhouses had double walls filled with gravel and carefully constructed loopholes closed by sliding shutters, the stairs up the watch tower were concealed inside the tower, the earthworks were six feet thick and up to twelve feet high above the surrounding ditch. And finally, to enter this singular road repair depot, the workmen crossed a drawbridge,' Parihaka historian Dick Scott writes.[42]

The commission rejected an invitation to come to Parihaka, and the Parihaka leaders would not leave their marae to attend commission hearings at Oeo or Hawera. The only Māori who appeared before the commission were those who believed that the best way to benefit their people was to 'paddle' the canoe of the government, rather than the canoe of Te Whiti and his followers.[43]

The commission was working in one kind of reality, Parihaka in another. In one of its three reports, the commission said: 'As on the Plains, even more so certainly at the doors of Parihaka, the establishment of English homesteads and the fencing and cultivation of the land, will be a guarantee of peace.'[44] The wilful blindness in this statement is ludicrous. As the commission knew only too well, it was precisely the fencing and the cultivation of land (by Māori around Parihaka) and the construction of large English homesteads (by Māori at Parihaka) that was causing all the unrest. Such activity, celebrated in English settlers, would not be sanctioned in Māori. In the miserable twentieth century that unfolded later, Māori in Taranaki and elsewhere would be scolded for not making productive use of their few scraps of remaining land.

Initially, Māori had again asserted their ownership of the plains by welcoming the 'road builders' with lavish gifts of food, drays loaded with chickens, pigs, peaches and potatoes. But as the number of troops increased, such gestures became impossible. Soldiers encircled Parihaka. By April 1880, Bryce had about 600 armed police and labourers building a new New Plymouth to Hawera road towards Parihaka from both the south and the north. Soldiers built a camp and stockade at Rahotu, just south of the village, and another fortification to the north at Pungarehu. They cut through crops and built redoubts, survey camps, parade grounds and rifle ranges.

In June, Bryce ordered his men to make gaps in fences around Parihaka clearings where crops were stored. Te Whiti sent out people to mend them. And so it started. One day, the soldiers would rip a hole in a fence, letting pigs out to destroy tender new crops; the next, Parihaka people would repair the damage.

The first fencers were arrested in July 1880. By September, 216 Parihaka fencers were in jail in the South Island, all sentenced to two years' imprisonment with hard labour. The jails were packed and the government could not afford to make any more arrests. All of Parihaka's fit young men were imprisoned, so it was only the elderly and the young boys who were left to put up slip-rails to 'keep stock out of their wheat paddocks but still allow free passage of the road'.[45] Six-year-olds were among those who repaired fences.

By the end of 1880, it was estimated that Parihaka had cost the government at least a million pounds, a quarter of a million more than the land that it wanted to acquire was worth.[46]

In early 1881, the Governor of New Zealand, Sir Arthur Gordon, wrote to the Secretary of State for the Colonies, Lord Kimberley, informing him that he would be unwilling to extend, yet again, the operation of the Māori Prisoners Trials Act, 1879. The legislation, he argued, was exceptional and set a dangerous example, 'for the precedent thus set may be hereafter far more easily followed with less reason, and its abuse afford a cloak to acts of grave oppression'.[47]

Gordon was Governor of New Zealand at the time of the invasion, and he was opposed to the colonial government's actions. Many historians and writers, including George Rusden, Dick Scott, Hazel Riseborough, Peter Walker and myself owe much to another kind of album, known as 'the Blue Book'. This patchwork of primary source documents – mainly official telegrams and the reports of pro-Māori newspaper correspondents – was put together by Gordon as proof of this 'grave oppression' at Parihaka and presented to the Secretary of State for the Colonies, Lord Kimberley, and the British Parliament in 1882.

Gordon understood that many of the community's actions had a kind of divine sanction. On the origins of the ploughing protests, he noted: 'It is far from improbable that the idea may have been suggested to Te Whiti, who is a most diligent student of the Bible, by the example of the mode employed by Samson to compel the attention of the Philistines to his grievances.'[48]

Māori grievances were noted, to a limited degree, by the West coast Commission which recommended in 1880 that the 400 ploughmen and fencers be released. In April 1881, the first of these men were allowed to return to Parihaka. Many were seriously ill. They had been imprisoned in barbaric conditions, up to thirty squashed in one room, and many had been beaten if they did not work hard enough. The violence of the arrests and imprisonment of Parihaka ploughmen is commemorated secretly in many Māori family names. Children were called Totoi (Toto for short), which means dragging, a reference to the way their forbear was dragged around a paddock 'because he wouldn't stop ploughing'. Other children were named Te Iwi Herehere (literally, imprisoned people), Te Kirihaehae (lashing), Matengaro (lost death or hidden death) and Ngarukeruke (discarded body).[49]

Figure 4. Laurence Aberhart, The Prisoner's Dream, (one panel from sequence of five) Taranaki from Oeo Road, under moonlight, 27–28 September 1999, *190 x 245 mm. Five silver gelatin prints, gifted by the artist to Parihaka Pā. Image courtesy of Laurence Aberhart.*

Figure 5. Laurence Aberhart, The Prisoner's Dream, (two panels from a sequence of five) View #3 Ripapa Island, Lyttelton Harbour, 14 March 2000, *165 x 245 mm, and* View #4 Ripapa Island, Lyttelton Harbour, 12 March 2000, *185 x 245 mm. Five silver gelatin prints, gifted by the artist to Parihaka Pā.*

After the commission's report was released, Bryce introduced legislation that would allow reserves but would also let the government imprison, without trial, anyone who interfered with survey parties or unlawfully fenced or ploughed land.

In mid-1881, Parihaka people had still not been informed about reserves, and the government began to survey, for sale, 15,000 acres of land between Parihaka and the sea. Again, people were sent out to cultivate and plant on ancestral land. It was getting close to the time for spring planting, and Māori continued on as if the hundreds of troops in the four constabulary camps that surrounded them were not there.

For instance, surveyor Hursthouse and W.J. Butler, a secretary to Bryce – both of whom spoke Māori – came upon a man and woman weeding a clearing on the cape. 'They told them their labour was in vain. They admitted they knew that the fence had been previously removed but said it was done foolishly by the Pākehā. They told us to go to Te Whiti and Tohu at Parihaka. The woman said 'Why cannot we cultivate together?'"[50]

Te Whiti and Tohu had not given up, and the government used a supposedly war-like speech given by Te Whiti at the September 1881 hui as an excuse to break up Parihaka by force. Taking advice, the government was told it could charge Te Whiti and Tohu with sedition. On 14 October, the government issued a proclamation ordering Te Whiti and Tohu to accept reserves sketched on an attached map, or they would lose everything. They were also ordered to submit to the authority of the Queen.

This was the first time the Parihaka leaders had seen evidence of any planned reserves. They did not respond to the proclamation. The troops moved closer. Something had to happen.

The ploughing and fencing protests had made headlines around the world. Parihaka had became a celebrated native trouble spot, a story reported in New Zealand, Australia, England and America.

Rightly or wrongly, the climax of this story, the defining moment in Parihaka's history, came on 5 November 1881, when 1589 government soldiers, militia-men, police and volunteers invaded the unfortified village. In an early example of media management, Bryce had declared a 'news blackout'; but several journalists, including S. Croumbie-Brown of the the *Lyttelton Times*, defied these orders and sneaked in.

Their reports describe how soldiers were greeted in what can only be described as an ambiguous fashion – by teams of children singing and dancing (some reports say the children were singing hymns, others that they were doing the haka) and skipping and playing with spinning tops. These children were known as tātarakihi (cicadas or locusts), a buzzing, chirping swarm that would plague

The story so far

the invaders. Many accounts use the childish welcoming party to argue for Parihaka's peaceful intentions; but to me, the children were a sign of scorn for the invaders, and their songs a pantomime of a military tattoo.[51]

Figure 6. Armed constabulary awaiting orders to advance on Parihaka Pā, November 1881, photograph by William Andrews Collis, Alexander Turnbull Library, reference number PA1-q-183-19.

Behind the children were women carrying warm bread baked for the soldiers. They offered no resistance, armed or otherwise. As Te Whiti had said: 'Are we not a small people, merely a handful. Is it likely, then, after all these years of peace, we should take up arms again?'[52]

The soldiers, led by Native Minister John Bryce, who reportedly rode on a prancing white horse, arrested Te Whiti, Tohu, Titokowaru and Hiroki (the man who was a suspect in the murder

49

of the surveyor). The place was then plundered. Over the subsequent weeks, soldiers forcibly dispersed most of the occupants, they raped women, they destroyed dozens of homes and significant community buildings and they stole taonga and livestock.

The evictions were described as 'weeding out' or 'extracting' natives, and soldiers compared their actions with 'drafting sheep' or 'culling ewes'. Not a pleasant process, certainly, but a necessary one.[53] Yet the soldiers found it difficult to disperse everyone because Māori refused to speak, to identify themselves, to step forward when ordered to.

'Time is no object to them,' a frustrated Bryce telegraphed to Rolleston. 'Consider, here are 2000 people sitting still, absolutely declining to give me any indication of where they belong to, or who they belong to, they will sit still where they are and do nothing else. My opponents in this game of chess will not move.'[54] The *New Zealand Times* reinforced Bryce's complaints:

> *The fact that they offer a perfectly passive resistance adds somewhat to the tediousness of their dispersal. It is impossible to use severely coercive measures with people who assume the characteristics of dumb, driven cattle and to compel those in authority to remove them almost bodily from the land they had kept so long and unprofitably encumbered.*[55]

Māori continued to offer no resistance to the invasion. Indeed, the historical record shows that they continued to offer gifts of hospitality, such as sacks of potatoes. On New Year's Day, 1882, Māori cooked soldiers a hangi of geese, pigs and vegetables, things nurtured on the land 'kept so long and unprofitably encumbered', the square miles of 'potato, melon and cabbage fields around Parihaka. They stretch on every side, acres and acres of land show the result of industry and care'.[56]

Te Whiti and Tohu, who had been under a gentlemanly kind of house arrest in the South Island (a punishment that included tours of various sites of settler modernity, such as the Christchurch cathedral and Canterbury museum), were allowed to return home in 1883.[57] Parihaka was a mess. None of the damage caused by the troops had been repaired.

In 1886, Te Whiti was again imprisoned for a new ploughing campaign on confiscated land. He spent six months in jail in Wellington. When he returned, he came with a new ally, a rich Te Āti Awa landowner from the Hutt Valley, Taare Waitara (Charlie Waitara). Together they rebuilt the village using Māori money and predominantly Māori labour. Parihaka became a site of modernity: gas lighting, a bakery, an abbatoir, many fine European style buildings, an inventive hydroponic water supply, a metalled road.

Parihaka residents continued to protest against the confiscation of land. In 1897, for example, ninety-two Māori were arrested for ploughing. Even so, the sting had apparently gone out of the place. In 1907, both leaders died and the village began a rapid decline, not arrested until a campaign of renewal began in the 1970s.

Some historians argue that the 1881 invasion of Parihaka signalled the end of the New Zealand Wars. Others say that this is not true, that the final act of white military aggression against Māori took place in 1916, when the New Zealand Police invaded Tūhoe prophet Rua Kenana's community at Maungapōhatu, in Te Urewera mountains. During the gun-fight that ensued, two Māori were killed and at least two more were wounded. Four police were also injured by the birdshot loaded in Māori guns. A third view, well-articlulated in a recent collection of essays edited by Danny Keenan, would be that the wars have never ended at all – witness, for example, the New Zealand Police's 2007 terror raids on Tame Iti and other Tūhoe in Te Urewera.

All stories require a beginning, a middle and an end; but the trouble with the story of Parihaka, the trouble with any of the hundreds of war stories connected with different iwi around

The Parihaka Album

New Zealand, is the way they resist this satisfying narrative arc. The stories bleed at both ends.

The Parihaka story does not really start with first ships and Bibles and guardian angels. A better beginning, perhaps, would be the one that Te Miringa Hohaia gives in his essay, 'The Foundation Story', written for an exhibition on views of maunga Taranaki. Hohaia relates that in the time before Taranaki arrived, the hapū were Kaahui Maunga. Many things were created by a union between Pukeonaki (an old name for Taranaki) and another mountain, Pouakai. Their offspring included 'mist, cloud, rain and sleet, springs, rivers, rocks, fish, birds, insects, animals and people, plants, trees, wind, thunder and lightning'.[58] With a beginning like this, a mid-point is harder to locate and a conclusion is even more difficult.

Parihaka is many things. It is a historic site, a place where war crimes were committed. It is a living community, impoverished, divided, dynamic. It is also an ideal, a yet-be-achieved utopia. For historians and others who write about the past, the greatest challenge is to resist the lure of the inevitable, the uncanny certainty that can arise about events once enough time has passed: first this, then that, then the next thing, and finally the conclusion.

But the story of Parihaka did not end with the 1881 invasion or the 1907 death of its two leaders. It is difficult, impossible even, to find the place to put the final full stop to the story of this place or the stories of many of Aotearoa New Zealand's other trouble spots. Our world is saturated with the unfinished past, and yet it is so easy to be blind to it all, to pretend that the past is not really there at all and none of these disturbing things really happened.

Open your eyes! Come with me on a road trip into the present past.

---

[1] For more information see Danny Keenan, 'Te Whiti o Rongomai III, Erueti ? – 1907" and Ailsa Smith, 'Tohu Kakahi 1828-1907', both in Claudia Orange, ed, *The Dictionary of New Zealand Biography* online *(DNZB)*, updated 22 June 2007, URL: http://www.dnzb.govt.nz, accessed 7 January 2009.

[2] Gyanendra Pandey, *Remembering Partition,* Cambridge: Cambridge University Press, 2001, 54.

³ Smith, 'Tohu Kakahi', *DNZB*.

⁴ Keenan, 'Te Whiti', *DNZB*.

⁵ 'Takiri te Raukura', a song performed with poi by the Ngati Mutunga poi team from the time of the invasion of Parihaka. Song transcribed and translated by Ngati Mutunga in 'Historical Account' in Deed of Settlement of the historical claims of Ngati Mutunga, signed 31 July 2005 at Urenui Marae, 49-50. Available online at http://www.ots.govt.nz/ accessed 7 January 2009.

⁶ Te Whiti, 1 November 1881, all quotes taken from J. Caselberg, ed., *Māori Is My Name: Historical Māori Writings in Translation,* Dunedin: John McIndoe, 1975, 135-136.

⁷ Bronwyn Elsmore, *Mana from Heaven: A Century of Māori Prophets in New Zealand,* Tauranga: Moana Press, 1989, 238-253.

⁸ Jane McRae, 'Māori Oral Tradition Meets the Book' in P. Griffith, P. Hughes and P. Loney, eds, *A Book in the Hand: Essays on the History of the Book in New Zealand,* Auckland: Auckland University Press, 2000, 6.

⁹ Danny Keenan, 'Aversion to Print? Māori Resistance to the Written Word' in Griffith et al., eds, *A Book in the Hand,* 17-29.

¹⁰ *Taranaki Herald,* 7 June 1879 and 23 August 1879, contained in typed notes at Puke Ariki (PA) museum and library, New Plymouth.

¹¹ George Rusden, *History of New Zealand,* vol III, London: Chapman & Hall, 1883 and Melbourne and Sydney: George Robertson, 1883, 413.

¹² Elsmore, *Mana from Heaven,* 247. This prophecy is also referred to in *Bryce v. Rusden,* Queen's Bench Division, High Court of Justice, London, 1886, 54. Ailsa Smith, 'Ko Tohu Te Matua: The story of Tohu Kakahi', unpublished MA Thesis, University of Canterbury, 1990, also refers to it. Smith writes: 'Te Whiti taught his followers that when the Lord put Pākehā where they belonged – in the sea – then the Māori dead would arise and repossess the country', 78.

¹³ Te Whiti, 18 September 1879, speech translated by Charles Hursthouse, Hursthouse diaries, Puke Ariki museum library.

¹⁴ Hazel Riseborough, 'Parihaka and the Historians', *Parihaka: Te Niho o Te Ati Awa Parihaka Seminars* no.1, 1993.

¹⁵ Tohu Kakahi, 1895. Speech recorded by Te Kaahui Kararehe, Te Mirigina Hohaia, 'Koorero Moo Parihaka', *Art of Passive Resistance,* 59.

¹⁶ Tohu Kakahi, 1895, *Art of Passive Resistance,* 59.

¹⁷ This is the opening portion of 'I Te Raa O Maehe' (On a Day in March): The Ploughman's Song, composed by Tonga Awhikau, a returned ploughman who died in 1957 aged 104. Song transcribed and translated by Hohaia, in *Passive Resistance,* 48.

¹⁸ Keenan, 'Te Whiti', *DNZB*.

¹⁹ For an account of this war, see James Belich, *'I Shall Not Die': Titokowaru's War 1868-*

1869, Wellington: Allen & Unwin and Port Nicholson Press, 1989.

[20] New Zealand Company, Terms Of Purchase For Lands In The Company's Settlements, 30 July 1839. Copy of terms in Wallace Papers, MS Papers 0108-8, Alexander Turnbull Library (ATL).

[21] J H Wallace, 'The First Settlement of Wellington', *Daily Advertiser,* 17 January 1871. Clipping in Wallace Papers, ATL.

[22] For a detailed history of these wars, see R.D. Crosby, *The Musket Wars: A History of Inter-iwi Conflict 1806-1845,* Auckland: Reed, 1999.

[23] James Belich, *Making Peoples,* Honolulu: University of Hawaii Press, 1996, 157.

[24] Crosby, *Musket Wars,* 168-69.

[25] Te Miringa Hohaia, 'The Foundation Story' in *Te Maunga Taranaki: Views of a Mountain,* New Plymouth: Govett-Brewster Art Gallery, 2001, 12-13.

[26] Patricia Limerick, 'Haunted America' in Limerick, *Something in the Soil,* 2000, 33.

[27] Lyndsey Head, 'The Pursuit of Modernity in Māori Society' in Andrew Sharp and Paul McHugh, eds, *Histories, Power & Loss,* Wellington: Bridget Williams Books, 2001, 97.

[28] For a map of the 'original confiscation boundary, see *The Taranaki Report Kaupapa Tuatahi,* Wellington: The Waitangi Tribunal, Legislation Direct, 1996, 2-3.

[29] See 'The Tataraimaka Tollgate', text board, in *Parihaka: The Struggle for Peace,* Puke Ariki, New Plymouth, September 2003-January 2004.

[30] Donald McLean, Third Report of the West coast Commission, Appendices to the Journals of the House of Representatives (AJHR), vol II, 1880, G-2, li.

[31] Riseborough, 'Te Pahuatanga o Parihaka' in Hohaia, ed., *Parihaka: Art of Passive Resistance,* 24.

[32] Riseborough, 'Te Pahuatanga', in *Art of Passive Resistance,* 19.

[33] Dick Scott, *Ask That Mountain: The Story of Parihaka,* Auckland: Reed/Southern Cross, 1975, 79.

[34] Surveyor Charles Hursthouse, diary, 17 September 1879, PA.

[35] Reports to the Royal Commissions – 'The Confiscated Lands Inquiry and Māori Prisoners' Trial Act 1879', AJHR, Vol II, 1880, G-2, 10.

[36] Te Whiti, cited in AJHR, Vol II, 1881, G-7, 7.

[37] Hazel Riseborough, *Days of Darkness: The Government and Parihaka Taranaki 1878-1884,* revised edition, Auckland: Penguin, 2002 (first published 1989) 81.

[38] Riseborough, *Art of Passive Resistance,* 28.

[39] Scott, *Ask That Mountain,* 69.

[40] Henare Tomoana, cited in Rusden, *History of New Zealand* vol III, 321. For a longer

extract from this speech, see John Caselberg, ed., *Māori Is My Name: Historical Māori Writings in Translation,* Dunedin: John McIndoe, 1975, 132-33.

[41] Riseborough, *Days of Darkness,* 104.

[42] Scott, *Ask That Mountain,* 69.

[43] See, for example, the testimony of Katene of Weriweri, West coast Commission proceedings and evidence, 11 February 1880, Hawera, AJHR, vol II, G-2, 5.

[44] West coast Commission third report, AJHR, Vol II G-2, 1880, lviii.

[45] Riseborough, *Art of Passive Resistance,* 33.

[46] Scott, *Ask That Mountain,* 81.

[47] Gordon to Kimberley, 26 February 1881, AJHR 1882, A-8, p. 11. For a similarly critical opinion of events at Parihaka, see Dom Felice Vaggioli, *History of New Zealand and its Inhabitants Vol.2,* translated by John Crockett, Dunedin: Otago University Press, 2000. The Italian original was published in 1897.

[48] Arthur Gordon, report to the Secretary of State for the Colonies, 26 February 1881, AJHR vol II, A-8, 1881, 10.

[49] See Amiria Matoe Rangi, 'Living Legacy' in *Parihaka: Art of Passive Resistance,* 69; 'Nga Ana a Puketai: The Caves', text panel in *Te Iwi Herehere: The Story of Māori Prisoners from Taranaki in Otago 1869-1882,* Dunedin Public Art Gallery 2002; and Ngati Mutunga Deed of Settlement, Historical Account, Office of Treaty Settlements, 7.87, 2004.

[50] Rolleston diary, 1 October 1881, qMS 1716, ATL.

[51] For examples of rather idealised accounts of these children as warriors, see Peter Walker, *Fox Boy,* 278-80 and John Hinchcliff, *Parihaka: A Novel,* Wellington: Steele Roberts, 2004, 300-306.

[52] Te Whiti, undated entry in Rolleston diary, 1881, q MS 1716, ATL.

[53] See Bryce to Rolleston, telegram 14 November 1881, telegram reprinted in Blue Book, *British Parliamentary Papers relating to New Zealand 1870-1882,* Colonies New Zealand (Shannon: Irish University Press, 1968), Native Affairs 1882 [c.3382], vol. 16, 593. 'This is not a pleasant process but we must plod on with it,' Bryce said.

[54] Bryce to Rolleston, telegram 11 November 1881, Blue Book, 588.

[55] *New Zealand Times,* December 1881, 'The Native Question', extract in Blue Book, 541.

[56] *Lyttelton Times,* 7 November 1881, Blue Book, 575.

[57] For an account of this unusual imprisonment/exile, see J P Ward, *Wanderings with the Māori Prophets Te Whiti and Tohu,* Nelson: Bond, Finney & Co, 1883.

[58] Hohaia, 'Foundation', 9.

CHAPTER 3

Illuminations

Road builders made me slow down. The surf highway switched from bitumen to shingle. The hire car, a shiny, gutless tangerine bubble, struggled along as smooth turned to rough. Slow. Stop. Slow. Men in fluoro orange safety vests were laying down a new surface. To the left was Taranaki showing off in the November sunshine, his summit dipped in snow, his lower reaches the same black-grey as you see in the famous bluestone laneways of Melbourne, my current hometown. To the right was the sea, sparkling blue water pounding into black sand and black rocks, the brilliant primary colours of my childhood. Between the mountain and the sea was the punk-rock green of south Taranaki paddocks. Along the road, next to the fences, were ancient cabbage trees crowned with creamy pom-pom blooms and hundreds of dark green spears.

    I had been looking at the names of the places and the roads. All were Māori. They flashed by like a poem: Omata, Oakura, Koru, Tataramika, Okato, Puniho, Warea, Ruakere, Te Kahui. Then one sign was in English. It pointed the way to the Cape Egmont Lighthouse. I had read about this lighthouse, I had thought about it, I had written about it but I had never seen it, not even a picture. Why not take a look? I swung the wheel and the tangerine bubble revved over the mountain of pebbles and sand that divided the two lanes.

Soon everything was quiet. The road was just a single lane. I wound down the windows and smelt cow shit and sunshine. The greenness was overwhelming. There were a few farmhouses, their gates marked by metal rural delivery flags. I saw a kid behind the wheel of a harvester, his happy competent face puzzled up high in the glass cab. Aside from him, there was no one.

I felt excited and a bit scared, the same pleasant, fearful feeling you get before meeting someone notorious for the first time. The road went on and on, the paddocks blazed in the afternoon sunlight, then suddenly there it was. I parked the car, stepped across the cattle stop and the rope and walked up to take a look.

There was a small wooden building on the right, bordered by overgrown red and pink geraniums. It was empty, unlived in. Purple Scotch thistle flowers, just like the ones on the Fleming's rolled oats bag, dotted the grass. Squawking little guinea fowl pecked at my feet. The noise and smell and presence of the sea was everywhere, just as it was when I was little and woke each morning to the sea out the front door and the mountain out the back.

Anyone who has swum in the west coast surf will appreciate the awesome tug of the tide, the way the sea powers in to the land, breaker upon breaker, and the way it greedily sucks itself back out, tugging you, dumping you, sweeping you up and under into a swirl of seaweed and sand, until your head bumps onto the seafloor and your hair makes a curtain between you and the ocean and finally you right yourself, half-dead, half-alive, coughing up snot and sea and little specks of gritty black, unsure of what has happened but happy that it is not happening any more and then another wave comes and sweeps you up again.

And now the sea has washed me up here, in a side road off the surf highway, next to this lighthouse looming up in front of me at the top of a small flight of uneven concrete steps.

Illuminations

Figure 7. 'I saw raised black letters near the red door: Simpson & Co. Pimlico London 1864', Cape Egmont Lighthouse, Cape Egmont, December 2007. Image: Rachel Buchanan.

The lighthouse was big and small all at once. It was in good nick. The twenty-metre-high cast-iron tower gleamed new white, and the padlocked door and skirting were bold blood-red. Between the tower and a water tank, cloud was starting to cover the mountain. I saw raised black letters near the red door: Simpson & Co. Pimlico London 1864.

Three small windows marked the tower's side, peep holes for anyone climbing the spiral staircase inside. There was a walkway at the top, below the glass tower for the fifty-watt lamp that flashes every eight seconds and can be seen nineteen nautical miles out to sea. A man used to tend this light, but these days it's all done by a computer in Wellington.

Maritime New Zealand had put up a sign. It said in part:

> *This light shone for the first time in August 1881. The lighthouse was originally placed on Mana Island north of Wellington in 1865. However, the Mana Island station was closed in 1877 following several shipping accidents and it was believed that this light was being confused with the Pencarrow light at Wellington Heads. In 1881, the tower was dismantled and carried in sections by the steamer* Hinemoa *to Cape Egmont and reassembled on this site.*

I read the sign many times and I touched the tower, and I looked out to the sparkling sea at the edge of the paddocks. I took 365-degree photos on my new digital camera as proof. I knew this lighthouse existed, but until I saw it, I didn't really believe that such a thing was possible: a tower cast in inner London, shipped out to the ends of the earth, put up on a small island near what settlers called Wellington, then taken down again, put on yet another boat, a steamer, sailed up a treacherous coastline in the middle of winter, lifted off the steamer and carried up onto land and reassembled here, on this cape, its upright white back to the silent mountain, its glowing face shining out to sea.

Illuminations

The sign made me angry. I wanted to tell someone why, but I was alone with my camera and my notebook and my silly little hirecar, trespassing, no doubt, on some stranger's farm. I could feel my breath getting faster, that jittery feeling you get just before it's your turn to speak in a school debate. Is it my turn now?

The thing is I couldn't dispute the facts presented on the sign, the longitude and latitude, the heights and the weights, the seconds and the dates; but even so, what the sign said was not really true. The lie of the sign, if I can put it that way, is in what it doesn't say, in the facts it leaves out.

―――

This light did not just happen to shine for the first time in August 1881. There is absolutely no coincidence in the date of this illumination. This light shone then because it was illuminated as part of the military campaign on Parihaka, only seven kilometres up the road from the cape. Soldiers erected this lighthouse, soldiers guarded it once it started to shine. They built the road I had driven on, and they installed the telegraph lines that allowed the men leading the campaign on Parihaka to communicate their thoughts, wishes and fantasies to politicians in Wellington. The road, the telegraph and the lighthouse – speed, safety, secrecy, enlightenment – all these things the soldiers installed, forcibly, in this formerly independent Māori place.

Under the leadership of Te Whiti and Tohu at Parihaka, Māori had resisted the ongoing theft of their land through inventive non-violent protests. By 1880, when soldiers on the *Hinemoa* helped unload the heavy bits and pieces of what would become the Cape Egmont Lighthouse, hundreds of ploughmen and fencers had been arrested and imprisoned, without trial, in the South Island.

In November 1881, three months after the light first shone on the wild sea, the soldiers marched up the track from the lighthouse and joined the force of 1500 volunteers, militia men and colonial troops who invaded Parihaka. The lighthouse is a blockhouse, a relic of war. Why doesn't the sign say so?

For me, after seven years of research and writing on Parihaka at Monash University in Melbourne and later at La Trobe, a doctorate's worth and then some, this sign and the neat, easy, safe, sensible and totally false story it told illuminated many of the contradictions in New Zealand history.[1]

This is not a simple matter of silence. No one can argue now that the Parihaka story has not been told or shared. Like other mythic stories in New Zealand and Australia, the landing at Gallipoli say or the anti-establishment activities of bushranger Ned Kelly, Parihaka has generated an excess of storytelling.

The Parihaka archive is a sensory feast. Pop a CD into the player and listen to its sounds. Fire up the computer and look at its people in digital images stored in the Alexander Turnbull Library's Timeframes database or the photo gallery for the annual peace festival held there each year. Visit the national archives and pour over secret telegrams written during the 1881 invasion. Read the books, visit the exhibition, take in the Treaty settlements, click through the websites, buy the poster, go to the festival.

Yes, Parihaka generates plenty of noise. Yet it is still possible to stand at the foot of this beautiful-ugly lighthouse and to hear only silence. One of this country's most iconic and important historic events is still totally hidden here.

A visitor to the capital, Wellington, can walk from the harbour to parliament and encounter, outside the railway station, a bronze statue of Gandhi, the twentieth century Indian hero of non-violent resistance. The statue was a gift from the nation's Indian community. It was erected in 2007, the 100th anniversary of the deaths of Te Whiti and Tohu. Yet there are no statues in the capital or anywhere else to commemorate their philosophies, struggles and leadership.

The problem, it seems, is not lack of information about Parihaka but lack of integration. History-making is segregated, subject to a kind of intellectual apartheid. Māori stories belong on one side of this artificial divide, Pākehā ones on the other. The work of the Waitangi Tribunal, so vital, important and fascinating in many respects, has created and reinforced this divide. Us and them. Māori and Pākehā. Victim and perpetrator. Colonised and coloniser. Then and now. When these kind of binaries provide the dominant framework for thinking about the past and present in New Zealand, it is difficult to see a lighthouse as a military relic.

The recent extraordinary rise of New Zealand as a film location for all kinds of other people's histories – mythic or otherwise – makes it even harder for Māori and Pākehā, for all of us in New Zealand, to see and hear our own histories, both the short, entangled ones that have unfolded post-contact, and the longer, but equally entangled iwi histories that preceded white settlement.

I witnessed the start of this, Hollywood's colonisation of our landscapes to tell its stories, when I was a cadet reporter at the Queenstown bureau of *The Southland Times* in the mid 1980s. Queenstown was one of the locations for director Ron Howard's 1988 movie, *Willow,* an epic story in which 'a reluctant dwarf must play a critical role in protecting a special baby from an evil queen'. One cold night in Arrowtown, I saw Val Kilmer (who played Madmartigan, a full-sized master swordsman) and other movie stars huddled inside a marquee in the main street. Another day, I rode in a helicopter over Cardrona to see one of the sets, a medieval village for dwarves built on the side of an Otago mountain more commonly known for its easy, wide-open ski runs.

Since then, New Zealand has been the location for many similar historical, fantastical or fictional past worlds: Middle Earth and Mordor (the *Lord of the Rings* trilogy); medieval Japan (*The Last Samurai*); Narnia (*The Lion, the Witch and the Wardrobe* and *Prince Caspian*); World War II Europe (*Bridge to Terabithia*); a Scottish loch (*The Waterhorse*); and a remote tribal African-ish village that is home to a giant gorilla (*King Kong*). During the Rings filming, Wellington became Wellywood. While Samurai was being filmed in Taranaki in 2003, it became Nakiwood. Matamata is now

Hobbiton, a transition that is not, perhaps, entirely unwelcome. In July 2008, I got a letter from my mother with two stamps informing me that the envelope came from 'Narnia New Zealand'.[2]

When so many other narratives are located in our backyards, where is the room for our own stories? What happens if we want to locate our histories in these places? If New Zealand has become a location for the deep pasts of a whole clutch of fantasy beings – all those dwarves and elves and ogres and beasts – what room is there for the real people who were here, for all the different iwi and their stories? Thinking about the more recent past, if history-making continues to be influenced by the segregated Waitangi Tribunal model, how is it possible to make necessary connections between Māori and Pākehā, between then and now, between here (Cape Egmont, New Plymouth, Taranaki, New Zealand) and everywhere else in the world?

Segregated history is weak history. It does not make necessary connections and fails to grasp the many daring possibilities that are offered by seeing how the past and the present connect in people and places.

Why not be daring? We all need adventures, the tickle and thrill of the unexpected, the uncanny, the ghostly, the hilarious, the sad. Aotearoa New Zealand's short and long pasts provide all of this and more. I grew up in New Plymouth, and my childhood was filled with adventure, some good, some bad and some just really crazy. One of the great adventures of my primary-school years was visits to the observatory and planetarium on Marsland Hill.

We would arrive after dark. Dad would park the Holden next to the strange small white building with the white dome on top like a giant egg. We'd bundle in and sit on the bench seats against the walls of the dome. A man would start to talk. The normal lights would go off. We'd point our chins at the ceiling and look at all the hundreds of pinpricks of simulated starlight, our very own Waitomo minus the scary boat trip. Behind the talking, soft music played – John Denver's *Calypso* or a John Williams guitar solo. The lights looked beautiful, but it was difficult to see the pictures and patterns the man was talking about: the crab and the scorpion, Sagittarius and the famous Southern Cross. Then lines would appear, joining up the dots, making the individual spots of light into something bigger, into star signs and constellations. Mysterious smudges and clouds of light made a milky way.

Thus primed, the great moment would arrive. The dome would part and the night would rush in, fierce and cold and black. An enormous telescope would be trained up and out at the darkness. The sky was never as perfect as the pictures on the ceiling of the planetarium, clouds and seasons and possibly even hemispheres interfered with all that, but it was still amazingly interesting, a book we could read, if only for a moment. Then we would all get a chance to press our small faces into the telescope's viewfinder, squinting in towards the lens. The distant, pure brilliance of a star would be exploded into an intimate swirl of gritty, milky vapours, pulsing and heaving, a soup of light and fathomless purpose. Brain spinning, I would pull my cold face back. John Denver and electric planets were less puzzling, more fun.

History is a telescope that can make distant objects and events appear both nearer and larger. It can be turned on the black holes of our private, local and national pasts and futures to find out what has fallen into these silent, dark spaces. What are the untold stories, the overlooked stories, the stories that are just too difficult or weird or obvious to think about?

You don't even need the metaphor of a telescope to explain the way the past can suddenly intrude on the present, a giant blurry pulsing brilliant *thing* that distorts (or corrects) your vision. A little knowledge is all it takes and a willingness to let yourself see a little more in the place you come from.

I had visited the lighthouse on my way back from New Plymouth to Wellington. That visit was strictly business, connected with my work as a historian and my plans for this book. I'd never seen the lighthouse before, and the strong feelings it evoked in me were not connected with any memory I had of that place. The lighthouse is part of my history, but it is not part of my past, that clouded universe of memories generated by our own lives. But earlier that same day, I had decided to spend a couple of hours visiting sites from my childhood. As I once heard Australian historian Rebe Taylor say: Every history starts with the historian.

I come from a big family. I am the oldest of eight kids and the younger sibling of a foster sister and her three sisters. My youngest brother was born a few days before I turned 14. Less than a year later, my family left New Plymouth and moved to Masterton. I've been back to my old home town maybe half a dozen times since then. First these trips were to see school friends, then they were about young adult nostalgia, then they were connected with my research, work that was squeezed in around the demands of babies and young children. The visits are always rushed. There's never enough time to do everything, see everything and everyone. This most recent visit felt luxurious, free of children and obvious deadlines. I decided to spend the morning going to some of the places I had enjoyed as a kid.

The first stop was Marsland Hill, site of the observatory, a carillon and two marble war memorials, one to the wars at home, the other to the wars overseas. As well as coming here at night, we used to visit during the day and have picnics on the hill, spending the afternoon playing monsters among the pōhutukawa trees or the tombstones in the cemetery in the churchyard down below.

Like many hills in New Zealand, this one used to be a pā. A sign explained that it was once Pukaka Pā, built by Taranaki iwi in the eighteenth century on the frontier of territory claimed by Taranaki and Te Āti Awa people. 'In 1760 Te Āti Awa regained possession of the area and Pukaka was abandoned,' the sign said. In 1855, colonial troops lopped the top off the hill and built their barracks on newly level ground. This hill – with its views of the sea and the mountain and all the land in between – changed from a Māori stronghold to a Pākehā one. Colonial troops lived here during the Taranaki wars.

In 1874, when the worst of the fighting was over and New Plymouth was secure enough to attract new settlers again, the barracks became an 'immigration depot' for these people.

I knew this hill had been a pā. I remember Dad telling us that. And I also knew it had been connected with fighting between Māori and Pākehā. I remembered both the memorials, the fountain with the fish at its base and the other much taller one with the soldier on top. I had never really looked at them. The inscriptions were all at adult height anyway. That morning I did.

The fish fountain commemorated New Zealand soldiers who died in the Boer War, and the other one talked about deaths closer to home:

To the honoured memory of the officers and men of Her Majesty's Naval and Military and Colonial Forces and loyal Māoris who fell in action and died in the Māori wars.

1845-47. 1860-71.

Erected by their comrades and fellow countrymen from all parts of the British Empire April 1909.

The memorial was inscribed on all four sides. The side facing the sea listed the Colonial forces that served in the New Zealand Militia. Volunteer loyal Māori came last, two down from volunteer military settlers (many of whom came from Melbourne).

This was one of the first memorials erected to the New Zealand Wars, put up as part of a jingoistic rush inspired by both the Boer War and by the fiftieth anniversary of various battles. An enormous crowd of settlers attended the unveiling; their flat caps and boaters and bowlers and brollies bobbed about under a bunting of large and small flags: England, Ireland, Australia and New Zealand.[3] Veterans paraded by, one of many now forgotten twentieth-century memorial marches and gatherings to commemorate the New Zealand Wars.

The Boer War started the national switch from seeing war as something integral to the settlement of New Zealand to seeing it as something that existed only outside New Zealand, something distant, foreign, tragic and inexplicable that occurred in Turkey or South Africa or France or Egypt or New Caledonia. When I was a kid, these rare memorials to the New Zealand Wars, commemorating only the men who fought for the government, not all the men who died opposing it, were hard to see. As Paul Ashton has observed in regard to Australia, and Annie Coombes in regard to South Africa, monuments and memorials stand out and disappear depending on the time and the context. 'There is nothing in the world as invisible as a monument,' Ashton writes.[4]

The wars at home weren't distant or tragic or inexplicable. They simply didn't happen. There was nothing in the world as invisible as these wars; yet the remains of these battles, some ruined, some functioning, were hidden everywhere in the everyday life of New Zealanders, including my family. Marsland Hill is just one of a mountain range of places in New Zealand towns and cities that were occupied first by Māori, then by Pākehā. Military barracks replaced pā, then hospitals or schools or asylums replaced the barracks. Every culture appreciates a good location, a nice view, a high point from which to conduct important business.

From Marsland Hill, I drove to Pukekura Park. I grew up next door to the park and the racecourse. These public spaces were our playground. Mostly we roamed around here unsupervised by adults, but sometimes, on the weekends, our parents would join us. On those occasions, the family would walk through the park and up to the Bowl of Brooklands, site of an outdoor performance shell and a small zoo. Entry free.

On the morning of my visit, the weather was perfect, sunny, windless and warm. Sprinklers tick-ticked over the cricket pitch. Everything looked film-set bright and clean. To eyes accustomed to Australian drought-brown grass, the terraces that surrounded the pitch were an enviable green. The cricket pavilion and clubrooms had been extended and renovated. I saw Martin Crowe get his first test century here, and I lined up at the pavilion to get his autograph. In another inter-province match, I saw Lance Cairns hit a six so mighty that it landed in the lake behind the pavilion.

It is a commonplace for people to say that they return to the places of their childhood, the school, the home, the playground, the park, and they find everything so much smaller and plainer than what they remember. For me it is the opposite. New Plymouth is bigger, deeper and more beautiful now than it ever was. My childhood home is a mansion. The sea is so much closer and wider, the sand blacker, the grass greener, the trees more luxuriant and twisting, the mountain so perfect that its ongoing existence seems to be some kind of miracle. The symmetry of Pukekura Park is deeply satisfying still. The smaller lake (where Lance Cairns's six is probably still buried) with the coin-operated fountain in the middle leads to the far bigger lake with its red walk bridges, wooden row boats for hire and duckies waiting for bread. All around are trees. A gap in the trees, created by the lake, provides a perfect opening for the mountain to show himself.

I decided to walk up to the Bowl. I passed the dim shed where all the boats were tethered together and came to the soundshell. It had been painted green and was fenced off, so I was unable to relive this particular part of my earlier years by leaping on to the stage and singing 'Waterloo' at full volume. I clambered up the steep hillside where we used to collect conkers and chuck them at each other's heads. Men were fixing steps, painting and hammering and mowing. Elton John was due to sing here before Christmas. Like the cricket ground and the park, the bowl was amazingly polished and well-tended; all the rough edges I remembered from the 1970s – the open stage, the manky pond, the flaking paint – were gone.

Panting after the climb, I could see that the zoo was still there. Adults pushed children on swings and goats nibbled the grass. As a child, I loved the zoo, especially the vivacious monkeys, but the best part of a walk to the Bowl was playing in the park next door. We would burst through the zoo gates, run onto a lawn dotted with enormous English trees and head for the stone chimney. I would grab onto the metal bar suspended between the two moss-covered stone walls, run my feet up the stones, hook them over the bar and hang upside down just like a monkey. After that, I'd climb onto the top of the chimney and see if there was any new graffiti up there.

The chimney was still there as I remembered it. I went over for a look. As a kid I had never considered what this chimney might have been part of or how the original structure had been destroyed. It was just really old and old buildings were like old people. Bits broke off or broke down and then they just died or disappeared.

Of course the home that the fireplace was once part of didn't just happen to disappear, just as the lighthouse didn't just happen to be illuminated. There was a sign here too: 'During the Māori war of 1860, the original Brooklands home of Captain King was burnt to the ground. This fireplace is all that remains of the original Brooklands homestead.' I don't know when that sign went up. I certainly never noticed it as a youngster. Who burnt the house down? What happened to the occupants? What happened to the people who did the burning? The Māori war? Weren't other people involved too?

I looked around at the herbaceous borders and the English trees and the soft, inviting lawn. A group of women pushed prams into the zoo. Children screamed. A memorial stone by the gate said: 'BROOKLANDS. The gift to New Plymouth of Newton King esq.' Just like the lighthouse sign, this one is true and not true. No connections are made, for instance, between this plaque and the one only fifty metres away, next to the ruined fireplace.

One thing the sign doesn't say is: To the victors the spoils. History decides who will win the right to be generous, who will be able to offer apologies and settlements and reparations and partnerships. But if you have taken something, is it yours to give? As a backpacker, I had visited the sites of world famous battles waged in my century and many centuries before – Gallipoli in Turkey, Culloden in the Scottish Highlands – yet until that morning, I had never seen the battleground in my own backyard.

Now, months later, when I read over this last paragraph, I am shocked at what I felt that day and at what I have written here. I get angry and then bored when settlers (in either New Zealand or Australia) profess ignorance, horror and surprise when they 'suddenly' learn (yet again) the 'truth' about historical dispossession and violence. I understand what Australian historian Chris Healy meant when he wrote in his book *Forgetting Aborigines* that remembering 'might be a way of non-indigenous Australians avoiding the arrogance of consciousness, the bad faith of asking Why weren't we told?, the fleeting outrage of discovering injustice and the quick-drying tears of indignation. Remembering a different kind of history-in-the-present can, I believe, help us fashion a more ethical future.'[5]

I know all these arguments, yet here I am doing the same old thing, writing about the things I didn't see in my own place. Shouldn't I know better? Maybe I am being too hard on myself. It takes time and effort to know and see and hear and feel something, to undo the many decades of effort that have been put into not knowing, not seeing, not hearing, not feeling.

As Elizabeth Jelin has observed, in relation to Argentina's military junta in the 1970s, societies have to work hard to forget, they have to decide not to pass on stories from one generation to the next, not to acknowledge a person or event as meaningful. But forgetting is not a void or a vacuum. It is the 'presence of an absence', 'the representation of what was once there and no longer is, the representation of something that has been erased, silenced or denied'.[6]

Touch these tender, hidden spots and surprising stories emerge. Where do you come from? What are your blind-spots? What are the stories behind your childhood places?[7]

The Parihaka Album

[1] See Rachel Buchanan, 'Village of Peace, Village of War: Parihaka Stories 1881-2004', unpublished PhD thesis, Monash University, 2005.

[2] For an exploration of these ideas, see Rachel Buchanan, 'The Powder Room', *Meanjin* vol 63, no 1, 2004, 54-59. For an analysis of 'the impact of the construction, commodification and virtualisation of the New Zealand landscape', see Thierry Jutel, 'Lord of the Rings: Landscape, Transformation, and the Geography of the Virtual', in Claudia Bell and Steve Matthewman, eds, *Cultural Studies in Aotearoa New Zealand: Identity, Space and Place,* Melbourne: Oxford, 2004.

[3] See Chris MacLean and Jock Phillips, *The Sorrow & the Pride: New Zealand War Memorials,* Wellington: Historical Branch, Department of Internal Affairs, 1990, 27-31.

[4] Paul Ashton, 'The Past in the Present: Public History and the City of Sydney', in Tim Murray, ed, *Exploring the Modern City: Recent Approaches to Urban Archaeology,* Melbourne: Historic Places New South Wales and La Trobe University, 2003, 8.

[5] Chris Healy, *Forgetting Aborigines,* Sydney: UNSW Press, 2008, 63-64.

[6] Elizabeth Jelin and Susan Kaufmann, 'Layers of Memories: Twenty Years After in Argentina', in T.G. Ashplant, Graham Dawson and Michael Roper, eds, *The Politics of War and Commemoration,* London and New York: Routledge, 2000, 106.

[7] Two other books have influenced my approach to this chapter. They are: Kate Fielding and Eve Vincent, eds, *Cover Your Tracks: Creative Histories by Young Victorians,* Fitzroy: Express Media 2001, and Kate Grenville, *Searching for the Secret River: A Writing Memoir,* Melbourne: Text, 2006.

CHAPTER 4

Road, telegraph, lighthouse

One of the most striking aspects of the Parihaka story is the way that both Māori and Pākehā were very aware of themselves as historical actors. The things they said and did and sang show that they were acutely sensitive to the way history – meaning accounts of their actions to be told in the future – would judge them.

Both Te Whiti and Tohu linked themselves with the biblical 'prince of peace', and both of them wanted to make a break with Taranaki's undoubtedly violent recent past and claim the mantle of non-violent peacemakers in the eyes of their contemporaries and in the eyes of generations to come.

Settlers wanted to claim this title too. They also wanted to be the princes, or perhaps the kings, of peace, the ones who would solve the west coast difficulty without any bloodshed, turning Parihaka into a re-run of the bloodless signing of the Treaty of Waitangi forty-one years earlier, creating a new foundational moment that would erase all the violence that had occurred in between.

The construction of utilities in Taranaki was one way to do this. The colonial government believed that ongoing Māori opposition to utilities was hampering the district's progress. The forceful completion of essential public works would be a show of European might against Māori, but it would also maintain the veneer of peace and reason that was so important to settlers and to the narrative of harmonious, just race relations that they were so eager to establish.

In its third report of August 1880, the West coast Commission said:

> Your excellency will perhaps remember that when the survey of the Waimate Plains was about to be commenced it was agreed at Parihaka that the lighthouse ought not to be opposed, though the site will hardly be six miles from Te Whiti's village. A very great political effect would now be produced upon the Natives throughout the coast if they saw the three things for which the government have so long contended, being done together; the road, the telegraph line, and the lighthouse.[1]

The road, the telegraph and the lighthouse would inscribe European modernity on Māori time and space. They provided the colonial government with powerful literal and symbolic signs of their mastery of this once staunchly Māori locality. 'I pushed the road within two miles of Parihaka,' Native Minister John Bryce said. 'In spite of the natives, I went where I liked. I showed I was the superior force. I did not care for their affront or objection.'[2] Installing the utilities was a potent step in the government's mission to gain control of Māori in central Taranaki, to colonise them, to create one law – British law – in a province where there had been two. Roads and lighthouses were gifts of modernity but they were barbed and loaded offerings. Once constructed, they could be pointed to as signs of 'European settlement', a settlement that has two meanings: European inhabitation of a particular location and European settlement of native difficulties through the installation of the structures of modern civilisation.

In reality, neither Māori nor Pākehā saw the construction of utilities as quite so beneficent. Beneath its civilising veneer, the extract from the West coast Commission contains a barely masked aggression, an aggression that is revealed by the responses Māori had long had to the construction of roads in other parts of the North Island and by the way settlers themselves understood the nature of their work. Roads, like railways, were pathways for the military. They established the military frontier. In 1861, the government started to build the Great South Road from Auckland to Waikato. This construction was a forerunner to the invasion of that hitherto independent Māori province, and Māori protested against it by sitting in the path of surveyors.[3]

Surveyors, too, understood the nature of their task. In 1901, when surveyor-general Stephenson Percy Smith retired, George Sturtevant presented him with a large watercolour testimonial to his life's work. One segment depicted labourers and surveyors cutting a new road through the bush. The caption reads: 'The first attack, Road-making'.[4] It may have been referring to the large trees being felled to clear a path for the road, but it is hard not to find a more deadly meaning in this war-like metaphor, because in the campaign to destroy Parihaka, road-making was, indeed, the first attack. The second attack was the construction of a web of telegraph lines at military barracks, the third the erection of a lighthouse. The final attack, the invasion of Parihaka, was made possible by these earlier acts of violence.

Illustrator Sturtevant's pointed reference to the 'attack' that road-making represented is rare. In general, settlers did not describe the construction of roads and other utilities as explicitly violent activities. Even today, such a description is unusual. In her insightful and comprehensive political history of Taranaki, Hazel Riseborough uses the metaphor of the 'road to Parihaka' to describe the chain of events that led to the invasion of the settlement. This road had 'begun with a failure to allot reserves and was continued in a determination to teach Māori who was master,' Riseborough writes. 'But Te Whiti would not oblige the ministry either by giving in or resisting. Baffled and uncomprehending, the government carried on their injustice to the *point of violence* ...'[5] But building the actual road to Parihaka was a violent act in itself, and the coast road is as much a material remain of war as the redoubts, blockhouses or grass-covered Māori fortifications that have been excavated, since the 1970s, on the Taranaki military frontier.

The road to non-violence

It is important to link the concept of violence with the road if we are to begin to destabilise the pervasiveness of the 'non-violent' label that settlers used to describe their actions at Parihaka and elsewhere in New Zealand, a nation that has long prided itself on its fair treatment of natives. Māori were violent in Taranaki in the wars of the 1860s, but their eventual non-violence was too easily co-opted by their opponents. The Pākehā soldiers and their Māori allies who invaded the village were heavily armed, but they did not fire a single shot. No one died there. The body count was zero. Parihaka was a village of peace, surrounded by blockhouses and redoubts. It was a war zone without a war. The colonial government was proud of its bloodless settlement of the 'Native difficulty' on the coast.[6] 'Parihaka was taken without a struggle and its occupation by the Colonial forces was a peaceful victory,' the *Taranaki Herald* reported in its Special at the Front.[7]

In the aftermath of the supposedly peaceful victory, the government was proud of the way that the Parihaka leaders, Te Whiti and Tohu, were treated during their exile and imprisonment in the South Island in 1882 and 1883. They were treated like gentlemen. Even though this gentlemen's confinement appeared to have had little impact on bringing Te Whiti and Tohu into 'a proper frame of mind', the government could have a clear conscience about its actions. The men's gaoler, John Ward, wrote: 'We shall know as humane men and British colonists that no effort of ours was spared to vindicate the laws of justice and humanity in dealing with the prophets of Parihaka.'[8] Minister Bryce echoed these sentiments in a London court when he denied that Te Whiti and Tohu were prisoners: 'They were treated more as guests than as prisoners … while travelling they were treated with the utmost kindness and consideration.'[9]

Linking the construction of roads and other utilities with more obvious acts of war – such as bombardment or shooting – is one way of exposing the violence that Arjun Appadurai argues is implicit in every foundational ritual, whether local or national.[10]

To settle Taranaki, to produce the Taranaki that exists today, the government had to assert the full range of its bureaucratic, military and domestic power over Māori. The 'trouble on the plains' could be ended only by the erasure of independent and stubbornly Māori forms of life there. But this erasure was to be represented as an act not of war, but of peace. In its third report, the West coast Commission said: 'As on the Plains, even more so certainly at the doors of Parihaka, the establishment of English homesteads and the fencing and cultivation of the land, will be a guarantee of peace.'

Eyewitness reports written by soldier road-builders reinforce the commission's wilful blindness to Māori farming and homes. By April 1880, 600 armed police and labourers (both Pākehā and Māori) had crossed the Waiweranui River (also known as Stony River) and were surveying and building a road south towards Parihaka only a few miles away.

The soldiers imagined the town as a sizeable block in the path of the progress. Private James Ledger, a volunteer soldier from Timaru, sketched the 'thickly-populated pa' of Parihaka, depicting a cemetery, a bank, a marae, fenced roads, bullock carts and a 'European house erected to receive the Governor had he wished to visit Te Whiti'.[11] The pā, he wrote, 'stood right in the way of the main road marked out to join Wellington and New Plymouth; and was one of the causes of trouble with the Natives of the West coast'. The soldiers drove their road aggressively so it ran straight through Māori places. The provocation was extreme. The West coast Commission noted that: 'When the road approached Titokowaru's clearings, his grass paddocks and his village, the surveyor, for engineering reasons that seem to us were inadequate, insisted on taking his road line in a direction where it cut into a large fenced enclosure sown with English cocksfoot grass, a yearly source of income.'[12]

Titokowaru's land was south of Parihaka. North of the village, similar incursions took place. Surveyor Stuart Newall had crossed the Waiweranui with the soldiers. In his delicate hand, Newall describes coming across 'new cultivations', 'old cultivations', 'extensive cultivations', 'Māori flagstaffs', 'Te Whiti's clearing', 'dray tracks' and orchards of peach and cherry trees.[13] Yet still the troops and the road-builders advanced. Telegraph poles were erected next to abandoned Māori villages. Military force replaced Māori landmarks with Pākehā ones. The work of the soldiers was more than symbolic though. They were literally destroying Māori food sources.[14]

Newall's notebook plots the flashpoints. Every time Māori 'fenced across a road', it was in an area of what Newall described as 'extensive cultivations'. Of a location near Pungarehu, he writes: 'Where the natives persisted so long in fencing across the road and where most of the arrests were made in 1880.' Of a site a little closer to Parihaka, a place Newall describes as Te Whiti's clearing, troops arrested a procession of Māori holding green branches. The first group of Māori fencers were arrested on 19 July 1880 near the Waitotara footbridge, an area that Newall had noted contained 'extensive cultivations'. Te Whetu, sometimes described as Te Whiti's lieutenant, was among them.[15] This land around Parihaka was the site of ancient cultivations. It was, Te Whiti told then Native Minister William Rolleston, the home of the 'cultivations of his ancestors'.[16] Rolleston made detailed notes of this meeting, which took place less than a month before the village was invaded. In the meeting, Te Whiti referred to the land as a garment – a cloak, a hat, a blanket – that was being torn apart by government policy, leaving Māori poorly clad.

Despite Te Whiti's concerns, the meeting put Rolleston at ease. In a confidential telegram to fellow minister Harry Atkinson, Rolleston said: 'I am glad to have seen Te Whiti – it relieves my mind as to his attitude and enables us to go to work with a good conscience of having done our best to settle differences.'[17] In the work of settlement, a good conscience was essential for Europeans. As the *Times* of London had reported, 'The Māori, like every primitive race, is doomed to gradual extinction … But though the result is inevitable it is our manifest duty to see that the process is kindly and just.'[18] These sentiments were challenged by thriving settlements such as Parihaka, a place characterised by rapid expansion rather than gradual extinction.

Swift words

As the soldiers destroyed Parihaka crops and set up military camps in their place, they also installed another technology – the telegraph – a technology that allowed men like Rolleston to make swift, secret reports on their activities. Like roads, telegraph lines were part of the equipment of the military. After the Waikato had been invaded by imperial troops in the 1860s, the first telegraph lines in the North Island were built between Auckland and the Waikato. In 1872, the colonial government paid the British army 2276 pounds for the line and planned to incorporate it into the North Island main trunk line down the centre of the island.[19]

The telegraph line on the west coast ran from Wellington to Whanganui, but in 1872, Māori from Taranaki prevented it from going any further than Opunake. Telegraph historian Frank Watters writes that when Māori in Taranaki discovered 'that the lines brought soldiers, they prevented their erection from Stony River, just south of Okato to Oanui, north of Opunake, a distance of 16 miles. However, a Māori runner faithful to the Queen carried telegraphic messages between the two points until peace came to the coast and the line was completed.' Māori had held the contracts to carry postal mail in Taranaki and so strong was Māori control of what was known as 'the old beach road' that 'scarcely a white man dared to pass up and down the coast'.[20] By 1876, when an alternative telegraph line was set up east of Mount Taranaki (Egmont), Māori control was aggressively being whittled away. The colonial government was extending its reach into Māori territory and out into the wider world. In 1876, New Zealand was also linked to Australia (and so on to England and Europe) by a telegraph line.

The telegraph was a European mechanism for mastering time and information. By the nineteenth century, Watters writes, the word telegraph had become synonymous with speed. Newspapers and coaches used 'telegraph' in their titles to denote the swiftness with which they delivered goods and information. Telegraphs had already been used in the military campaign against Māori from Waikato and they were also used in Taranaki to relay everything from secret political information – some of the telegrams are in code – to requests for better wheelbarrows or building supplies such as drain pipes, gravel, tōtara bridge timber and stormwater pipes or reports on the purchase of tents for soldiers.[21] Between 1879 and 1881, the telegraph and the military advanced together, surrounding Parihaka. Offices were opened in Pungarehu, Rahotu, Cape Egmont, Oeo, Pukehinau and Waihi. None of these offices were open to the public. They were all set up in armed constabulary camps and as the troops advanced closer to Parihaka, the telegraph offices closed behind them.

The office at Pungarehu, the village closest to Parihaka, opened in 1880 and closed on 30 November 1881, a few weeks after Parihaka had been occupied. The office at the Cape Egmont Lighthouse opened in October 1881 and closed in January 1882.[22] On 17 November, less than two weeks after Parihaka had been invaded, Bryce issued orders that a telegraph wire was to be run right up to the township. Newspaper correspondents were delighted because the Parihaka wire would save them from running to Pungarehu to send their daily reports from the front. The telegraph offices were tools of warfare and once the village had been invaded – and a telegraph office had been installed there – they were no longer necessary. The overwhelming profusion of telegraphs that were tapped out from these military posts in 1880 and 1881 suggest that the surveyors, soldiers and politicians who sent them were conveying more than mere military information.

Telegraphs were a weapon that gave European forces and their Māori allies an edge over their Māori opponents. They were used to convey strategic information and requests swiftly and secretly. But reading these telegraphs, something else is evident. The senders display a kind of childish glee about the technology itself and by the things this technology represented for them: a mastery of time and space, an all-encompassing sense of advancement.[23] The telegraph was a disembodied form of communication and advancement. There was no longer any need to rely on a Māori runner to convey messages from one point to another around the increasingly settled North Island. Words could fly, unheard and unseen, through the air. Space and time had been shrunk to fit sleek and often brutal new dimensions of a white New Zealand, a nation seeking to assert itself after it had been 'abandoned' by England when imperial troops withdrew in the late 1860s.

The installation of the telegraph lines was an example of the peaceful and resourceful nature of the orphaned New Zealand colonists. A quiet pride in the colony's achievements towards building modernity is reflected in a public works statement from 1890. The statement, which ends with a map of the dense star-burst of telegraph and telephone lines that had by then been established all over Taranaki, reads: 'At the critical stage in the history of New Zealand, when the colony was left by the Mother-country with a Māori war on its hands, the colonists adapted what was called a "self-reliant policy" and successfully fought their own battles. In the more peaceful operations of colonisation we may well follow their example, and meet the elements of further settlement from our own resources.'[24]

The light of civilisation

The road and the telegraph, two of the 'more peaceful operations of colonisation', rapidly increased European mastery of the land.[25] After Parihaka had been invaded, Bryce excitedly reported to Rolleston his plans to run a telegraph wire up to the Parihaka armed constabulary camp. He also promised that within a week, the road would be quickly run in two miles or so landward of Parihaka and out to Parapara. 'I think we have now come to a distinct stage of the settlement of the West coast difficulty and I am intensely grateful it has been reached without bloodshed, which could not have been avoided by any other means than that we have employed,' Bryce telegraphed Rolleston.[26]

The lighthouse is the final utility in the trinity that formed the beginnings of the Parihaka campaign. Captain Robert Johnson, the chief of New Zealand's Marine Board, had first recommended a lighthouse at Cape Egmont (the site 'hardly six miles from Te Whiti's village') in 1861. The black sand beaches of Taranaki were littered with dozens of wrecks, settler ships that had been dashed on the rocks in wild west coast winds. The first documented European ship to sink on Taranaki shores was the *Adventure,* captained by whalers John Love and Richard [Dicky] Barrett. In 1828, local Māori helped whalers push the stranded boat back into the sea, then proceeded to help themselves to the ship's cargo and stores. During the unloading, a cask of pork fell through the bottom and the boat sank. The stranded Love and Barrett ended up marrying 'high-caste Ngati Te Whiti women' and, with their help, set up a whaling station at Nga Motu, the place that would soon be renamed New Plymouth.[27]

The fate of the *Adventure* set the pattern for subsequent wrecks in Taranaki. Boats, passengers and freight became Māori property, and any Europeans on board depended on Māori goodwill for their survival. In late April 1834, the barque *Harriet* was shipwrecked at Cape Egmont. All those on board – the twenty-three seamen, the whaling gang, captain John Guard, his wife Elizabeth and their two children – got off alive. A few days later, a small party of Māori appeared and two seamen deserted and joined them. A week later 200 Māori, armed with muskets, tomahawks and spears, attacked the survivors and killed 10 of them. Mrs Guard and her children were spared, but were held by the Māori, and the rest of the party escaped. Mr Guard got to Sydney and the governor dispatched two ships, one carrying sixty-three troops from the Queen's Own Regiment, to Taranaki to rescue the *Harriet* survivors.[28] By September 1834, the soldiers had arrived, 'hostilities broke out' and the survivors were rescued. This was the first armed warfare between Māori and Europeans in Taranaki.

The wreckings continued. In 1841, the *Amelia Thompson* left Plymouth for 'New' Plymouth, carrying settlers from Devon and Cornwall, enticed southwards by the promises of the Plymouth Company. The settlers' freight and luggage were carried on another ship, the schooner *Regina,* but a gale drove it ashore 'near the landing place, on a reef below the northern end of Queen Street. The schooner was wedged in between two rocks and deeply embedded in sand, the sea breaking over her as high as the masts.' It was a total wreck. In the next year alone, 1841, thirteen ships were wrecked along New Zealand coasts.

Settlers had erected the first coastal beacon in New Zealand in 1842 at Pencarrow Head, the entrance to Wellington Harbour. In 1861, when Marine Board head Captain Johnson proposed the lighthouse at Cape Egmont and twelve other treacherous locations, the war between Māori from Taranaki and the British Crown thwarted any construction plans there. Then on 1 September 1862, another ship, the inter-colonial steamer *Lord Worsley,* was wrecked just a few miles south of the cape. It was one of twenty-six boats wrecked in New Zealand that year, but Ingram reports that it 'claimed particular attention owing to the fact that her complement were in imminent danger of massacre by the hostile Taranaki Māoris'.[29]

In 1862, this coast was Māori territory. Settlers from New Plymouth tried, unsuccessfully, to pay a toll and reach the scene of the *Lord Worsley* wreck. A Māori messenger had spread the news in a besieged New Plymouth that the sixty passengers had been saved and were under the protection of Wiremu Kingi Matakatea, a local chief and ally of Te Whiti. Warea residents, including Te Whiti and Tohu, provided horses and drays to take the survivors and all their luggage to New Plymouth, an incident that is often used as evidence of the beginnings of the men's conversion to passive resistance.[30]

'Māoris behaved very well to the unfortunate, shipwrecked people. All private property was respected and passengers were permitted to removed their luggage … every kindness which was in their power to bestow was freely shown,' Ingram writes. The power to bestow kindness and to offer (or withhold) hospitality and protection was one of Māoridom's most potent weapons in the battle for continued possession of Taranaki. In 1862, when white people were still at their mercy, this power was great indeed.

In 1880, a detachment of troops marched to Cape Egmont and supervised the unloading of the *Hinemoa*. It carried a ninety-tonne iron tower and lantern – built in Britain in 1864 – from the dismantled Mana Island light in Wellington.[31] By then, Māori protection and hospitality was no longer so necessary for vulnerable European sea or land travellers. Māori had not agreed to surrender any land for the lighthouse, but their opposition was overridden by force. The armed constabulary fenced off paddocks on the cape that were old clearings where melon and sweetcorn grew. These fences were removed and Māori continued to clear the land in preparation for planting.

Under the guard of the armed constabulary, the 'Egmont light' first appeared over the sea on 1 August 1881. It illuminated a stretch of coastline that owed its name to Captain Cook, who in 1770 sailed round the cape, saw the mountain Taranaki and named it Egmont, after the man who was then Lord of the British Admiralty. Europeans had named the cape; now they would flood it with light. Ross writes of the 1881 illumination: 'For some time after, the detachment remained on the site to protect the light and its keepers, but since those troublesome days Egmont has continued to peacefully serve its purpose.'[32]

Europeans brought the 'light' to Taranaki, a province 'troubled' by the presence of independent Māoridom at Parihaka. Europeans introduced the light (of God, civilisation, safety, progress, order and, above all else, peace) and they were the keepers of this light too. Some settlers believed that Māori fanaticism had kept that race in the dark but, with the installation of the road, the telegraph and the lighthouse, and the subsequent invasion of Parihaka and dispersal of its residents, Māori had been enlightened. The 'spell' cast by Te Whiti and Tohu would be broken.[33] A new light of rationality and modernity had dawned on Taranaki, and the bringers and keepers of this light were prepared to defend their accomplishment vigorously.[33]

On 7 November 1881, two days after the village had been invaded, journalist and politician Edward Wakefield telegraphed William Rolleston to congratulate the former Native Minister on the way he and Bryce had overcome the 'blasted fellows' at Parihaka. 'I don't want to dictate but since you have gone so far I think you might as well make the most of the opportunity and smash the native difficulty altogether.'[34]

On 22 November, Bryce excitedly reported his plans for a telegraph line to be run right up to Parihaka and for a road to be run through the bush behind the village. 'I think we have now come to a distinct stage of the settlement of the West coast difficulty and I am intensely grateful it has been reached without bloodshed, which could not have been avoided by any other means than that we have employed,' he said.[35]

Later, Bryce would boast: 'I made the roads and I made them without the consent of Māori; I completed the telegraph line which Te Whiti resented; I caused the lighthouse to begin, to which Te Whiti had refused his consent … This is a small country, too small to hold two separate authorities … I must say the authority of law shall, from this time forth, prevail at Parihaka as well as elsewhere.'[36]

After the invasion, the government knew that the 1544 residents it had evicted could face starvation because they were returning to degraded kainga where no crops had been planted. The government offered these people rations. They were given passes to allow them to return to Parihaka with bullock carts to collect potatoes and other crops. Bryce also, rather cruelly, offered evicted residents work building roads.

The ark of Parihaka had not saved these people from the flood of colonisation, but Māori who had chosen to sail in the canoe of the government were not safe either. In the weeks that followed the march on Parihaka, dozens of other Māori homes and settlements around Taranaki were also invaded, searched and looted. As Lyndsay Head has eloquently put it, it did not matter whether Māori were neutrals, loyals or rebels, because 'colonial predation ... fell, like biblical rain, on all alike'.[37]

Many of the Māori from Taranaki who had not joined the community at Parihaka had fought for the government against other Māori during the 1860s. In 1875, for instance, Donald McLean had given Motu, of Puneho near Okato, a Union Jack as a reward for his loyalty. After the invasion of Parihaka, Motu's settlement was also raided. Twenty-four guns, mostly fowling pieces, were taken. After the guns had been taken, Motu had told an interpreter: 'I have another kind of gun in the big house [rununga]'. Then he threw the Union Jack at the feet of the commanding officer and shouted, 'You'd better take that too!'[38] He told the *Lyttelton Times* reporter Croumbie-Brown that once he had been given the flag, the Queen had entered his house 'and since then good has been taught under her protection, adding with intense scorn, "and now this is the treatment I get for my loyalty".' The actions of the government transformed the Union Jack from a symbol of authority and justice into a symbol of violence, a flag for the gun.

Other men who had nothing to do with Parihaka were also punished. Ramaha, who lived north of Waitara, had three guns taken and said 'he had never seen Te Whiti and had no sympathy for him'. Epiha had a family heirloom, a tiki, taken and had reported the theft to the Waitara police. Three of Tom Preston's guns were stolen and everything in his whare was tossed about and smashed. He had been loyal but now declared he must 'give up the government'. He said the soldiers might as well burn his whare over his head and be done with it. George Kukapa wept as he recounted the pillage he had suffered. 'He was one of those who fought for us against the rebels and had given good service. Governor Browne had sent him a gun telling him to hand it down to his son or heir. It was a reward for his valour and he prized it. This had been taken from him and his whare damaged.'[39]

Kukapa, Preston, Epiha and Motu had remained in their homes for the duration of the west coast difficulty. Further, they had demonstrated their loyalty to the government by either remaining neutral during the fighting of the 1860s or by fighting for the government. Yet their raft sank too.

Scarcity and excess

This excessive settler response to any kind of Māori presence in Taranaki reveals just how unsettling the community at Parihaka had become. The prophetic utterances of the prophets, and the disciplined protests of their followers, were described as examples of fanaticism.

The word fanatic – that is, people 'filled with excessive and mistaken enthusiasm, especially in religion' – was constantly invoked in connection with Parihaka. One element of fanaticism, its excessive nature, was particularly potent. Māori who lived at Parihaka were believed to have had excessive religious beliefs, and excessive numbers of them occupied an excessive amount of land. Further, Māori consumption of food, clothing and equipment was excessive.

Excess is a strong theme in the Proclamation issued to residents of Parihaka fourteen days before the settlement was invaded. The Proclamation warned Māori either to accept the 25,000 acres comprising 'the Parihaka block', which the government had set aside for Parihaka people, or to expect to suffer, innocent and guilty alike. All pretence at road-building as a peaceful, beneficial activity was abandoned. The proclamation said: 'Should the Natives be so infatuated as to disregard this warning, the Government will proceed to make roads throughout The Parihaka Block and to lay off lands for European occupation inland of the main road.[40]

The document distils many settler ideas about Parihaka. It positions Europeans as the group seeking peace on the west coast, and Māori as the ones preventing its attainment. Te Whiti, in particular, was stopping any progress towards a peaceful settlement of the district and his *words* were depriving Māori of their land. When Te Whiti and Tohu were arrested in November 1881, they were charged with using 'seditious language', language that undermined the authority of the state. Māori should forget the words of Te Whiti and listen to the 'word of the Government'. If they failed to heed this warning, the proclamation asked, 'who can distinguish between those who desire peace and those whose work leads to disaster?'

Māori were accused of being wasteful of their own resources. By their protests, they had forced the government to 'incur great expense' – to waste money – on Armed Constabulary. They were improvident, communal, neglectful and unsettled. Unsettlement encompassed both the mental and physical condition of Māori. They had unsettled minds and they were unsettled in their homes, constantly leaving their places of residence to journey to Parihaka. The Proclamation said:

> *Month after month, Natives are assembled from a distance. They are making themselves poor by contributing to useless expenditure upon feasts which take them away from their own homes; and they are led to neglect the cultivation of their own lands. At these meetings Te Whiti has spoken in such a way as to turn aside the people from listening to the proposals of the Government, and the sound of his voice has unsettled the minds of the people. Recently his words were such as to promote angry feelings and incite open resistance to law.*

These accusations of 'useless expenditure' mirror earlier reports of Māori excess. They are typical of broader colonising discourses that described natives as improvident, wasteful, careless and ruthless.[41] Taranaki newspapers were scornful, or perhaps envious, of the abundance of Māori life at 'The Parihaka Parliament'. Well-dressed Māori rode through the main street of New Plymouth on their way to Parihaka meetings in 'large numbers'.[42] Settler visitors to the meetings were overwhelmed by the plentitude of everything. Visitors were offered wood pigeons, fried meat, European condiments, bottled beer and brandy. After eating, 'European dancing' was accompanied by an accordion. 'It is thus that a great portion of the money obtained for the grass seed harvested by the natives from the Waimate Plains – nearly 4000 pounds – has been squandered,' the Herald reported. The rest had been spent on dresses, saddles, a threshing machine, bright new riding habits in 'the latest fashion', buckskin pants and top boots and 'natty cut-away coats'. Māori had purchased all the saddles from one Hawera shop.[43] The surveyor Hursthouse, who often attended Parihaka meetings, also depicted the town as a site of wealth, abandon and excess. In September 1881, Hursthouse wrote, Tohu addressed a crowd of 2500, and after the talk the gathering feasted on '9000 birds', mainly pigeons, kākā and tui.[44]

As anyone who has visited a marae will know, hospitality is central to Māori culture, and the Māori language contains dozens of sayings relating to every aspect of providing for guests.[45] Less than a decade before Hursthouse and the *Herald* were constructing their condemning reports, another surveyor, Thomas Kingwell Skinner, had relished this famous Taranaki Māori hospitality. 'Like the patriarchs of old, their hospitality cannot be exceeded,' Skinner wrote in the field. 'They could not be more hospitable to angels, they could not entertain an angel with greater luxuries than they do a stranger. They open their doors to you and you are welcome, yes welcome, to everything they have in a reasonable kind of manner.'[46]

On 5 November 1881, the government and its soldiers decided to help themselves to everything Parihaka had. At midnight, all the residents of Parihaka, including the returned prisoners, were roused and called to gather on the marae. They knew the troops were coming. At 2 a.m. everyone ate together and waited for the soldiers to arrive. At 5 a.m., women were told to prepare more food and at 6 a.m. Parihaka people ate together again. Everyone wore their best clothes. Many had raukura in their hair. At 7.15 a.m., they glimpsed the oncoming soldiers. Their weapons gleamed in the sun. Journalists reported that residents had pulled down some of their fences to clear a path for the troops. A group of children, about 200 of them, were sent out to greet the troops with a haka. Older girls jumped over skipping ropes. The children were described as gleeful, bold and unafraid.

Even when the constabulary marched straight towards them, the children kept singing. Soldiers were offered warm bread. Throughout that day and the terrible ones that followed, other gifts of food would be offered to them too. One senior resident complained about soldiers killing Parihaka pigs and stealing potatoes. It was strange, the man said 'that after refusing a present of potatoes made to the constabulary ... a few hours afterwards they stole from their pits and pulled up their growing crops, the potatoes of which were no larger than walnuts.'[47] Still people kept on singing...

> *Ko te kupu a Te Whiti*
> The statement of Te Whiti
> *Korikori e te iwi*
> People take action
> *Kia ngāueue a tauiwi e*
> To unsettle the colonisers
> *Mehemea, ko te ra tēnei*
> If this is to be the day

Road, telegraph, lighthouse

O te whakangaromanga
When all is to be lost
E te iwi kia manawanui rā e
People take courage
Ka manawanui auē
I am of stout heart
Ka manawanui au i hei ha
I am indeed of stout heart
Ka manawanui au i hei ha
I am indeed of stout heart
Ka manawanui au i hei ha
I am indeed of stout heart
Ka manawanui au i hei ha
I am indeed of stout heart[48]

---

[1] West coast Commission, August 1880, AJHR, G-2, 14.

[2] Bryce quoted by Gorst in *Bryce v Rusden,* 219-200.

[3] Giselle Byrnes, *Boundary Markers,* Wellington: Bridget Williams Books, 2001, 107.

[4] George Neville Sturtevant, 'The First Attack, Road Making 1901', reproduced in Byrnes, *Markers,* 103.

[5] Riseborough, *Darkness,* 178. The emphasis is my own.

[6] The words 'bloodless' and 'bloodshed' appear in many settler documents about Parihaka. On 17 November 1881, for example, the former Native Minister, William Rolleston, responded to a critical letter from a Mr Fitzgerald (probably the former superintendent of Canterbury): '… the government has so far succeeded, possibly by an abnormal course of action, in avoiding the terrible consequences of Bloodshed. For myself and colleagues we have taken the only straight course to save the Māoris from their own infatuation and from the bad consequences of foolish action …' Rolleston correspondence, MS-Papers-248-05/3, ATL.

[7] *Taranaki Herald,* 7 November 1881.

[8] John Ward, *Wanderings with the Māori Prophets,* Nelson: Bond, Finney & Co, 1883, 136.

[9] Bryce being cross-examined by Sir John Gorst, *Bryce v. Rusden,* 102.

[10] Arjun Appadurai, 'The Production of Locality', in *Modernity at Large,* Minneapolis: University of Minnesota Press, 1998, 183-184.

[11] Private James Ledger, *Pen and Ink Sketches of Parihaka and Neighbourhood,* Dunedin: New Zealand: Fergusson & Mitchell, 1883.

[12] Second report of West coast Commission, AJHR vol II 1880, G-2, xxvi.

[13] Stuart Newall notebook, 1880, Ms Z526.92, PA.

[14] In November 1881, Rolleston relayed a message he had received from Bryce on to the Prime Minister. The message referred to the consequences of the destruction of crops. Bryce warned that the government might still expect trouble from the Ngāti Ruanui tribe of the Waimate Plains (Titokowaru's people). 'They may give us temporary annoyance by interfering with fences and so on. There are a few places in which they may get short of food and in these cases I should like to give them road works. Free rations have a bad effect and of course we could not let them starve.' Telegraph, 19 November 1881, Rolleston Papers, ATL.

[15] Newall's notebook and Riseborough, 120-121.0

[16] Te Whiti, quoted in William Rolleston Diary 1881, qms – 1716, ATL.

[17] Rolleston to Atkinson, confidential telegraph, 8 October 1881, Rolleston Papers, 77-248-05/1, ATL

[18] *Times,* London, 27 October 1881, cited in Rusden, *History of New Zealand* vol III, 410.

[19] Frank Watters, *New Zealand Telegraph & Telephone Offices,* Auckland: Postal History Society of New Zealand, 1973, 9. The first telegraph lines in New Zealand were built in the South Island, between Christchurch and Lyttelton, in 1865. The lines were part of a package of superior modernity that these two (mainly white) towns claimed, a modernity that the colonial government showed off to Te Whiti and Tohu during their South Island imprisonment in 1882 and 1883.

[20] *Lyttelton Times,* 12 November 1881. Article reprinted in 'The Blue Book', 587.

21 See, for example, Hursthouse telegraph book III, January to May 1881, ARC 2003 213, PA. Also Rolleston to Bryce, 31 October 1881, 77-248-05/3, Rolleston Papers, ATL. On 30 October, a distraught Bryce telegraphed Rolleston to complain: 'We are, however, getting so many more volunteers than expected and are so short of canvas kits etc that there will be considerable embarrassment.'

[22] Watters, 15, 22, 47, 54, 60, 68.

[23] Richard Dyer, *White,* London and New York: Routledge, 1997, 31.

[24] Conclusion of Public Works Statement, AJHR 1890, Vol II, 3-D.1,13.

[25] As if to prove this, Te Whiti and Tohu were taken to a surveyor's office in Dunedin during their 'imprisonment' in the South Island in 1882 and 1883. They were shown maps, surveys and equipment. Their gaoler, Ward, writes 'But Te Whiti and Tohu looked at this things … as so many devices of the evil one, for by the aid of these diabolical things, and the men who work them, they surveyors, the land is being swallowed up,' *Wanderings with the Māori Prophets,* 37.

[26] Bryce to Rolleston, telegram, 22 November 1882, 'Blue Book', 610.

[27] Charles Ingram and P.O. Wheatley, *New Zealand Shipwrecks 1795-1960,* Wellington: Reed, 1961 3rd edition, 7. The descendants of John Love and Rawinia Waikaiua are prominent Te Āti Awa people in Wellington and Taranaki today. Morrie Love, for example, was a CEO of the Waitangi Tribunal and his brother Ngatata was the head of Te Puni Kokiri, the Ministry of Māori Affairs, and is now head of the Port Nicholson Block Treaty settlement negotiation team. The daughters of 'Dicky' Barrett were the subject of the first known daguerreotype taken in New Zealand. For a discussion of whalers as colonisers, see Rebe Taylor, *Unearthed: The Aboriginal Tasmanians of Kangaroo Island,* Adelaide: Wakefield Press, 2002.

[28] For a wonderful fictional re-imagining of these events see Fiona Kidman, *The Captive Wife,* Auckland: Random House, 2005.

[29] Ingram, *Shipwrecks,* 68.

[30] Peter Walker, *The Fox Boy,* 208; Scott, *Ask That Mountain,* 16; Riseborough, *Darkness,* 17-18.

[31] John Ross, *The Lighthouses of New Zealand,* Palmerston North: Dunmore Press, 1975, 88-89. The boat that brought the light, the *Hinemoa,* was the same vessel that in 1882 carried Te Whiti and Tohu to the South Island for their 'imprisonment'. See, also, 'Cape Light', text board from 'Parihaka: The Struggle for Peace' exhibition, PA, September 2003-January 2004.

[32] Ross, *Lighthouses,* p. 89.

[33] In a telegram to Prime Minister John Hall on 19 November 1881, William Rolleston passed on Bryce's report of the dispersal of 'alien' natives at Parihaka. He wrote that large numbers of women and children, had, at last, been induced to 'come out of the pah – without being brought – to accompany their husbands. Over 1300 have now been extracted. – John Bryce (no 2). I believe the spell is broken here.' Rolleston to Hall, 19 November 1881, Rolleston Papers, ATL. Two days later, Bryce wrote: 'I intend to pull down a number of whares around the marae tomorrow and shall put them into the marae so as to deprive it of its sacred character and break the magic spell.' Rolleston to Hall, 21 November 1881, ATL.

The Parihaka Album

[34] Edward Wakefield to Rolleston, 7 November 1881, Rolleston correspondence, ATL.

[35] Bryce to Rolleston, telegram 22 November 1882, Blue Book, 610.

[36] Bryce, quoted by Sir John Gorst in *Bryce v Rusden*, 57.

[37] Head, 'Pursuit of Modernity', 97.

[38] *Lyttelton Times,* 21 November 1881, Blue Book, 604.

[39] *Lyttelton Times,* 21 November 1881, Blue Book, 606-607.

[40] 'A Proclamation', W. M. Rolleston, 19 October 1881, copied from AJHR 1882, contained in Rolleston papers, 77-248-os/2, p.2.

[41] For a fascinating discussion of waste and 'racial tropes of colonisation' see Deborah Bird-Rose, 'Decolonizing the Discourse of Environmental Knowledge in Settler Societies', in Gay Hawkins and Stephen Muecke, eds, *Culture and Waste,* Oxford: Rowman & Littlefield, 2003, 53-72.

[42] 'The Parihaka Parliament', *Taranaki Herald,* 16 March 1878.

[43] *Taranaki Herald,* 23 March 1878

[44] Hursthouse, 20 September 1881, Telegraph Book 1881, PA.

[45] Two examples will have to suffice here. With regard to finery, a nineteenth-century Te Āti Awa poi chant, sung in the style of a lament, contains the lines: 'Adorn your raukura/ Ah! Adorn, Adorn/Adornment Adornment/ Ah! It is so good … Oh! Your beautiful garments people', translated by Hohaia, in *Art of Passive Resistance,* p. 50. With regard to food, a saying that describes the generosity of Te Āti Awa people as hosts is: 'Ko te Ati Awa ko Tahuaroa/ Te Ati Awa, rich in food resources,' in Hirini Moko Mead and Neil Grove, eds, *Nga Pepeha o nga Tupuna, The Sayings of the Ancestors,* Wellington: Victoria University Press, 2001, 266.

[46] Thomas Kingwell Skinner, diary entry, 8 January 1873, ATL.

[47] *Lyttelton Times,* 7 November 1881, Blue Book, 579.

[48] 'Takiri te Raukura', a song performed with poi by the Ngāti Mutunga poi team from the time of the invasion of Parihaka.

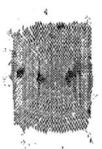

CHAPTER 5

After the invasion

The campaign against Parihaka and the way that Māori responded to this campaign has never been a set of solid, agreed upon narratives of a single set of events, with a standardised beginning and end. Since the nineteenth century, various narrators have retold the story in many ways.

'A most dangerous lot of men'

In 1882, Ngā Puhi chiefs from the far north included the invasion of Parihaka and the imprisonment of the leaders and their followers in a petition to the Queen complaining about Treaty breaches. Of the invasion of Parihaka, the petition said, in part: 'We have pored over the Treaty of Waitangi to find the grounds on which these evil proceedings of the government rested but could find none.'[1]

In their petition, Ngā Puhi leaders compared the bloodless invasion of Parihaka with the far from bloodless invasion of the Waikato and 'rape of Waitara' in the 1860s. Certainly, the invasion of the settlement was the event that most threatened the rational, reasonable and non-violent reputation that the colonial government wanted to establish for itself in the settlement of Taranaki affairs.

Most settlers had supported the invasion. The government had been overwhelmed with volunteers. Troops had been seen off from their hometowns like heroes – 4000 farewelled the

180-strong contingent from Manawatū, and thousands of people lined streets and wharves to farewell troops in Taranaki itself, as well as in Thames, Whanganui, Wellington, Wairarapa, Marlborough, Nelson, Canterbury and Timaru. Most volunteers were Pākehā or tauiwi. The foreigners were adventurers such as Swiss man Anton Fromm, lured from Melbourne by the generous pay and promise of three meals a day with meat and vegetables.[2] Others were foreign mercenaries who had fought against the Hindus in India and the Indians in America. A few, including an Alexandra Cavalry trumpeter described as 'Bugler Brookes', as well as other unidentified men captured in photographs, were Māori.[3]

A vocal minority of settlers were opposed to the invasion and mocked the massive display of military force used against unarmed people at Parihaka. The reasons for this opposition included political rivalry and the multicultural nature of New Zealand society, a place that included anti-English people from Ireland and Scotland. Irish people, in particular, saw many parallels between Māori struggles to keep their land and their own battles against English colonisers. Geography played a part too. In the South Island, far from any 'Native difficulty', the invasion was subject to a 'good deal of burlesque sentiment'. Bryce and his men were lampooned in satirical ballads and poems that drew on the reports of radical or liberal newspaper articles.[4] In 'The Charge at Parihaka', Jessie Mackay asked the cutting question of the 1200 or more soldiers who participated, parodying Tennyson's famous poem glorifying the charge of the Light Brigade in the Crimea: 'When can their glory fade?/Oh! The wild charge they made/New Zealand wondered/Whether each doughty soul/Paid for the pigs he stole: /Noble Twelve Hundred!'[5]

Yet time and retrospective wisdom could quell even criticisms such as these. In 1883, the civilising work of the surveyors and road-builders was challenged in a more confrontational and violent way by Te Mahuki Manukura, a Ngāti Maniapoto follower of Te Whiti and Tohu, who had built a replica of Parihaka village in the King

Country and established his own community there. Te Mahuki and many of his followers had lived at Parihaka and had been arrested and imprisoned for their part in the fencing and ploughing protests. Te Mahuki's followers called themselves Tekau-mā-rua, the Sacred Twelve, a reference to Christ's twelve disciples or the twelve tribes of Israel.[6] Since the invasion, they had been forbidden to return to Parihaka, so they lived in the King Country – so named because of the Māori king – a region that the government was keen to open up to the railway.

In March 1883 at Te Uira, Te Mahuki and his men stopped a railway survey party, led by Charles Hursthouse, from proceeding. Hursthouse was the man who surveyed the Waitara block, an action that sparked the 1860 war. He and members of his party, including a Mr Newsham and his 'native' escort, Te Haere, were attacked and robbed. Newsham and Hursthouse were bound with chains and ropes for forty hours. Eventually, Te Kooti, the former East Coast rebel leader, rescued the surveyors.[7] Te Mahuki and twenty-two of his followers were arrested, tried and imprisoned for their crime. The case, which was said to display 'the impotent, but violent fanaticism which has sprung up, through the demoralisation of the barbarous remnant of the Māori people', received extensive newspaper coverage.[8] It seemed to prove, retrospectively, the wisdom of the government's actions at Parihaka two years earlier. The *New Zealand Herald* reported:

> *The strange outbreak of Te Mahuki and his followers must considerably affect the judgment passed by many people upon the Parihaka affair. It was then contended that the display of overwhelming force that was made in the arrest of Te Whiti and the dispersion of those who were gathered at the settlement was absolutely useless, and a good deal of would-be comic literary talent has been expended in attempts to ridicule the gathering of the volunteers and the bloodless arrest of Te Whiti. The prophet and his followers have been represented as harmless, peace-loving, religious people, into whose minds no thought of outrage or lawlessness ever*

> entered, and the armed parade, which it was thought necessary
> to make has been stigmatised as an unseemly and cowardly farce.
> The natives were spoken of as peaceful, dignified and calm, while
> Mr Bryce and the other Ministers were accused of getting up a
> vulgar, useless and expensive show. But there can be no doubt now
> that the natives assembled at Parihaka were a most dangerous lot
> of men, and it may fairly be concluded that but for the display of
> overwhelming force that was made, there would have been a very
> different result.[9]

In 1886, only a few years after Te Mahuki's imprisonment of a surveying party had so conveniently provided a retrospective reinforcement of the government's actions at Parihaka, Māori had a chance to explain to a national and international audience why they considered Bryce and his troops to be 'a most dangerous lot of men'.

The forum for these stories was the libel trial of a retired senior public servant living in the colony of Victoria, G.W. (George) Rusden. Drawing on public documents, newspaper accounts (especially those published in the pro-Māori *Lyttelton Times*) and on information gathered during visits to New Zealand in 1878-79 and 1881, Rusden had written a three-volume history of New Zealand.

In public and in private, Rusden had made no secret of his opposition to the New Zealand government's treatment of Māori. Two weeks before Parihaka was invaded, he wrote a concerned letter to William Rolleston. From the comfort of the Melbourne Club, he wrote:

> I can not express the pang which it gave me to see that you had
> resigned the post of Native Minister and had been succeeded by Mr
> Bryce. It would be impertinent of me to advise, but it may interest
> you to reflect upon what must be the judgment of posterity if the
> marauding schemes of the New Zealand company – the robbery
> of Waitara ... the confessed broken promises on the West coast –
> are wound up by an attack upon Te Whiti – because he preaches

and preaches with more eloquence than his enemies (or) some of them who advocate war. Had I but a trumpet tongue I would cry to the world but I have not, and I appeal to you as one who has until now maintained the manners of an English gentleman though brought into contact with strange Englishmen, civilised savages abroad, as well as with 'naked savages' as the New Zealand company called the Māoris.[10]

Rusden did, in fact, have something of a trumpet tongue. It soon got him into trouble. His history of New Zealand reached New Zealand and Australia in 1883. The final volume, Volume III, was largely devoted to a highly critical narrative of the invasion of Parihaka. Volume II contained a brief account of a massacre at settler John Handley's Woolshed near Tauranga Ika Pā in central Taranaki in 1868, at the peak of the government's war with Titokowaru.

This, broadly, is what happened there: A section of the Kai Iwi Cavalry, under the command of Lieutenant John Bryce, were riding back to their camp after an expedition, when they spotted a small party of Māori down below them near the woolshed. They fired at them. This enemy party was actually a group of about a dozen unarmed boys, aged between about six and ten, who had been trying to kill a pig. After shots were fired, the children ran for their lives. As the men on horseback got closer, they could see their quarry were children – a soldier told a later inquiry, 'it struck me that they were children – big and small boys'. Without waiting for orders, the men charged on. They killed two boys, Kingi Takatua, aged ten, and Akuhata Herewini, an even younger child, and seriously injured at least four others. Both Kingi and Akuhata were shot first and then attacked with sabres. A cowering Kingi was hit with such force by farmer-turned-soldier George Maxwell that his head was 'split in two halves, one half falling down over his shoulder'.[11]

Rethinking this murderous brutality, re-reading accounts of it, renews my admiration for those brave children who were the little frontline troops in Parihaka's 'welcome' of the invading force in

1881. Were those children, perhaps, thinking about stories they had heard about white soldiers killing unarmed children thirteen years ago? Or were they unafraid because they believed themselves protected by Te Whiti and Tohu, by the sacredness of their community?

Twentieth century accounts of the butchery at the woolshed, especially James Belich's retelling, make it clear that Bryce himself did not actually fire on the children or attack them with his sword. It appears that the men were fired by some horrendous blood-lust and just decided to chase and kill the children. Once Bryce overtook Sergeant Maxwell, he ordered all of them to retire. But this story was not nearly as clear in the nineteenth century, when memories of the brutality were still raw and oral testimony was perhaps more powerful than written accounts. In his history, Rusden wrote of the woolshed killings: 'Some women and young children emerged from a pah to hunt pigs. Lieut. Bryce and Sergt. Maxwell dashed upon them and cut them down gleefully and with ease.'[12]

Bryce sued Rusden for defamation, and the case went to the Supreme Court in England. In 1886, Baron Huddleston found that Rusden's accusation was baseless, and the historian was ordered to pay Bryce 5000 pounds damages, an enormous sum at that time. All remaining copies of his history were withdrawn from sale.[13]

'Bryce – the murderer'

The Māori witnesses in the Rusden case were questioned at a court in Whanganui, and their evidence was tabled in London. Their testimony reveals that although the entire Cabinet had endorsed the government's decision to invade Parihaka, it was Bryce who had become a figurehead for Māori outrage. He embodied everything that Māori saw as uncivilised, reprehensible, duplicitous and destructive about Pākehā. His role at Handley's Woolshed was one reason for this.

Drawing on memories of Bryce's behaviour during the massacre at the woolshed and his role at the head of the invading troops at

Parihaka in 1881, Māori had given the Native Minister a nickname: Bryce – he tangata kōhuru (Bryce – the man who murders). According to Rusden's history, Bryce earned this nickname because he murdered women and children at the woolshed.

As Belich notes: 'There had been no women at the woolshed and Bryce did not cut anyone down himself. But he was fully aware that his men had done so, and that very young boys were their victims, and he took no disciplinary procedures against them. Poor Rusden had got the right tragedy and the wrong details.'[14] In evidence put forward at the trial, former cavalry volunteers attempted to claim that those killed had been men, not boys. Māori, on the other hand, testifying for Rusden, said that members of the Kai Iwi Cavalry, not Bryce himself, had killed children at the woolshed.

Why did Māori describe Bryce as a murderer when the evidence, including the evidence of Māori witnesses themselves, suggests that this label was not strictly 'true'? In giving Bryce this damning label, Māori wanted to indicate that Bryce had authorised or, at least, condoned the killing of the children at the woolshed. He had certainly never condemned his men's actions.

Likewise, at Parihaka, Bryce's men did not literally murder anyone; but their actions murdered a community, a people, a movement. The eviction of so many people, the destruction of crops and theft of livestock, all these things led to starvation and suffering. The label 'Bryce – the murderer' contained both symbolic and literal truths. It was intended to foreground the violence in the supposedly non-violent solution to what the government called the west coast 'difficulty'.

Māori understood that nicknames stick. For instance, Tame Iti called his installation for the 2000 Parihaka exhibition at Wellington's City Gallery (mixed media, including a musket, albatross feather, table, two bullets, golf club, mirrors, golf balls) *Kohuru Tangata*. Peter Walker's 2001 history of a Māori child who was abducted during Titokowaru's war in the 1860s, and raised by William Fox, repeats, uncritically, Rusden's claim that

John Bryce was known as 'Bryce – kōhuru' or 'Kōhuruhuru' – 'an intensified form of the word, which means simply Wickedness or Black Murder'. Walker draws uncritically on spurious and rather ridiculous stories contained in Rusden's history, such as the 'fact' that Bryce had acquired a reputation for cruelty when he worked as a cowboy and had been seen 'throwing stones at the eyes of a patient cow'.[15]

Kōhuru is a word that has many dictionary meanings, including to 'kill by stealth', to 'ill-treat grievously' or to 'deal treacherously'.[16] Through these more subtle meanings of the word, rather than the literal description of a man who takes another's life in an act of murder, Māori expressed their responses to the non-violent colonisation of Taranaki.

The testimony of former MP Wi Parata, of Waikanae, exposes the different interpretive strategies at work when settlers and Māori described colonisation. Parata began his testimony by talking about the fighting that had occurred in Taranaki in 1881.

> Q: *When you said now that there had been fighting, I understand you to mean that there had not been actual fighting but that some people were armed?*
> A: *When people carry arms we speak of it as fighting.*

Parata then explained that Bryce was known as a 'tangata kohuru': 'he was a murderer, a man that murdered'.[17] Parata, who was at Parihaka in 1881 when it was invaded, said he first heard that description of Bryce then.

> Q: *Did you ever hear it said that the action of Mr Bryce or the soldiers was murder at that time?*
> A: *Yes, Mr Bryce went there with his guns and the Māori had no guns. That was a murderous action.*
> Q: *You said that the term 'kohuru' you heard applied to Mr Bryce at Parihaka; do I understand that it was a consequence*

of something that had taken place at Nukumaru [Handley's Woolshed] or something that happened at Parihaka?
A: For both. They were coupled together.[18]

Bryce's libel case was concerned with just two lines in Volume II of Rusden's history, but as Parata's testimony suggests, most of the case was concerned with what happened at Parihaka in 1881. For eight days, an often rather puzzled London court became a stage on which Māori and Pākehā and their supporters or detractors could narrate alternative versions of the history of the place that was now called New Zealand. Both sides were deeply concerned with proving the morality, or otherwise, of colonisation.

'The trial has laid bare, here before the English public, the history of the struggle between the colonists and the Māories [sic]. In New Zealand, two policies have been long face to face – what might be called the colonial and native policies,' the *Times* reported.[19] In this history, the invasion of Parihaka functioned as the kind of ultimate test case of the morality of colonisation. It was a site where the court could debate whether colonists had behaved like gentlemen or whether their actions had been far less worthy. Did British colonists in New Zealand respect the faiths and superstitions of native peoples as much as colonists in India and other parts of the empire did? Were Māori an exceptional race of 'aborigines' with special qualities of chivalry, generosity and bravery, or were they as barbarous as 'aborigines' everywhere else?[20]

For settlers in New Zealand, much was at stake. In 1883, Bryce had told the New Zealand parliament that Rusden cared nothing about Bryce as an individual, rather 'what he is meaning to do is to prove that the New Zealand colonists are villainous in their entirety and so when he refers to me, he merely does so to show that when the colonists are so entirely vile to the core, they will select persons of that kind to administer their affairs'.[21] In taking his case in London, rather than Wellington, Bryce was seeking to be examined

103

and exonerated in the birthplace of civilisation itself. He would clear any slander not only his name, but that of the colony too.

Counsel for Bryce, Sir Henry James, opened his case by emphasising the barbarity of the New Zealand Māori, a savagery demonstrated by the 'native outbreak' of 1868 in Taranaki. Māori, he argued, were cannibals, and they staged a 'war of brutality' with the aim of 'exterminating' European life and property. In his address, he constructed a narrative in which Europeans, rather than Māori, were a besieged minority, victims of a superior, barbaric force.[22] The residents of Parihaka were fanatics of another sort, but dangerous just the same. Therefore, Bryce's skill in dispersing 'the assemblage without bloodshed' was remarkable.[23]

Sir John Gorst, counsel for Rusden, sought to depict Bryce as a vengeful man who used the Parihaka campaign to get revenge against Titokowaru, who had humiliated him in battle in 1868. Bryce had ignored the rights of Māori during the Parihaka campaign, and the laws he had introduced to detain Māori without trial rivalled the worst excesses of the French Revolution.[24] The invasion of Parihaka and the confiscation of Taranaki land that had proceeded it had breached the Treaty of Waitangi, Gorst argued, and he said that Bishop Selwyn (New Zealand), Bishop Lichfield (England) and Justice Martin all supported this view.[25]

Gorst's narrative emphasised the hospitality and peaceful intentions of Parihaka residents and suggested that the bloodlessness of the Parihaka raid was due to Te Whiti's calming influence, rather than to the weaponry and troops assembled by the government under Bryce's leadership. In cross-examination, Bryce continued to reassert that Parihaka, in fact, represented the worst case of fanaticism in New Zealand history, and fanaticism in the Māori race 'was of an exceedingly dangerous character. The instances we have had of it have generally been accompanied by bloodshed and enormous atrocities'.[26] Yet an exchange between Gorst and Bryce shows that Bryce, like Māori, could find violence in episodes where there had been no bloodshed:

Gorst: In the fanatical movement of Te Whiti from the first to the last there was the most absolute submission on the part of the natives to the executive government?
Bryce: Not at all; there was absolute defiance of the government.
Gorst: Not by violence?
Bryce: Not by bloodshed.
Gorst: Only by passive resistance.
Bryce: I should not like to say that. I am quite willing to say not by bloodshed.[27]

Nineteenth-century Parihaka narratives are knotted up in exchanges such as this. What Māori and their supporters might label as 'absolute submission', settlers chose to see as 'absolute defiance'. The problem was one of definition. Who was violent? Who was peace-loving? What sort of resistance, if any, might be legitimate? What sort of behaviour was excessive, what sort might be reasonable?

Histories emerge from these debates, literally. (It was the monumental transcript of this libel case that set the young Dick Scott off on a search for Parihaka in 1953, a journey that led to his self-published first book, *The Parihaka Story,* and his best-selling second one, *Ask That Mountain*.)[28] As time passes and new events take place, reputations are reassessed, emphasis is changed, meanings shift. Bryce, it seems clear, was labelled a murderer only after the invasion of Parihaka.[29] Another member of Rusden's defence team, Sir Richard Webster, told the court that it was only after his actions at Parihaka that Māori found it necessary to re-examine Bryce's early actions, at places such as Handley's Woolshed, for example.[30]

The Parihaka Album

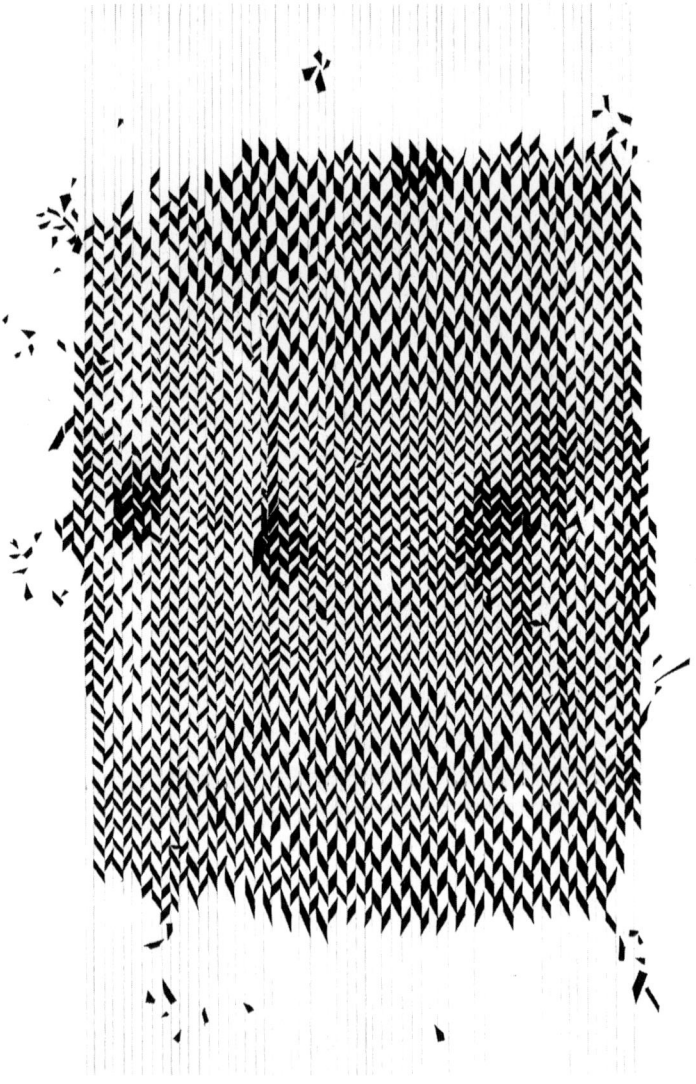

Figure 8. The story fractures: 'The problem was one of definition. Who was violent? Who was peace-loving? What sort of resistance, if any, might be legitimate?' Benjamin Buchanan, 'Untitled', vinyl adhesive on paper, 305mm x 200mm, 2009. Image courtesy of the artist.

After the invasion

For Māori and those settlers who supported them, the bloodless installation of the lighthouse, the telegraph and the road and the bloodless invasion of Parihaka did not mask the government's violent intentions. They sought to broaden the definition of violence and war beyond the firing of guns and cannons, into a domain that would cover violent intentions. They sought to debunk, subtly, the arguments that war-like behaviour was actually intended to bring peace. 'It was suggested by Mr Bryce that it was necessary to do something which had the appearance of war in order to avoid war,' said Webster, Rusden's counsel. 'That it was necessary to take up an armed force, an Armstrong six-pounder – to seize guns and pull down houses and to take people's property, to avoid war.'[31]

In 1886, after eight days of detailed evidence, the English jury took just fifteen minutes to decide that the history of New Zealand constructed by Rusden, a history that displayed a deep sympathy with Māori, was libellous. Bryce's reputation had been vindicated. One newspaper noted that Rusden's history had argued that the government had been brutal and treacherous towards Māori, but it believed the native policy in New Zealand had been 'at once patriotic and forbearing to the point of generosity'. As for Bryce, he was 'one of those honest, energetic and straightforward persons of whom England produces so many for the conduct of affairs abroad and retains so few for the management of affairs at home'.[32] New Zealand, in other words, was lucky to have him.

Although the court found in favour of Bryce, Rusden ensured that he had the final word. He donated his copy of the proceedings of the libel case to the State Library of Victoria. The 638-page volume is richly annotated. It waits, in the stacks, to be discovered by researchers like me.

More than 100 years after the decision, Rusden has his own sly reply. On page 429, he has underlined several lines in an address by Sir Henry James, in which James outlines his views on where Rusden acquired the slanderous information about Bryce's actions at the woolshed. James alleges that the 'foul slander and untruth' came from Sir Arthur Gordon. He accuses the defendant of seeking Gordon's protection 'in whining tone'.

'What a foolish fib!!' Rusden has written in the margins. 'Why James himself grumbled in other passages because of my insisting and not whining.' He has signed his little note 'GWR'.

[1] Rusden, *History,* vol III, p. 478. For Te Kooti's perspective on the invasion of Parihaka, see Judith Binney, *Redemption Songs: The Life of Te Kooti Arikirangi Te Turuki,* Auckland: Auckland University Press, 1995, 292.

[2] Anton Fromm, diary, PA. Fromm notes that the armed constabulary were paid £10 per month. In his entry for 22 September 1881, he describes rushing to New Plymouth where he found a throng of men who, like him, wanted to become armed constabulary. 'At last … came a telegram from Wellington, from the Minister of War, Rolleston, with the strict order not to enlist any more people in the Armed Constabulary as there were already more than required.' See 26 September and 1 October entries for admiring description of camp conditions – a good library and several billiards and playrooms – and food, making this army 'pretty well off compared with the European military'. See also *Lyttelton Times,* 17 November 1881. The reporter noted that volunteers were beginning to protest about their pay. They had believed they would be paid for two months, but apparently they had misunderstood instructions that they had to be prepared to serve for two months. They were to be paid only for their time on the front. Blue Book, 600.

[3] Brookes or Brooks, whose first name is not given in sources I have examined, was a bugler or a trumpeter. He was described as a 'half caste'. See *Lyttelton Times,* 12 November 1881 and *New Zealand Times ,*15 November 1881, extracts Blue Book, 587 and 556. Several Māori men are prominent in the foreground of 'Armed Constabulary Camp near Parihaka', c.1881, photographer unknown, TP, reproduced in *Art of Passive Resistance,* 184.

[4] The *Lyttelton Times,* through the work of its correspondent Croumbie-Brown, was consistently critical of the government's actions at Parihaka. For a fascinating discussion of 'multicultural' poetry that criticised the invasion of Parihaka, see Jane Stafford, 'To sing this Bryce and bunkum age' in Hohaia et al., eds., *Parihaka: The Art of Passive Resistance,* 179-185.

[5] Jessie Mackay, 'The Charge at Parihaka', *The Spirit of the Rangatira and Other Ballads,* Melbourne: George Robertson, 1889, 30-32. Stafford, citing this poem (in *The Art of Passive Resistance,* 180) that it was first published in a Christchurch newspaper not long after the invasion of Parihaka.

[6] Elsmore, 'The Tekau-mā-rua Movement', *Mana from Heaven,* 297-302.

[7] Te Kooti had been 'pardoned' by Native Minister Bryce in February 1883. For an account of why he intervened and freed Hursthouse, see Binney, *Redemption Songs,* 312-314.

After the invasion

[8] *New Zealand Herald*, 7 April 1883, clipping contained in Māori Affairs, File 23/5, Archives New Zealand (ANZ).

[9] *New Zealand Herald*, 28 March 1883, File 23/5, ANZ. For a different perspective see Binney, *Redemption Songs*; after Te Kooti had been pardoned by Bryce, the *Christchurch Star* noted the paradox that the pardon had been extended by 'the bully of Parihaka, the oppressor of Te Whiti and his unfortunate people' (Binney, *Redemption Songs*, 311).

[10] Rusden to Rolleston, 21 October 1881. Rolleston correspondence 1831-1903, 82-355-03/2, ATL. Rusden's letter ends with a request for archival material on the West coast, to help him with the history of New Zealand he is preparing.

[11] For a detailed account of this awful event, see James Belich, *Titokowaru's War,* 190-211.

[12] Belich, *Titokowaru's War,* 204. This version of events has been expunged from the copy of Rusden's history held at La Trobe University. The second edition of Rusden's history, published in 1895, noted that the children were charged by the order of a Captain Newland. Bryce is not mentioned at all in connection with the main narrative about the massacre, but the libel case is referred to, obliquely, in a footnote: 'A historian cannot often procure the aid of a Commission of the High Court of Justice in eliciting truth, but when it has been thrown in his way he would be ungrateful if he were to neglect it.' See *History of New Zealand,* vol II, second edition, 553.

[13] Detailed eyewitness accounts of what happened at the woolshed can be found in the appendixes to *Bryce v Rusden,* High Court of Justice, Queen's Bench Division, 1886 before Baron Huddleston and a special jury, London: 1886.

[14] Belich, *Titokowaru,* 204.

[15] For the murderer nickname information, see P. Walker, *The Fox Boy,* London: Bloomsbury, 2002, 147. Later in the book Walker repeats, uncritically, Rusden's unsourced gossip about Bryce as a cruel cowboy, 241.

[16] H.W. Williams, *Dictionary of the Māori Language* Wellington: Legislation Direct, reprint of seventh edition, 2001, 127. The first edition of this dictionary was published in 1844. The seventh edition, which I use, was revised and augmented by the advisory committee on the teaching of Māori language, Department of Education. Of course, Māori speakers in the nineteenth-century, and native speakers now, will have further meanings and understandings for a word like 'kohuru' too.

[17] The exact exchange is as follows. Q: Have you heard the natives apply any term of opprobrium to Mr Bryce. A. Yes, I have. Q. What was that term? A. It is said that he was a murderer; a man that murdered. Q. Give us the Māori expression? A. Tangata Kohuru. (The interpreter then explained that this expression means murderous man or murderer), *Bryce v Rusden,* 625.

[18] Wi Parata, *Bryce v. Rusden*, 622-626

[19] *Times*, 13 March 1886, extract printed in *Bryce v Rusden,* 506.

[20] See *Bryce v Rusden,* pp. 123-148 for exchanges that cover these questions.

[21] Bryce cited by Sir John Gorst, *Bryce v Rusden,* 33.

22 Sir Henry James, *Bryce v Rusden*, 2-3.

23 *Bryce v Rusden*, 15-32.

24 Gorst quoted Sir George Grey on Parihaka to make his point: 'We say in the worst days of the French Revolution such a power was never sought, never given and never attempted to be taken,' *Bryce v Rusden*, 78.

25 *Bryce v Rusden*, 213.

26 *Bryce v Rusden*, 118.

27 *Bryce v Rusden*, 119.

28 See Dick Scott's memoir, *A Radical Writer's Life*, Auckland: Reed, 2004. Scott's books are cited as motivating forces for dozens of artists, singers and writers, including James K. Baxter, Jacquie Sturm, Tony Fomison, Colin McCahon, Marti Friedlander, Dinah Hawken, Ralph Hotere, Gordon Walters, Tim Finn, Barry Brickell and Michael Smither. See *Art of Passive Resistance*, especially 192-202.

29 In his summing up, Sir James said: 'With the exception of one witness, nobody ever heard that term [kohuru] before 1881,' *Bryce v Rusden*, 445.

30 *Bryce v Rusden*, 399.

31 *Bryce v Rusden*, 409.

32 *St James Gazette*, 13 March 1886, extract *Rusden v Bryce*, 513.

CHAPTER 6

Pictures

One of the most recycled artefacts in the Parihaka archive is a small, hard-covered booklet with black pages, similar in size and shape to old-fashioned autograph books. An anonymous New Plymouth settler put Parihaka invasion photographs in this booklet, and the Alexander Turnbull Library has labelled it 'The Parihaka Album'.

The photographs contained in its pages have been reproduced in historical monographs, such as Riseborough's *Days of Darkness*; best-selling popular histories, such as Scott's *Ask That Mountain*; commissions of inquiry, such as the Waitangi Tribunal's *Taranaki Report*; and art show catalogues, such as the one produced for the City Gallery's millenium exhibition. Post-1881 pictures that are not contained in this souvenir album itself but are part of the broader archive of nineteenth-century Parihaka images have also inspired artists, such as Ralph Hotere, Michael Shepherd, Anne Noble and Seraphine Pick.

The 1881 photographs are a valuable visual record of New Zealand's wars. As far as I am aware, there are sketches and paintings but no photographs of earlier acts of war in Taranaki. There are no photographs of Titokowaru's war against the Crown in 1868 or of the Crown's war against Taranaki people, which began in Waitara in 1861. There are no pictures of atrocities, such as the slaying of children by settler volunteers at Handley's Woolshed.

The Parihaka Album

Parihaka was invaded at exactly the right moment to be captured not only by writers, but by artists and photographers too. In 1881, photographs were beginning to replace sketches and paintings as a documentary medium. This doubling up has resulted in the abundance of Parihaka images: shirt-sleeve sketches and post cards, stereographs and oil paintings and all those haunting photographs.

In 1881, photographers were travelling New Zealand looking for subjects that would sell. The arrival of the wet-plate collodian process had allowed inexpensive prints to be made from a single glass negative. As technology developed, so did the paraphernalia associated with viewing it. The invasion and restoration of Parihaka dovetailed with the emergence of the photo album, and later the stereograph, as essential items in the middle-class Victorian home.[1] Stereographs were twin photographs printed on cigarette-card sized bits of cardboard and viewed through an optical instrument that looked something like opera glasses. The two images melded into one of greater depth.

Figure 9. Stereographs were twin photographs printed on cigarette-card sized bits of cardboard and viewed through a gadget that looked like opera glasses. The Alexander Turnbull Library describes this image as 'Stereoscopic photograph of a family sitting in an open car, parked at Parihaka, ca 1890', black and white original photographic print, photograph by Arthur Schaef, Alexander Turnbull Library, reference number PA4-0553.

Pictures

Figure 10. Stereoscopic photograph of a parked car at Te Whiti's Monument, Parihaka, black and white photographic print, photograph by Arthur Schaef, 1909, Alexander Turnbull Library, reference number PA4-1053.

Commercial photographers documented the November 1881 invasion as well as the time, from 1885 onwards, when the village was rebuilt and modernised and became a significant local tourist attraction, drawing large numbers of Pākehā to its monthly meetings. Parihaka was an ideal subject for these men because it was a site of fascination, an anomaly, a place for the notorious. Post-1885 Parihaka and the people who lived there were a tantalising blend of modern and traditional. What gave Parihaka photographs their spark was their status as symbols of these imagined markers of progress and decline. Women wore feather cloaks over Victorian dresses. They had white feathers in their hair but carried silver teapots. A boy wearing a sailor's suit jacket and a grass skirt played a little pipe, a natty fife, while next to him, a man in a grass skirt was a blur of tongue, flesh and eye-whites as he performed a haka.

Outside, the village was a collection of fine wooden buildings, ornate gas lights and raupō huts, a blend of architecture that resulted in novel images with titles such as 'Europeanised buildings in the

Parihaka Village'. In photographs, Parihaka interiors were formal, almost austere: the dining room of Te Niho had tongue and groove panelling, starched white table-cloths, silver cutlery, crystal vases filled with elegant stems of flax, bentwood chairs. In stereographs produced in the early twentieth century, delighted Parihaka children posed inside open-topped motorcars, parked right outside the magnificent Raukura meeting house.

In one very famous image, reproduced perhaps more than any other Parihaka picture, a brilliant, thick, white comet streaks from the heavens down towards the summit of Taranaki. The mountain is looking his stunning best: his slopes are symmetrical and cloaked in snow all the way down to the foothills. At his feet, there is a forest; in front of the trees is Parihaka, a village of dozens of raupō huts, all neatly fenced, and one conspicuously European style building, the twin-gabled Miti Mai Te Arero. Te Whiti used this building as a meeting house and reception room. Visual and written evidence suggests that this was the first European-style house at Parihaka; it was built by Parihaka men, under the supervision of of Te Whetu Moeahu, in about 1879. Sketches and notes made by Private James Ledger, a member of the invading force, describe a 'European house erected to receive the Governor had he wished to visit Te Whiti'.[2] Paintings by George Sheriff and G.C. Beale also depict a twin-gabled house on a rise to the left of the settlement.[3]

For settlers looking at the photograph, the twin-gabled building among the whare was, perhaps, a source of amusement, a bit of Māori play-acting; for Māori, the building was a deeply political gesture, a structure imbued with meaning. The building's name means to 'defiantly protrude one's tongue'.[4] This was a building that was meant to speak. So were the ones that followed it, such as Te Niho o Te Āti Awa, the teeth of Te Āti Awa. Arero or tongue is also the word for the 'upper point of a taiaha, carved in imitation of a human tongue'. The tongue is highly symbolic in Māori culture. When a man pokes out his tongue during the haka, for example, the gesture is a sign of his mauri, his life force, vitality and power. The construction of a European-style house called Miti Mai Te Arero, therefore, was a pointed and slyly aggressive show of the mana of Parihaka. A taiaha is a spear-like 'weapon of wood'. The building mimicked the civilisation that Europeans were so eager to inflict on Māori at Parihaka, but it was a fierce structure, intended to be a weapon, just like the words spoken by the leaders who used it.

The photographic postcard, captioned 'Parihaka, Mt Egmont & Comet Oct 1882', depicts the comet that streaked across the New Zealand skies in 1882, the year that Parihaka's leaders spent in imprisonment/exile in the South Island. I love this image, the trinity of mountain, comet and village. Te Whiti's name refers to the flight path of a comet, so the photograph has great appeal because it captures the prophet's spiritual presence at Parihaka, a sort of celestial homecoming, even though he was actually still imprisoned down south and would not return home until 1883. In 2003, when I visited the Alexander Turnbull to look at some Parihaka material, this picture was one of the items on my wish-list. Did the library have the original glass-plate negative? Or a print? Could I see it?

In the library catalogue and in publications, the image is attributed to T.S. Muir, who was either an assistant to well-known photographer Alfred Burton or a member of the invading force identified in a photograph taken at Rahotu redoubt.[5] I started talking to John Sullivan, the Turnbull's curator of photography, about it and he said, quite casually, that the photograph was almost certainly a fake. In 1882, there was not a camera in this world with a shutter speed fast enough to catch a streak of light in the night sky, let alone in broad daylight. The comet, Sullivan believes, was probably painted on the glass-plate negative. In a later email, Sullivan observed: 'Mt Taranaki, when it appears at all in photographs of Parihaka (it is normally obscured by cloud) is not as large as this.'

The library does not hold the original of the photograph, but a digitised copy of the copy is available on the Timeframes website. The catalogue description gives no indication of the photograph's dubious provenance. When I asked Sullivan about this on another research trip in 2007, he said the picture could now, most correctly, be described as a composite image.

It is a surprise to learn that photos could be faked in a pre-Photoshop world. Perhaps digital technology has made us more suspicious of photography's special truth claims, but it's still common to believe that a photograph is more objective and truthful than a written document, that it is somehow both 'a transcription of an actual moment of reality and an interpretation of that reality'.[6] Then and now, the Parihaka comet image was welcomed because people (including me) wanted to believe what it supposedly depicted – a moment in which this village was touched by the divine.

To really see what is happening in this picture requires the viewer to let go of some of the myths about Parihaka and consider some rather more prosaic factors, such as camera shutter speeds. The comet over Parihaka picture appears to be absolutely self-explanatory, but it's not. What it does show is people's willingness (then and now) to believe in the magical powers of Parihaka.

It is often observed that a picture is worth a thousand words. Pictures appear powerful because they can be read by anyone, even the illiterate. Their language, supposedly, is universal. But pictures don't really speak. Without captions, they are mute.[7]

Unanchored from the century in which they were created, the audience they were created for and the site in which they were displayed and studied, the Parihaka photographs placed in The Parihaka Album become the most flexible of documents. By the late twentieth century, the photographs had become both accusation and proof of a serious crime. In her book, Hazel Riseborough reproduced the pictures with pithy captions, statements made by settlers, politicians or journalists in 1881. The captions cleverly mock the intentions of the soldiers. The Waitangi Tribunal report, however, gives the images sober captions, as befits documents that were published as proof of the extent of settler war crimes in Taranaki.

Pictures

Figure 11. View of a comet in the sky above Mt Taranaki (Egmont) and Parihaka, 4 October 1882, composite image by an unknown photographer, black and white original negative, Alexander Turnbull Library, reference number 1/2-003184-F.

The Parihaka Album

But what happens to these photographs if you look at them more closely, if you see them as a beginning, rather than an end, of inquiry?[8]

The comet photograph almost certainly owes a debt to a picture taken by William Andrews Collis on the day that Parihaka was invaded. Collis's famous photograph of Parihaka, which the Alexander Turnbull Library dates to November 1881, depicts a throng of people sitting in the space in front of their homes. Like the comet photo, it is also uncanny – the centre portion is curiously overexposed, leaving a miasma of light dancing over the middle of the settlement, where the residents gathered to wait for the soldiers. The photograph shows a village comprised of hundreds of fenced whare raupō, paths and roadways, bullock carts and snuffling pigs. Outside one whare, clothes hang on a line.[9]

Figure 12. The Alexander Turnbull Library describes this photograph as 'View of Parihaka, Taranaki, photographed at the time of the Armed Constabulary invasion, ca November 1881, by William Andrews Collis. In the centre background, to the right, the inhabitants of Parihaka may be seen seated'. Albumen print 16.7 x 24.1 cm mounted in The Parihaka Album, Alexander Turnbull Library, reference number PA1-q-183-18. To the far left is Miti Mai Te Arero, the first 'European-style' house built at Parihaka. To the right is a small structure with a gable, the settlement's bank. The one word caption, 'Parihaka', was inscribed by the settler who compiled The Parihaka Album.

Two wooden, self-consciously European structures can be seen in the photograph. One is a small gabled building, the settlement's bank, Nuku Te Whatewha (Shift the Space).[10] The other, on a rise, is 'Miti Mai Te Arero', the house that was European in appearance but Māori in purpose. It was a whare rūnanga, a public meeting house, a place for assembling to discuss important matters. After such a meeting, participants would all eat together. Miti Mai looked like a homestead, but it functioned more like a parliament, as a ceremonial, semi-public space. The European homesteads that the West coast Commission wanted to set up 'at the doors of Parihaka' were quite different. These houses would have carefully divided public and private spaces, interiors where few, other than the closest family, were welcome.

As European military settlers advanced further into Taranaki, they forced Māori to retreat deep into the interior of their home. Māori fled to the isolated headlands of rivers, far from Pākehā settlement, or they journeyed inland into the deep bush that so overawed surveyors and soldiers. When people had run out of hiding places or got too hungry, they arrived at Parihaka where the Māori interior – the place for private learning and living – was nourished and protected by Te Whiti, Tohu and the collective weight of their followers. As the Pākehā nation-home was being developed, as Aotearoa was becoming New Zealand, there was no room for these competing interiors.

Michael Shepherd's reworking of this Collis photograph, into an unfinished image he calls 'Negative', makes a clever twenty-first century statement about the nature of photography and the nature of colonisation. But in the 1880s, few, if any, settlers would have been able to see this photograph in this way. Rather, in The Parihaka Album, 1881 photographs of the advance on Parihaka are used to tell a story of the domestication of 'a vast and unpredictable universe, setting its pleasures and terrors into a pattern of knowledge and experience inextricably linked with the self'.[11] The unpredictable and terrifying universe of Māori Taranaki was domesticated through the successful defence of the settler house and home against the threat (symbolic and real) represented by the Māori house and home at Parihaka. This 'domestication', the contents of the album suggest, was achieved through a 'bloodless victory' of the sort Bryce described.

While the military campaign on Parihaka generated a significant body of photographs, it is a lopsided record that remembers the successful defence of the settler home, while forgetting the violence involved in this defence. Apart from the Collis shot of a (largely hidden) crowd of Māori waiting for the soldiers to arrive at Parihaka, the pictures in The Parihaka Album depict Bryce's army only in camp or performing military manoeuvres. Like Roger Fenton, who took famous photographs of the Crimean War, Collis has rendered war 'as a dignified all-male group outing', in tableaux that required subjects to be absolutely still for the fifteen seconds of exposure that was needed for the image to take.[12]

In Collis's images, the invaders are everywhere, but the invaded are absent, ghostly. In this pictorial geography, the people-less Parihaka is almost a model village, a collection of native show homes, an empty place waiting to be enlivened by the presence of predominantly Pākehā soldiers and their swags, dogs, bayonets, blankets and marching bands.

The violence of the invasion is masked by the absence of victims. If the inhabitants are invisible, so is their suffering. We can see the troops parading in their Parihaka camp; but we cannot see them tugging at the support posts of people's homes to tear them down. We cannot see them stealing Māori food and treasures or attacking Māori women.

Art critic Alan Sekula notes that every photographic image, every collection, tells a story about the power of the collector. Therefore, historians working with photographs might ask: 'How is historical and social memory preserved, transformed, restricted and obliterated by photography? What futures are promised; what

Pictures

futures are forgotten?'[13] What did the compiler of The Parihaka Album want to remember? What did they want to forget?

The first two images in the album are war photographs taken by William Collis. 'Rahotu volunteer camp' depicts three spectators in the foreground looking at a great mass of men and volunteers snaking across a hill in the middle distance. Behind them are the white bell tents.[14] The next photograph is of 'Officers' quarters at Pungarehu'. It depicts two raupō huts, very similar to the homes at Parihaka. There is a neat path between them and, in the background, a smaller hut, a long-drop toilet or washhouse perhaps. It is a homely scene of little houses and well-tended paths. Without the caption, it could well be a portion of Parihaka.

Figure 13. Volunteer camp, Rahotu. ca 1881, black and white original photographic print, mounted on album page, photograph by William Andrews Collis, Alexander Turnbull Library, reference number PA1-q-183-01.

The next two photographs depict picturesque scenes: a waterfall, 'Bells Falls, Mt Egmont', and a white family having a picnic at 'The Meeting of the Waters'. In the Bells Falls photograph, the photographer's cumbersome mobile darkroom can be seen in the foreground. A Māori child – the photographer's assistant perhaps – is in the right foreground.[15]

Figure 14. View of Bells Falls, Mt Egmont, Taranaki, ca 1878, photograph by William Andrews Collis. The photographer's darkroom may be seen in the foreground. Black and white original photographic print, albumen print 21.6 x 26 cm, mounted on album page, Alexander Turnbull Library, reference number PA1-q-183-03.

Then there are seventeen more photographs of the Parihaka campaign. They begin with several images of Parihaka itself, followed by a selection that demonstrates the size of the force massed against the village: the 'Pungarehu A.C. station', the 'Taranaki Rifles camp', the 'Nelson Camp', 'A.C. Officers' and the 'Wellington Navals', dressed in sailors' suits and sailors' hats, adrift in a brown paddock.

As well as the men, Collis has photographed the fortifications. The Rahotu and Pungarehu redoubts can be inspected from several angles, including a back view, which shows a large, smooth, thatched wall snaking over a hilltop. Among the fortification photos, there is also the famous Collis image of residents crowded onto the marae.

One of the distinctive features of many of these images, especially the ones of the soldiers' camps, is the blasted, burnt-off landscape. The trees are dead, the grass stubble. This ruined land is so different from the lush world of nature presented in the images that follow the Parihaka photos in the album. We see the ocean and the Sugar Loaf rocks, a fern gully, a merry river.

In 'Raupō Whare', a white woman in a ruffled black shirt and skirt nurses a child outside a hut that resembles the houses at Parihaka.[16] This photograph is a hybrid image. The title points out that although the picture contains certain signifiers of the settler home – the lace curtains, the pram, the window – it is nonetheless foreign. The whare mediates the photographs of Parihaka at the start of the album and the images of white civilisation that end it. It is followed by a picture of Waitara, the place where the Taranaki wars began, in which all traces of conflict (and obviously Māori occupation) have been erased. Waitara is progressive and Waitara is white, the photograph says. It has a wooden bridge and wooden buildings and a small dock and neat fishing boats. There are no whare raupō.

The Parihaka Album

Figure 15. View of a mother and infant sitting outside a raupō house in Taranaki, 1875–1885, photograph by William Andrews Collis, black and white original photographic print, albumen print 13.6 x 20.2 cm, mounted on album page, Alexander Turnbull Library, reference number PA1-q-183-25-2.

Waitara is followed by images of the Taranaki settler capital, New Plymouth, with the mountain in full view behind it (as it is in so many pictures of Parihaka). New Plymouth is clearly bigger than Waitara. It has a dense collection of buildings with gables and widows' walks, walls made from solid wood, probably rimu or kauri.

The Parihaka Album ends with a very specific collection of images. 'View of an Interior' shows, in exquisite detail, a settler's parlour. A sideboard gleams, ceramic figurines raise a sword and club in a symbolic battle over a display of family silver, a dining table is draped in a velvet cloth. A landscape painting depicts a tumbling waterfall, an echo of the photograph of 'Bells Falls' included earlier in the album.

Pictures

Figure 16. Defence of the interior. This photograph is the last image in The Parihaka Album. The Alexander Turnbull Library describes is as 'View of a dining room of a large house, probably in New Plymouth, photographed in the period 1880–1895, probably by William Andrews Collis, albumen print 13.6 x 20.3 cm, mounted on album page'. Alexander Turnbull Library, reference number PA1-q-183-42-2.

Three more images of New Plymouth follow – Devon Street, with the enormous White Hart hotel hugging the corner, the Roman Catholic convent and an 'English church' – before the final shot, another 'View of an Interior'. This interior is even more lavish than the first. Ferns and other native foliage spill from a vase in the fireplace, which is ebonised in what was known as the Pompeian style. The mantelpiece is decorated with a Japanese vase and Royal Doulton figurines. Above the dado is a leafy, glossy wallpaper. Next to it is a chaise longue, with carved, shapely legs, a suitable place for reclining in this lush, state-of-the-art interior. This is the home of a rich, fashionable person.[17]

So the album begins with the Collis photograph of the Rahotu volunteers camp and ends with the settler sitting room. It tells a story in which the invasion of Parihaka was a defence of settler house and home. The presence of Miti Mai Te Arero, Parihaka's defiantly European building, does not change that narrative. Māori at Parihaka lived in mere huts – they didn't even have lace curtains – whereas settlers lived in homes, places that contained rooms decorated with vases, figurines and flowers. Māori lived in one-roomed shelters, whereas wealthy settlers lived in multiple-roomed homes with neat white exteriors and dark, ornate interiors piled high with evidence of an individual's leisure, money, taste and refinement. The defence of this interior was an act of patriotism. The defence of the other one was rebellion.

The album also lays the townscapes of Parihaka and the settler communities of Waitara and New Plymouth side by side and finds the Māori town wanting. Collis's photographs often show Māori vegetable gardens, or perhaps urupā (burial grounds), enclosed by handmade fences. When these enclosures are viewed next to modest raupō huts, they appear to signal something that is makeshift and impermanent, easily destroyed, so different from the wooden enormity of the White Hart Hotel or the English church in nearby New Plymouth. Far from home, the soldiers who invaded Parihaka lived in the most impermanent home imaginable, a tent, but these hundreds of tents were merely the advance guard for the permanent base of the European home.

The album tells a Parihaka story in which the narrator, a settler, has domesticated Taranaki. The taming of Taranaki encompasses the invasion of Parihaka and the transforming of wild landscapes – such as Bells Falls – into objects of picturesque admiration. These victories protected and bolstered the 'white house' of settler New Zealand, from the streets of New Plymouth and Waitara to the hushed interiors of the settler family home. Military force had ensured that the 'white house' would follow the lighthouse in central Taranaki.

The language of buildings

While settlers were telling one story with their buildings and their pictures, Māori were determined to tell another. Te Whiti's and Tohu's exile in the South Island ended in March 1883, when they were allowed to return to Parihaka. The township was dilapidated, and once they got home, the leaders started to rebuild the pā and repair the damage done by the invading forces two years earlier.

This work was initially funded by Raniera Ellison of Otakou in Southland. Ellison (Erihana) was born at Warea, Taranaki, in 1839, the son of Englishman Tom Ellison and Ngāti Moeahu woman Taikairaua. In 1862, he found gold on the Kawarau River in Otago and made his fortune.[18] Māori from as far off as the Chatham Islands also sent generous gifts of food and money.[19] Māori sold horses, cattle and land so they could give money to Te Whiti, and guests at the village's monthly meetings always left a shilling on their plates after breakfast to help pay for hospitality and upkeep.

Later construction work was funded by Waitara, the Te Āti Awa landowner from the Hutt Valley. John Bryce introduced Waitara to Te Whiti in 1886, while Te Whiti and Titokowaru were serving a six-month sentence in Wellington. The men were imprisoned because 500 Māori from Parihaka and other places along the coast had built raupō whares on 'settler' farms around Hawera and moved in.[20] From the time they met, Waitara paid for whatever the chiefs needed. The pair were 'handed over to him' when they were released, and Waitara paid for them to get back to Taranaki.[21] Waitara went back to Parihaka with them, and in 1889, he married Te Whiti's daughter Ngaruaki Pereni.[22] Waitara spent 'thousands of pounds of his own money' on rebuilding Te Whiti's part of Parihaka.[23]

It is unclear what happened to Miti Mai Te Arero and the settlement's bank after the November 1881 invasion. Telegraphs and government reports do not mention Miti Mai by name as one of the structures that was pulled down, but it seems unlikely that the soldiers would have spared Te Whiti's council chamber in their destruction of the village.

In 1981, with the support of the Parihaka Pā Trustees, Vivian Hutchinson and Matarena Rau-Kupa prepared a script to go with a photographic survey on Parihaka. The script says that Miti Mai Te Arero was rebuilt when Te Whiti and Tohu returned to Parihaka after their exile. A new twin-gabled dining room, Te Niho o Te Āti Awa, was built to support it.

The reconstruction of Miti Mai and the construction of Te Niho were preludes to a more extensive modernisation of Parihaka, a project that challenges many still-potent ideas in which authentic indigenous people must remain in a ghetto of tradition, an ossified place where no new traditions can be invented. Parihaka's modernity overturns these cruel historical exclusions. Parihaka was a new kind of pan-tribal Māori settlement, established in response to the ravages of colonisation in Taranaki. At Parihaka, Te Whiti and Tohu self-consciously rejected some aspects of the traditional past (such as armed warfare) and embraced some aspects of technological advancement (such as ploughs, threshing machines and electricity).

Pre-invasion Parihaka was already different from other Māori settlements because the prophets discouraged traditional carving and rafter patterns. The buildings at Parihaka, like the teachings of the prophets, were intended to reflect new ways of thinking. In 1880, the gable of one whare was decorated with a carving of an owl looking down on a stalking cat. The owl was ruru (the morepork, a symbol of the God of Peace), and the cat, an introduced predator, was the Pākehā.[24]

From 1883 onwards, many more European buildings were constructed among the raupō whares that still predominated in the village. The rebuilding spoke to three audiences: Māori at Parihaka, Māori outside Parihaka and Europeans.[25]

Building Miti Mai Te Arero had been an act of defiance towards settlers. The reconstruction of Parihaka continued to demonstrate the mana of Māori and their mastery of the architecture of European modernity, but the reconstruction was also part of a vigorous and divisive internal negotiation of how far Māori should move towards this modernity and how modernity might coexist with tradition – including the Old Testament traditions that had influenced the thinking of Te Whiti and Tohu.

The paradox of Parihaka as a place that was supposed to represent both the death of tradition and its maintenance is revealed in speeches made by Te Whiti and Tohu in 1885. According to the aptly-named government translator, Charles Messenger, Te Whiti said:

> *The people are dead and the land is dead. This gathering here today is the gathering that was scattered to be destroyed but here we are today. The only work for this generation is work like this table today, and we shall live. The trouble is past and gone and lost sight of, it will never be seen any more – never, never again till the end of the world.*[26]

This speech implies that the Māori and the land of old are 'dead' – killed by colonisation, yet the community of Parihaka, a community that 'was scattered to be destroyed' in 1881, endured.

Tohu also described Parihaka as a place where Māori tradition would endure. He said that the trouble had gone, and the protests of the past were no longer worthwhile, but the people remained:

> *We will gather in this marae. This will not be done away with till the end of the world. Weeds will never grow in this marae, but I will keep it for my people to gather in. Waikato, Taranaki, Ngati Ruanui, don't say: 'This is what he says to day, but tomorrow he will tell us different.' No; not tomorrow – next month – a year – it will be the same; we shall live; this generation will not be lost sight of.*[27]

The Parihaka Album

Messenger's interpretation of these speeches displays an accord in the thinking of Te Whiti and Tohu, but the two men developed different ideas about how Parihaka should remain dynamic enough to ensure that 'weeds will never grow on this marae'. Both a source of innovation and a keeper of tradition, Parihaka was a community pulled in two directions. Could any place cope with such a tension?

Figure 17. Meeting at Parihaka Pā, with Te Whetu Moeahu, 17 March 1896, photograph by William Andrews Collis, black and white original negative, glass negative, Alexander Turnbull Library, reference number G-12103-1/1.

Ironically, it was when the restoration and modernisation of Parihaka was at its peak – when the settlement appeared most prosperous and successful to its many visitors – that a division developed between Te Whiti and Tohu and their followers.[28] As Taranaki kuia Matarena Rau-Kupa has narrated: 'Perhaps 50 years of constant change and pressures on Parihaka finally took its toll as feelings of resentment began to turn within. The prophets had a dispute between themselves in 1890, and thereafter lived on separate parts of the marae.'²⁹

Photographs taken at this time depict a thriving place, but beneath the bustling village were deep fissures and damage. The leaders remained inspirational, but one of the casualties of war was the accord between them. The men and their followers paid a high price for the 'peace' they had secured.

In a thesis seeking to restore Tohu to a central role in the Parihaka story, and in a subsequent entry in the *Dictionary of New Zealand Biography*, Ailsa Smith has argued that Te Whiti and Tohu had different responses to the European places and things that they saw during their South Island imprisonment. Te Whiti had been impressed with 'Pākehā refinements', while Tohu wanted to keep Parihaka's original 'policy of self sufficiency'.³⁰ Money was also a factor. The 'Day of Reckoning' funds – money that would be used once Māori had re-inherited their land – were kept in the settlement's bank in Tohu's part of Parihaka. The money was collected, in part, from donations at the monthly meetings and from levies of up to seventy-five percent on the wages Parihaka people earned from growing grass seed or picking mushrooms. Waitara's money was not put in this common fund, and Smith argues that this money contributed to the tension between the two leaders.³¹

Tohu said the division between himself and Te Whiti had less earthly causes. In an 1895 speech recorded by Parihaka scribe Te Kaahui, Tohu said:

> *Listen to me, my people. This is to enlighten you on the subject of the separation between Te Whiti and myself. It was Jehovah who broke apart the yoke binding us together, men did not break our yoke apart. We two were anointed by Jehovah, by our God. It was our doing alone that we broke up and are now separated …*³²

Whether the split between the two men was caused by material or spiritual forces, one symbol of this split was the decision by Tohu's followers to stop wearing the raukura feather. Instead, Tohu's people were known as the pore (polled or dehorned) because they did not wear the feather. They chose to be identified by what they did *not* display. An absence was their sign. This difference is reflected in the way the burial places of the two prophets are marked. While Te Whiti's resting place – on the site where the demolished Miti Mai once stood – is marked by a large monument paid for by Waitara, Tohu is buried in an unmarked grave at Parihaka in a little-known location.

Writing about Te Whiti, Danny Keenan acknowledges the stories about the arguments between the two men and how each, apparently, claimed to be the true prophet, then goes on to note: 'Yet they and their histories are largely inseparable. That differences emerged between their followers in the 1880s and 1890s was, and remains, the source of some sorrow. Both men regularly sought each other's counsel; descendants speak of the men as complementary, two figures sharing a titanic burden.'[33]

The split between the two men is part of the history they share. In 1889, they began separate projects to build new meeting houses. Waitara, a master builder, erected Te Raukura with the assistance of Te Manuera (Emmanuel Dix), a Māori-Portuguese carpenter born on the Chatham Islands, and returned prisoners. The men had spent much of their confinement building walls and causeways; they used the skills gained during their imprisonment to reconstruct Parihaka. Te Manuera also helped to build Tohu's two-storied meeting house.

Although Smith has stated that the size and location of the houses demonstrated further tensions between the leaders, the names that the men gave to these magnificent buildings were concerned with togetherness and resolution of conflict and suggest that they still had hopes for a united community. Te Whiti named his house Te Raukura, after his feathered emblem of peace; Tohu called his Rangi Kapuia (Draw the People Together, or Gather the Skies). The balcony of Rangi Kapuia was decorated with playing card symbols, similar to those used by East Coast leader Te Kooti.[34]

Figure 18. Pākehā men and women photographed in front of a whare at Parihaka with Māori children. Many of the visitors are wearing white feathers, ca 1895–1900, photographer unknown, gelatin silver print mounted on album page, Alexander Turnbull Library, reference number PA1-0-405-13.

Te Raukura was built on a raised marae. Its centrepiece was a large meeting room that could hold two hundred. A cottage was built for Te Whiti, and also a home for his pigeons – he had taken up keeping them after his exile in Christchurch. There was also a house for the twelve 'apostles' who had been sent to live at Parihaka by the Māori king Tawhiao. As on other marae, residents of Parihaka often ate together in large communal dining rooms.

Both Tohu and Te Whiti also hosted large groups of visitors and served them sweets, puddings and cakes, along with more traditional Māori food (such as hāngi). A Pākehā cook, 'who knows more of the mysteries of making pudding and other luxuries', was employed at Raukura.³⁵ Pākehā visitors commented on the style of entertainment. In 1885, Lieutenant Colonel J.M. Roberts attended a 'great dinner' given by Tohu and noted that the feast was 'entirely different to the ordinary run of Māori foods … everything [was] carried out in European style; waiters in attendance &c'.³⁶ However, no beer or spirits were allowed.

Other innovations abounded. The Parihaka fife and drum band, an amalgam of European and Māori styles of music-making, entertained visitors. A bakery, staffed by Māori bakers, sold bread to Parihaka residents and white settlers who lived nearby. After an epidemic of typhoid fever, Waitara had invented an ingenious water supply system. A hydraulic ram pumped clean mountain water down to the village from two concrete reservoirs on a hill above it. Parihaka had an abattoir, butchery and bank, and it was one of the first places in New Zealand to have street lights. From 1900, the settlement generated its own electricity, using the overflow from the reservoirs.

The symbolic and practical importance of road building in and around Parihaka did not end with the 1881 invasion. In 1885, Te Whiti and Tohu organised large hīkoi (marches) of up to 2000 'chanting, poi-swinging Māori' who walked around Taranaki tribal boundaries, going from village to village and enjoying immense feasts at each place. These journeys were reportedly meant to 'establish peace among Māori now that peace had been firmly established between Europeans and Natives'.³⁷ The hīkoi constructed symbolic roads that linked different Māori groups in Taranaki.

Māori also demonstrated their mana and their mastery of peace by building real roads. In 1885, Parihaka scribe Te Kaahui built a road through the Ngatihaupoto Block at Rahotu (a small settlement close to Parihaka) and named it after himself. At the opening of Te Kahui Road, the leader told a deputation from Parihaka: 'Here is work, here are wheelbarrows, picks, adzes, bullocks; these are the prized possessions of peace, and Kahui Road is here as an example.'³⁸

Pictures

Figure 19. Piping the haka. Man with taiaha doing a haka, Parihaka, ca 1896, photograph by John Feaver, Feaver collection, Puke Ariki, New Plymouth, ARC2003-558.

Unable to resist a chance to possess peace, Te Whiti and Tohu decided to rebuild the road inside Parihaka. The 'beautifully metalled bye road', completed in 1896, was a joint effort: the followers of Te Whiti built the top portion and the followers of Tohu built the lower part.[39] The whole may have been a combined effort, but different Māori brass bands celebrated each segment. Newspapers reported that the Manukorihi fife and drum band played for Te Whiti, and the Upper Whanganui brass played for Tohu. Just one year earlier, the Whanganui band had played military leader Te Rangihiwinui (Te Keepa or Major Kemp) into Parihaka. Te Rangihiwinui had come to Parihaka to try to broker a resolution between Te Whiti and Tohu. The band had marched to Tohu's side, but Te Rangihiwinui's band went to Te Whiti's. The next year, Te Keepa came again; this time Tohu intercepted his party outside Parihaka and made the strategically important first offer of hospitality. Smith relates that by the next night, a slighted Te Whiti had still refused to acknowledge Te Keepa.[40]

In 1897, a year after the Parihaka road had been built, Te Rangi Hiroa (Peter Buck), then aged twenty, visited the settlement. Buck – who went on to become the first New Zealand-trained Māori doctor after graduating from Otago University in 1904 – had been born in 1877 and raised in Urenui, in north Taranaki, but his mother's family were Te Āti Awa, and he had spent time at Parihaka as a child. Buck wanted to compile a report on Māori of Taranaki for his old school, the Christian college for Māori boys, Te Aute. The young man was impressed with these signs of 'advance to civilisation', but he was less happy about some of the other signs of 'civilisation' that were also evident. Parihaka had two billiard-rooms and two 'houses where intoxicating liquors are sold secretly, without licence'. There was no church either, Buck observed. (Nor were there any schools as Te Whiti forbade them.) Despite his concerns about drinking and gambling, Buck was astounded at the transformation in the village and fascinated by Te Whiti's knowledge of world affairs, particularly European politics, which he gained through reading *The*

Taranaki Herald, the Auckland *Weekly News* and another Auckland daily. Each night, Buck observed, 'a young half-caste translates the more important passages out of the papers to him'. During his visit, Buck also helped translate some articles. He could not recognise the village he now saw before him, writing:

> *Parihaka, as I had seen it years ago, was a large pā full of dirt and all manner of filth. The houses were almost entirely built of raupō and toetoe, there being very few wooden buildings. But all this was changed. Branching off from the main road, a beautifully metalled bye road (made by the Māoris themselves), leads right up to the pā. They carted and broke the stones, dug the drains, leveled and built up the earth, and metalled the whole road for themselves … [we] saw Parihaka below us nestling in a small hollow. Wooden buildings rose on all sides. On the banks of the small stream which flows through the village stood a large, well-built wooden house, the residence of Tohu. On the left on a terrace stood the house of Te Whiti himself, while behind it was a handsome residence of some other Taranaki chief. The latter is the best house in Parihaka, fitted up in the most up-to-date Pākehā style, with dining-rooms, bath-rooms, and everything that the Māori thought was after the European fashion … I think Parihaka will soon resemble a Pākehā township.*[41]

Photographs of Parihaka in the early twentieth century suggest that Buck's prediction had come true: they show a place thick with wooden buildings of the sort found in any other New Zealand town. Few whare raupō remain.[42]

Yet as had been the case with Miti Mai Te Arero, appearances at Parihaka could deceive. Parihaka did resemble a Pākehā township, with houses and streets built 'after the European fashion', but the residents continued to engage in active resistance campaigns over the management or ownership of Māori lands. The year Buck visited, ninety-two Parihaka men were arrested for ploughing in protest at the native trustee's management of native reserves. Settlers' thirty-year leases on Māori land were being converted into perpetual titles.

The prisoners returned to Parihaka in 1898 and were welcomed back by large groups of women and children adorned with raukura and swinging poi.[43] The village had been rebuilt 'after the European fashion', but the wars that led to its foundation had not been forgotten. Regular political meetings continued to be held at Parihaka on the eighteenth[th] and nineteenth[th] of each month, and residents continued to push for at least some control over their land.

Figure 20. Parihaka, view towards the south, showing Rangi Kapuia, ca 1898, photograph by John Feaver, Feaver collection, Puke Ariki ARC2003-559.

Perhaps the cruellest outcome of the wars in Taranaki and the campaign on Parihaka was the fact that although some confiscated land was returned to Māori, they could not use it or care for it. Without land, there was no money to sustain Parihaka, to pay for its upkeep and to feed its residents and visitors. While Victorian buildings are renovated, painted and restored in New Zealand towns and cities, often under the authority of the Historic Places Trust, a visitor to Parihaka today will find little evidence of the Victorian modernity that once flourished there.

In the early 1950s, Dick Scott went to Parihaka and found a collection of houses of late Victorian design. He walked 'the grass streets past empty doorways and blank windows, past sagging verandahs and a fallen roof'.[44] I too saw Victorian ruins when I visited as a schoolgirl.

When I went back in 2002, Parihaka was even more run down. Physically, it is such a poor place. The toilet block leaked, and buildings were boarded up. One kuia, who was quite sick with asthma, lived in a mobile home not much bigger than a caravan. The only remaining traces of the village's Victorian magnificence were two brass and iron gas lights, stamped with the insignia of the New Plymouth Gas Works; Te Whiti's marble monument; a dilapidated Rangi Kapuia; and the monumental concrete slab for Te Raukura, where children were practising taiaha. Te Raukura burnt down in 1960, in a fire that claimed the life of caretaker George Te Kahui Pokai Aitua. At the time of the fire, Aitua and others had been seeking funds to reblock and refurbish the run-down building.[45]

History and tradition are such strange things. In 1881, colonial troops demolished so many whare (and a European-style house) to make way for the 'European homesteads' that would bring peace on the plains. In the two decades that followed, Māori rebuilt their home, replacing at least some whare with wooden houses, and installing the infrastructure that made Parihaka one of the most modern towns in New Zealand. Almost 100 years after the invasion, young Māori demolished the rotten old European-style parts of the settlement as part of the village's renewal, a renewal that included building 'a traditional ponga whare'.[46]

The Parihaka Album

[1] Asa Briggs, *Victorian Things*, London: B.T. Batsford, 1988, 132-134.

[2] Private James Ledger, *Pen and Ink Sketches of Parihaka and Neighbourhood*, Dunedin: Fergusson & Mitchell, 1883. Scott, *Ask That Mountain*, says released prisoners built the house 'used as a dining and reception centre by Te Whiti and Tohu' in 1881, and relates how some people said the house had been 'put up to receive the new Governor, Sir Arthur Gordon', 91.

[3] G.C. Beale, 'Parihaka, 1881' and George Sherriff, 'Parihaka 1881', reproduced in *Passive Resistance*, 22 and 25.

[4] For information on this house, see Hohaia, 'Te Whetu Moeahu', text panel, *Parihaka: The Struggle for Peace*, PA or Vivian Hutchinson and Matarena Rau-Kupa, 'Parihaka: A Photographic Survey', script for audiovisual presentation, caption 88, catalogue no: 2003-497, PA. This script was made for Taranaki Museum – and eventually broadcast on local station 2ZP – to commemorate the centennial of the sacking of Parihaka. Written by Hutchinson with the approval and support of Parihaka Trustees, it was co-narrated by Hutchinson and Rau-Kupa, a Taranaki kuia.

[5] T.S. Muir photograph, ARC2003-564, PA. This image inspired Ralph Hotere's 1972 work *Comet over Mt Egmont (Taranaki) and Parihaka*, *Passive Resistance*, 126. Peter Walker uses the comet photograph as a metaphor of both victory and loss in *The Fox Boy*, 310-311.

[6] Susan Sontag, *Regarding the Pain of Others*, New York: Farrar, Straus and Giroux, 2003, 26.

[7] Sontag, *Pain of Others*, 29.

[8] Philip Gourevitch and Errol Morris, *Standard Operating Procedure: A War Story*, London: Picador, 2008, 148.

[9] The ATL describes this photograph as: 'View of Parihaka, Taranaki, photographed at the time of the Armed Constabulary invasion. In the centre background, to the right, the inhabitants of Parihaka may be seen seated.' This photograph was the basis for Michael Shepherd's 'Negative', *Art of Passive Resistance*, 94. The one-word caption, 'Parihaka', was inscribed by the settler who compiled what the ATL describes as 'The Parihaka Album'. Black and white albumen print mounted on album page, William Andrews Collis, 'View of Parihaka, Taranaki, photographed at the time of the Armed Constabulary invasion.' Albumen print mounted on albumen page, November 1881, The Parihaka Album, PA1-q-183-18, ATL.

[10] For a photograph of the bank, see Scott, *Ask That Mountain*, 159. Scott says the bank was dated Hane (June) 1881.

[11] Martha Langford, 'The Album As Collection' in *Suspended Conversations: The Afterlife of Memory in Photographic Albums*, Montreal and London: McGill-Queen's University Press, 2001, 63.

[12] Sontag, *Pain of Others*, 47.

[13] Alan Sekula, 'Reading an Archive', in B. Wallis & M. Tucker, eds. *Blasted Allegories* Cambridge, Mass: MIT Press, 1987, 113.

[14] Rahotu Volunteer Camp. Black and white albumen print mounted on album page, William Andrews Collis, PA1-q-183-01, ATL.

[15] The ATL notes: 'This photo was probably taken in February 1878 during a climbing expedition on Mt Egmont undertaken by Collis and a group of other young men. Photographs of Mt Egmont and Bells Falls taken on this trip were reported in the *Taranaki Herald* of 7 March 1878.' Black and white albumen print mounted on album page, Collis, PA1-q-183-03, ATL.

[16] ATL describes the photograph as: 'A mother and child sit outside this raupō house close to the child's pram, at the Rahotu Redoubt, Egmont … Raupō, a marsh reed, was a traditional building material of the Māori. The raupō was tied in bundles and lashed to a wooden framework with flax. The roof was then thatched. These homes were cheap and quick to build, and relatively weathertight. They were, however, highly inflammable and were eventually forbidden in towns. The imported doors and windows would later be transferred to a more permanent home.' Black and white albumen print mounted on album page, photographer unknown, PA1-q-183-25-2, ATL.

[17] My thanks to Walter Cook, assistant curator photography at Alexander Turnbull Library, for his insights into late nineteenth-century home decorating. The ATL describes the photo as: 'View of the dining room of a large house, probably in New Plymouth.' Black and white albumen print mounted in album, William Collis, PA1-q-183-42-2, ATL.

[18] See Hohaia, 'Another Parihaka leader: Raniera Erihana (Daniel Ellison)', text panel, Puke Ariki Parhiaka exhibition. Hohaia writes that Raniera maintained his links with Taranaki and in 1865 invited Taranaki tohunga Piripi Te Kohe south to share Te Whiti's teachers. In 1880, Raniera went to Parihaka to welcome men who had been imprisoned in Dunedin, and in 1882 he was granted permission, by Parihaka authorities, to celebrate the 18th (Te Whiti's day) at Otakou Marae on the Otago Peninsula. For information on other Ellisons, see Bill Dacker, 'Nga Hononga: connections', text panel from *Parihaka: The Art of Passive Resistance* and 'Te Iwi Herehere: the story of Māori prisoners from Taranaki in Otago 1869-1882', Dunedin Public Art Gallery, 2002.

[19] Smith, 'Tohu Kakahi', *DNZB*, and Riseborough, *Darkness*, p. 210. Riseborough notes that in 1885, a European on the Chathams saw 'some 2000 tuna drying and another 5000 in drays drawn by 14 bullocks, and thought there would be "quite 20,000 eels in all for Te Whiti".' For another account of Chatham Islands (Ngāti Mutunga) support of Parihaka, see Evelyn Tuuta, 'Feast or Famine: Customary Fisheries Management in a Contemporary Tribal Society', in Michael Belgrave, Merata Kawharu and David Williams, eds, *Waitangi Revisited: Perspectives on the Treaty of Waitangi,* Melbourne: Oxford University Press, 2005, 171.

[20] Scott, *Ask That Mountain,* 150-153.

[21] Te Miringa Hohaia, 'Taare Waitara', text board, Parihaka: the struggle for peace, PA.

The Parihaka Album

[22] Hutchinson and Rau-Kupa, 'Parihaka: A Photographic Survey', caption 84, 1981, PA.

[23] 'Te Whiti Case Claim for Trust-Fund Accounts', *Taranaki Herald*, 18 March 1926.

[24] Scott, *Ask That Mountain*. The gable decoration was sketched in 1880 by W.F. Gordon, p. 28. Ngati Mutunga use the owl and the cat as symbols of friend and foe in a song they performed before the Sim Commission. See 'Ko Waitara', Ngati Mutunga Deed of Settlement, OTS.

[25] Parihaka was one of a number of competing centres of Māori power. In 1885, for instance, Te Kooti said: 'There are two stars still standing, that of the East and that of the West.' Binney interprets this as a reference to Te Whiti as the 'star of the west', and says it implies there was a developing rivalry between Te Kooti's Ringatu faith and the faith of followers of Te Whiti. *Redemption Songs*, 425.

[26] Charles Messenger, telegram No.2, from J.M Roberts to the Under-Secretary, Native Office, Wellington, 1 July 1885, AJHR, vol II 1885, G-8 and G-8a.

[27] This speech was also translated by Messenger in telegram No.2, from J.M Roberts to the Under-Secretary, Native Office, Wellington, 1 July 1885, AJHR, vol II 1885, G-8 and G-8a.

[28] See Scott, *Ask That Mountain*, 163. In a fascinating footnote, Scott explains that in 1890, the Taranaki Holiday Guide listed Parihaka as a tourist attraction. Visitors were advised that the village was 'exceptionally large', but they were warned not to get lost down the lanes and alleys. Scott also notes that Frederick and Agnes Simeon, who had supported the cause of Parihaka prisoners in 1881, became the owners of the Rahotu Hotel in 1893, and one of the pub's charms was its proximity to 'historic' Parihaka.

[29] Hutchinson and Rau-Kupa, 'Parihaka: A Photographic Survey', caption 81.

[30] Smith, 'Tohu Kakahi', DNZB.

[31] Smith, 'Ko Tohu', 126-7.

[32] Tohu Kakahi, cited in Smith, 'Ko Tohu'. Smith has translated this speech from Ruka Broughton's MA thesis on Titokowaru, 1984, 49.

[33] Keenan, 'Te Whiti', *DNZB*.

[34] See D. Duncan, 'View of Tohu Kakahi's house, Rangikaapuia, at Parihaka Pa', ca. 1920, black and white photograph, W.A. Price collection, ATL, reproduced in *Art of Passive Resistance*, 58. For a discussion of playing cards and other iconography on Māori buildings, Pai Marire poles in Taranaki and flags, see Binney et al., *Mihaia: the Prophet Rua Kenana*, 1979 and Binney, *Redemption Songs*, 42-43 for poles and 198-200 for an analysis of flag symbolism.

[35] Peter Buck, 'The Taranaki Māoris: Te Whiti and Parihaka', Te Aute College Students' Association Conference, Papers and Addresses, December 1897, reproduced in J.B. Condliffe, *Te Rangi Hiroa: The Life of Sir Peter Buck*, Christchurch: Whitcombe & Tombs, 1971, 42.

[36] Lieutenant-Colonel J.M. Roberts, 'Native meeting at Parihaka in June, 1885', G-8A, AJHR, vol II, 1885.

[37] Riseborough, *Days of Darkness*, 210. Riseborough cites comments made to Wilfred Rennell of the New Plymouth Native Office by a man he described as a 'very intelligent Native chief'.

[38] Smith, 'Ko Tohu', 131.

[39] Buck, 'The Taranaki Māoris' in Condliffe, *Te Rangi Hiroa*, 41.

[40] Smith, 'Ko Tohu', 134-35.

[41] Buck, 'Taranaki Māoris' in Condliffe, 41.

[42] See 'Parihaka in 1907', black and white photograph 'taken at the time of Te Whiti's death', 188-189, Scott, *Ask That Mountain*. Photograph published in *Weekly News*, 28 November 1907, collection of Auckland Institute & Museum Library.

[43] William Collis, 'Reception of prisoners at Parihaka, 1898', black and white photograph, ATL, reproduced in *Passive Resistance,* 115. In an undated photograph, which may have been taken that same year, Collis photographed the magnificent Te Raukura, with its latticed balcony and three chimneys, and many other 'European' buildings at Parihaka; see *Passive Resistance,* 39.

[44] Scott, Foreword, *The Story of Parihaka,* 1954.

[45] For graphic archival evidence of the village's physical decline, see Marti Freidlander's 1967 photographs of the village, taken during a visit with Dick Scott, *Passive Resistance*, 169-172. See, also, Trevor Ulyatt's 1972 photographs taken for the National Museum and now in the collection of Te Papa, e.g. 'Old house situated North West of Mount Rolleston'; 'Door of Maniapoto family house – Nameplate reads: 1899, Hepetema 27, Tauakira'; registration numbers B.012208 and B.012209. Also, 'Detail of door from old deserted house east of main settlement'; 'Plough (circa 1880) in a swamp east of main settlement'; and 'Remains of a cart, situated in a swamp east of the settlement', numbers B.012226, B.012227 and B.012228. The descriptions are Te Papa's.

[46] Scott, *Writer's Life,* 284. Scott writes that he helped to build one such whare.

CHAPTER 7

The wrong that was done

Te Whiti and Tohu both died in 1907. It is difficult to resist telling a story in which their passing marks the end of Parihaka as a radical, non-traditional, non-violent community. One of the orators at Te Whiti's tangi was Maui Pomare, and he certainly saw things this way.

Pomare's parents had been followers of Te Whiti, and he had been at Parihaka in 1881 when it was invaded. He would have been only five or six years old then, and legend has it that he lost a toe under the hoof of Bryce's horse.[1] Pomare was the first Māori to become a medical doctor – he trained at a Seventh Day Adventist college at Battle Creek in the United States and qualified in 1899. In 1901, he took the post of Māori health officer and began his vigorous campaign to upgrade living conditions for Māori by improving water quality and sanitation and by reducing 'overcrowding' at places such as Parihaka – overcrowding, he pointed out, that had been caused by land confiscation.

Like his fellow doctor, Peter Buck, Pomare's prescription for the ailing Māori race was what he called progress and modernity. The two men saw that the province they both came from, Taranaki, was an especially diseased part of the body of Māori people, and it was Parihaka that was the cause of this illness. To their eyes, Taranaki was 'backward'. In 1905 Buck, too, became a Māori health officer.

145

He had been overawed by the modernity of Parihaka in 1897; but no traces of this admiration remained in a report he wrote six months into his new job.

Buck wrote that the influence of Parihaka meant that Māori from Taranaki were 'two generations' behind other tribes: 'As long as Te Whiti and Tohu are alive the majority of people will maintain their isolation and reserve, which any attempt at force will fan into active opposition, as it has done in the past. Here are a people cherishing a delusion which many force themselves to accept because their fathers have died believing it and handed it on as a sacred cause.'[2]

His words echoed those of Pomare, who had complained in one of his early reports for the Health Department that Te Āti Awa were the most backward and demoralised of all tribes. 'There are two main causes that keep them back: first, Te Whitism; second, prejudice against the Pākehā. The first cause will only end when Te Whiti dies and it will be useless to do anything radical until then …'[3]

Pomare's methods of health reform for Māori were sometimes brutal. In his first three years, he ordered that 1900 derelict, rotting whare – places that were 'breeding grounds' for rats – be burned down.[4] He also recommended a Tohunga Suppression Act to outlaw the work of tohunga, skilled healers who used indigenous plants and incantations to treat physical and mental illnesses. Buck prepared a report to support Pomare's proposal. The report said the tohunga of old had been 'the priest and learned man of the tribe who had graduated in the ancient schools of learning. He was versed in the medical knowledge necessary for the treatment of the few ailments of those healthy times …'[5]

Their concerns for Māori health were more than justified. The new illnesses that had arrived with white settlers meant that the present was less than healthy. In 1884, for instance, the year after Te Whiti and Tohu returned, Parihaka people suffered from psoriasis, chest troubles and erysipelas, and 'many children had died'.[6] Both the prophets had asthma.

The wrong that was done

Buck and Pomare were worried about the rise in charlatans who claimed to be tohunga but had none of the traditional skills. Pomare's great-granddaughter, Ngāti Toa Treaty claims coordinator Miria Pomare, recently explained that Sir Maui was not opposed to 'the tohunga of old, who practised in the best interests of Māori and cared for their spiritual needs'.[7] Rather, he was worried about the fakes who either dunked people in cold water to cure them or prescribed alcohol as medicine. She said some of these fake healers had learnt Pākehā values and decided to 'make money out of the sick'. In one pā, Pomare wrote in his 1904 report, seventeen children with measles had died because of the 'wanton practices of a tohunga in whom many natives have faith'.

Education and hygiene, they believed, would save Māori lives. Their approach might be criticised as hostile to Māori tradition, but Māori were certainly more likely to die of disease than Pākehā; for instance, it is estimated that 2160 Māori died in the 1918 flu epidemic, a death rate seven times that of Pākehā.[8]

One of the communities decimated by this epidemic were the several hundred Te Āti Awa people who had withdrawn from Parihaka and established a community at the headwaters of the Waitara River.[9]

Another Māori supporter of the proposed Tohunga Suppression Act was James Carroll, who was elected as the member for Eastern Māori in 1887, and in 1893, won a 'European seat' in Parliament.[10] The Act was passed in 1907, the year Parihaka's prophets died.

At Te Whiti's tangi, Pomare praised Te Whiti's leadership skills, but he then suggested that in these present times, when Pākehā necessarily dominated, such skills were redundant:

Now that the Pākehā has come the iron has taken the place of the stone. The lightning flash of the Pākehā's wisdom [the telephone] speaks far and near. The old order has changed; your ancestors said it would change. When the net is old and worn it is cast aside and the new net goes fishing. I do not want to blame the old net, it was

> *good in its day ... but the old net is worn with time and we must go fishing with the new net our brothers have brought us. We must advance by work, for therein lies our salvation.*[11]

Pomare suggested that Māori would be saved by the 'new net' of work, but what opportunities were there for Māori who wanted to stay close to tribal kāinga such as Parihaka?

By the time the leaders died in 1907, many younger residents, including Te Whiti's son Nohomairangi, had already moved away. Influenced by the rhetoric of the Young Māori Party – of whom Buck and Pomare were leading members – many were working as dairy farmers elsewhere in Taranaki. Smith has argued that many families sought to 'shake off the Parihaka influence' by working away from Parihaka and no longer attending the monthly meetings there. They wanted their children to get a Pākehā education and learn trades.[12]

Some Parihaka people did become farmers. Momona Tamihana, who was one of the children who had greeted the invading troops in 1881, became involved in several successful farming ventures and was a member of the Taranaki Jersey Breeders' Association.[13] Tioko Atua, who was remembered at his Parihaka tangi as one of the small boys who 'opposed the advancing troops with psalms of praise to God', was a spiritual healer, a devout practitioner of the Rātana faith and a successful farmer in the Rahotu-Oanui district.[14]

But these stories were the exception. The Māori modernity that had flowered briefly at Parihaka in the post-invasion reconstruction period gave way to a time of poverty, in-fighting, despair and anger. At its peak, Parihaka was home to 2000 people. By the 1920s, there were only about 200 permanent residents left, and visitors recalled a 'ghost town'. The one high point was the restoration and reopening of Tohu's meeting house, Rangi Kapuia, in 1927. Te Whiti's house, Te Raukura, meanwhile, was described by one Pākehā journalist as 'a castle of decaying charm', a place maintained by Te Whiti's daughter Pereni, featuring a sleeping room 'in beautiful order, its walls graced with paintings of Te Whiti and other old chiefs, just such a room as one would find in the seat of an old English family'.[15]

Figure 21. Opening of the house Rangi Kapuia, Parihaka Pā, 1927, photographer unknown, black and white negative, part of the John Reginald Wall photographs, Alexander Turnbull Library, reference number 1/2 -017411-F.

The only wealth that remained was spiritual or mythical. School children told stories of a large stash of gold currency hidden somewhere in the village, while others believed that the fabled sword of Major Gustavus Von Tempsky had been buried under the settlement's bank. Von Tempsky was shot by Titokowaru's men at the 1868 battle of Te Ngutu o te Manu.

Followers of Te Whiti and Tohu had been divided during the years of prosperity and expansion, and elements of these divisions remained in the less prosperous time that followed their deaths. Impoverishment bitterly divided families, including Te Whiti's family. In 1926, in the Supreme Court, Nohomairangi Te Whiti, Wi Kupe and Wiremu Daymond alleged that Waitara's widow, Te Whiti's daughter Pereni Te Whiti, had held £4000 in a trust fund for Raukura (followers of Te Whiti), and she had fraudulently converted this money for her own use.[16] Maui Pomare and his older brother Tewai both appeared as witnesses for the plaintiffs in the seven-day trial.[17] Nohomairangi and other plaintiffs won the case. Justice Reed found that a 'bitter feud' existed between what he described as sections of the Raukura (followers of Te Whiti). He found that a trust had existed and that Pereni owed £1810 to it. He further ordered that Pereni be 'removed from the trusteeship'.[18]

Residents were united, however, in their ongoing grievances over land confiscation. Although Pomare had indicated that Māori should give up the 'old net' of tradition, such as adhering to the beliefs of the leaders of Parihaka, he most certainly did not advocate that Māori give up their land. Four years after his 'new net' speech, he was elected to parliament as an independent member for Western Māori.

World War I began in 1914. Although some iwi (notably those from the Waikato and Taranaki) refused to sign up for service in protest at the invasions of their territories in the 1860s, many Māori did fight alongside Pākehā (Buck, for example, was an army doctor at Gallipoli). Māori were quick to see the leverage that their participation might give them in settler society.

In 1923, Pomare, Apirana Ngata and sixty-eight other Māori leaders visited Native Minister Joseph Coates to request an inquiry into confiscated land. They found a sympathetic ear in Coates, who was amazed to discover that Māori had visited England many times to vent their grievances over land confiscation and breaches of the Treaty of Waitangi.[19] Coates spoke a little Māori, and he considered Apirana Ngata, the brilliant Ngāti Porou Liberal politician and academic, to be a close friend.[20] The friendship between Coates and Ngata, men from opposing political parties, allowed them to work together to persuade Waikato leader Te Puea Herangi to support the confiscation commission. Convinced a commission was necessary, Coates then approached Pomare and other Māori MPs for help with gathering evidence. He asked them to encourage Māori in their electorates to prepare petitions stating their grievances, making 'specific allegations', claims and charges that would be investigated by a commission.[21]

Dozens of Māori petitions were presented to parliament in 1925. With these in hand, Coates started to lobby his colleagues. In an argument that reflected the views of Pomare, Coates told Cabinet that 'the backwardness of a large section of the Māori people in education and social and moral conditions' could well have been caused by 'the sense of grievance they feel, rightly or wrongly, that an injustice was done to them in the past'. These grievances had become a tradition, 'handed down through the generations so that the youth of the tribes have, in addition to other difficulties, to overcome a pervading feeling of discontent'. Coates was worried that it might be too late to find an effective remedy for the alleged injustices, but felt it was important that the Crown and its representatives, 'who also represent the ideals of British justice and fair-play, afford the opportunity, even at this late date, for the ventilation of these alleged grievances before a tribunal'.[22]

He won his argument. Three men – Hon. Justice Sim, Hon. V. H. Reed and Mr W. Cooper, a 'native associate' – were appointed to run the 1927 Royal Commission into Confiscated Lands (known as the Sim Commission). The commission's chair, William Alexander Sim, was a seventy-year-old Supreme Court judge and noted legal scholar, who had been knighted for his work chairing the 1924 royal commission into taxation.

In a lightning few months, Sim's commission toured the North Island and heard testimonies from Māori in Taranaki, Waikato, Bay of Plenty, Auckland and Wellington. In Taranaki, the commission's hearings took place at Waitara. In his opening address, counsel for the Māori claimants, David Smith, linked the wars of colonisation with the recent war in Europe. Waitara, he said, was a place of 'sacred importance' to Māori because of its connection with confiscated land; it was 'the Sarajevo' of the Māori war, and the confiscation that followed the war in Taranaki was still discussed today in all native settlements.[23] Confiscation, he said:

> ... had exercised a powerful influence on practical affairs. There was vivid evidence on all sides of a sense of deep wrong and injustice. After the Great War, when the flower of Māori manhood fought shoulder to shoulder with their white brethren on the slopes of Gallipoli and the plains of Europe, it was felt that the Government would listen to their grievances. Petitions poured into Parliament, and deputations approached Ministers, and as a result the Commission had been appointed.[24]

A prophecy fulfilled?

Many Māori from Taranaki saw the Sim Commission as a belated fulfilment of Te Whiti's prophecy, proof that the peaceful protests of Parihaka residents had finally been rewarded by an inquiry into confiscated lands. Māori counsel Smith explained that Te Whiti's pacifist teachings had averted war in Taranaki – thus inverting the predominant story in 1881, that it was the size of Bryce's army that had prevented war. Smith said Te Whiti had promised his followers that if they used peaceful means to resist encroachments upon them, an inquiry would be held into the confiscations. 'It may be surprising to you, gentlemen, to know that in these circumstances, the members of the Commission sitting here today in Waitara are regarded by the Māori as the commissioners and arbiters appointed by the government in fulfillment of Te Whiti's prophecy.'[25]

Tamati Whanganui's Parihaka petition had explained that the fencing and ploughing protests of Parihaka residents had been intended to force the government to investigate the confiscations of the 1860s. But like many of the other Taranaki petitioners, Whanganui asserts, mistakenly, that land between Parininihi and Waitotara was not part of the 1865 confiscation. Rather, he understood this land had been confiscated to punish Māori for their actions at Parihaka.[26]

The central part of Whanganui's petition is a vivid account of the events leading up to the plunder of Parihaka. It reads, in part:

> *In spite of this intimidation by the Government (imprisonment of fencers without trial), the tribe did not flinch nor did they abandon the hope to regain their lands. Following upon the 'Plunder' at Parihaka took place. Mr Bryce, acting on behalf of the Government, ordered the surrender of Te Whiti, Tohu and their people within fourteen days, otherwise men, women and children would be wiped off the face of the earth. When Te Whiti and Tohu did not surrender to the Government, the Parihaka Pā was besieged by Mr Bryce and his soldiers. Whereat Te Whiti said, 'If you shoot me I will surrender, but if your gun does not fire you will surrender yourself to me'. Following upon this, Mr Bryce laid hands on Te Whiti and Tohu and imprisoned them. Then the Government soldiers plundered the houses of the people at Parihaka, smashed open boxes containing valuable greenstone goods and other things held dear to Māori. The Māoris were driven like pigs into their homes and were followed up by the plundering soldiers. Finally their lands were confiscated.*[27]

This account is biblical and apocalyptic. Bryce is depicted as a kind of omnipotent Old Testament wrathful God, a figure who threatens to wipe 'men, women and children … off the face of the earth'. His touch condemns. He arrests Te Whiti and Tohu, not with handcuffs, but by merely 'laying hands' on them. Then he unleashes the forces of vengeance, the plundering, violent soldiers. Once he has trapped and robbed Māori, he then exiles them from their homes: 'their lands were confiscated'.

Alongside this narrative runs the thread of Māori belief – in the face of this injustice, Parihaka residents neither flinched nor abandoned hope. Further, although the angry deity, Bryce, may have appeared to have had all the power during the 'plunder', in fact he was hypocritical and weak. His violence was both real and unreal. He was prepared to wreck homes and steal land and belongings; but the symbolic power of the unarmed force at Parihaka meant that he was not prepared to kill ('If you shoot me I will surrender, but if your gun does not fire you will surrender yourself to me').

The site of the Taranaki hearings was significant. They were held at Manukorihi, a marae near Waitara. During the 1860 wars, Manukorihi had been one of the most heavily fortified pā in Taranaki. Between then and 1927, the *Taranaki Herald* reported, Europeans had not been welcome in that place.[28] Hundreds of Māori from Taranaki and beyond attended a hui (meeting) to mark the start of the hearings, and men and women performed songs composed by Te Whiti.[29] Some Māori wore raukura and greenery in their hair; others wore fashionable hats on a jaunty angle. Manukorihi hosted a 'queer mixture of the civilised and the savage' that day, one newspaper reported.[30] Haka groups and a drum and fife band supported the singers. 'Ko Waitara', a song performed by one Taranaki tribe, Ngāti Mutunga, before the commission, explains the critical importance of the inquiry:[31]

Ko Waitara (Waitara)

Ko Waitara, Ko Waitara	Waitara Waitara
Ko te rā tēnei i mate ai te whenua	This was the day the land was lost
I mate ai te tangata	And people were killed
Ka pēwhea tātou e te iwi?	What should become of us?
Kua hutia reretia nei te whenua i raro i o tātou kumu	The lands have been wrenched from beneath our very seat
Ka tōrona ketai ki runga ki te maunga teitei – aue pākia	Cast upon the lofty mountain I exclaim
I te mea kua huakina nei	Because it has been opened
Kāhore he tangata māna e tūtaki	There is no one who is able to close it
I te mea kua tūtakina nei	Because it has been closed
Kāhore he tangata māna e hūaki	There is no one able to reopen it
Ka huakina, ka huakina	It will be opened, it will be opened
Ka tohungia e au he tangata mō te ao	I will appoint someone to put our case
He ruru rānei, e koia tēnā	If it is an owl, so be it
He ngeru rānei, e koia tēnā	If it is a cat, so be it
He ngārara rānei, e koia tēna, e koia tēnā, e koia tēnā	If it is a lizard, that will do, so be it, so be it, so be it

Māori often use the native owl (ruru), with its sharp night vision, as a metaphor for themselves. The predatory cat (ngeru), an introduced species, is often used as a metaphor for Pākehā. The lizard (ngārara) is something more alarming and supernatural than a cat. A lizard often represents death. The word ngārara also describes reptiles, monsters, creeping insects and – more recently – computer viruses. The song explains that Ngāti Mutunga were unsure what the outcome of the commission's inquiries would be; but they were so determined that their case would be opened that they would accept any advocate, even one that was monstrous and reptilian.

Whichever category Māori had placed the commissioners in, they gave them a powerful welcome at Manukorihi. Pomare translated the speeches made by senior Māori, and his status as a medical doctor may have prompted the metaphors – about bodies, healing and death – that Māori chose to use.

Ngāti Ruanui petitioner Pouwhareumu Toi greeted guests with Tihei Mauri Ora! Sneeze and Live! 'Word was left that the time would come when I should behold this day,' he said, referring, perhaps to the prophecies of Te Whiti and Tohu. 'The day is here! Welcome exceedingly because the power has been conferred upon you to remedy this evil. You are the doctors sent to us. It is my desire that the child should not be stillborn.'[32]

Rangi Matatoro Watene urged the commission to bring justice and honour with them. 'The corpse has been buried 67 years,' he said, referring to land confiscated at Waitara. 'Today it is resurrected.'[33] In his opening address, counsel Smith also used metaphors of death and resurrection to describe the inquiry. He argued that enough time had passed to allow a 'dispassionate survey' of the past; but the events under consideration were not so distant that they should be obliterated and buried.[34]

The exhumation was marked by a supernatural omen. Early on the first day, a loud thunderclap was heard above the hall where the commission sat. It was followed immediately by sunshine, and 'older natives considered it a traditional good omen, saying that it was the voice of the gods exhorting them to be strong and go on'.

Invasion day stories

The story of the invasion of Parihaka was told by Te Whiti's son, Nohomairangi, Rangi Matatoro Watene and Kapinga. Watene, the first man to be called, identified himself as a follower of Te Whiti. He explained that Māori had ploughed land to force the government to inquire into the confiscations that followed the war in Waitara. Fences had not been erected as a protest, but simply to repair damage done by European soldiers.

> *Mr Smith: Do you remember the time when the natives began to plough the lands of the settlers? Watene: I remember that time.*
>
> *What was the cause of the ploughing? – It was on account of the non-completion of the Waitara hearing.*
>
> *There was ploughing and other things: were there roads put through by the Government at that time? – Yes.*
>
> *Did the natives pull down the fences? – The natives there had cultivations all fenced in and the Europeans came and pulled down their fences.*[35]

In response to Smith's questions, Watene explained that about 100 children were playing, skipping and spinning tops as the soldiers approached Parihaka. Bread, potatoes and other food had been prepared for the soldiers. His story highlighted the violence of the soldiers during the invasion and after it, when residents were afraid of being pricked by a bayonet:

> *When Captain Tuke was on the parapet and Bryce was on the horse, and the people were in the pa, Bryce called out to the interpreter what was going on. Mr Bryce said that the people would be punished by King George. After that their war bugles*

> *sounded and the soldiers surrounded the pā and they attacked the pā, overrunning the women, children and everybody in the courtyard. The soldiers were tramping over the people in the direction where Te Whiti and Tohu were standing.*

Smith showed Watene a photograph, possibly the William Collis photograph of people gathered on the marae, and this image prompted further memories.

> *Yes, that is a picture of the first day showing the people and the soldiers in the courtyard. They arrested Te Whiti and took him away. Te Whiti exclaimed: 'I request you to be brave and stick to your souls, to be patient and long-suffering.' He then referred to the Scriptures, Isaiah: he referred to a sentence in the Bible: Glory to God on high, peace on earth to men.*
> *What happened after that? – Then he said this peace that you have sustained so long would be a peace with you and with the world as a whole.*
> *He told the Natives to be an example to the world? – Yes.*

Counsel for Māori, Smith, did not follow this line of questioning to seek elaboration on Parihaka as a village of peace. Nor was he interested in stories about the reconstruction of Parihaka. Rather, Smith's questions were designed to elicit information on what the soldiers stole and how much these stolen goods were worth. Whenever the witnesses threatened to stray from this narrative, they were reined in. For instance, Kapinga was asked what work he was doing the day of the invasion, and he responded that he would like to say something 'about the commencement of our occupation in the pa'; but Smith just asked him again to describe his work. Nohomairangi Te Whiti was asked if he saw any damage done by the soldiers, but he responded: 'Would I not be permitted to explain the reason of the raid. It would be long.' He was told that the commission understood the reasons for the raid, and so Nohomairangi moved on to explain what was taken from his father's house, including a cloak so valuable that 'money could not buy it', and how his mother wept for a week over all she had lost.[36]

Watene told Smith that troops had taken guns, gunpowder, greenstone, money, cloaks, mats, tiki, mere ('I had three greenstones and a tiki which were all taken'), horses, pigs and cattle. Kapinga, who was a waiter 'supplying the food for the people in the courtyard' at Parihaka, said 600 double-barreled guns were stolen from the pā, a figure triple that of the government report at the time.[37] The guns had been used for shooting birds and other game. They were highly prized, costing between twenty-fve pounds and thirty pounds each.

Smith asked Kapinga if Parihaka residents had discussed, at the time, the worth of the things that were stolen. The reply he received indicates how people who were used to having things taken from them viewed yet another theft. Kapinga said: 'There was no discussion took place: the only thing said was 'Let those things go as confiscations by the Europeans.' Smith: Do you mean that it was a sort of sacrifice? – That is so, because we were living peacefully and we did not want any fighting.'[38]

Two of the men told stories about women being sexually assaulted during the occupation and sacking of Parihaka. As Watene said:

> *The soldiers went on to the cultivations, and went there to get food. The women folk were gathering food for the people in the pa, for us, and the soldiers were assaulting the women folk. Some of those women got children through the soldiers, some of the soldiers married the women, and their children are living round about the place.*[39]

When Nohomairangi was asked what the soldiers did 'as far as the women were concerned', he responded: 'They took the women and made use of them, cohabited with them, the outcome of which is that their offspring are living now. I can mention one of them. I saw the assault by the soldiers on the women.'[40]

A doctor who worked in Taranaki corroborated these allegations. One of Dick Scott's informants in 1953 was Dr Pohau Erihana Ellison, the son of one of the men who had funded the restoration of Parihaka. Ellison became angry when he recalled the invasion. 'There was looting and debauchery,' he told Scott. 'In my work as a young man I saw cases of congenital syphilis in Taranaki, and that was the result of the occupation of Parihaka.' Another informant, Reverend Paahi Moke, told Scott that in 1931, he had met 'quite a number' of elderly Māori women who 'had children from Pākehā soldiers'. Rangi Kapo, of Opunake, claimed that a senior soldier, Colonel Wynyard, was his father.[41]

It is no coincidence that the word Māori use to describe the invasion of Parihaka is pahua (plunder or rape), and the annual commemoration of this day is called Te Ra o te Pahua (the day of plunder). The invasion was an assault on the body of Māori people as a whole. During the hearing, Crown counsel Taylor asked Watene: 'After the soldiers came to Parihaka you were taken away from Parihaka by them?' Watene replied: 'After the rape we were all brought back here (to Waitara) and to Waihi.'

A final feature of the testimonies were the stories about the destruction of Parihaka houses. All the important houses were pulled down, Watene said. Soldiers tied ropes to the houses and one lot pulled one way and the other lot pulled another way and the houses fell down.[42] Houses were carefully selected for destruction. Nohomairangi Te Whiti said: 'The soldiers were sent out to pull down the houses at two or three in the morning. Marking the doors of the houses, the indication being that where one was put on the door it meant that there was one man in the house, and where they put a two there were two men there. But at that time the people were afraid to go back into their houses: they lived together in the courtyard.'[43]

The commission's findings were sympathetic to Taranaki. It declared that of the 1.275 million acres initially confiscated, 557,000 acres had been purchased by the government and another 256,000 had been returned to Māori.[44] The remaining 462,000 acres had been 'finally confiscated' land, an action that the commission found to be unjust because, in the eyes of Māori, 'their fight was not against the Queen's sovereignty but a struggle for house and home'.[45] The commission recommended that 5000 pounds a year be paid to a Taranaki trust board in compensation for 'the wrong done' in confiscating this land. Te Whiti's son, Nohomairangi, was the board's first chairman.[46]

As well as investigating confiscations, the commission inquired into claims and allegations made by 56 petitioners from Hawke's Bay, Te Arawa and Taranaki. The sacking of the village was outside the scope of an investigation into confiscated lands, but the evidence presented to the commission was so compelling that it felt 'duty-bound' to inquire into it. The evidence, as shown, comprised the petition written by Tamati Whanganui from Puketapu and others, the testimony of three Māori eyewitnesses and the accounts of the invasion contained in the work of journalist James Cowan and historians Shrimpton and Mulgan, Irvine, Alpers and William Pember Reeves (the son of the owner of the *Lyttelton Times*, New Zealand's most 'philo-Māori' newspaper, which published dozens of reports mocking the government after the invasion of Parihaka).[47]

The commission made a separate finding in relation to Parihaka, declaring that looting had indisputably taken place and that the government was responsible for the destruction of homes and crops. Further, it was responsible, 'morally if not legally', for the theft of stock and personal belongings. In the absence of native records about individual losses, the commission decided that, 'according to good conscience and equity', a one-off payment of 300 pounds should be made to Māori at Parihaka in acknowledgment of the wrong that was done.[48]

The wrong that was done

Reading the report and the archival material associated with it, I cannot doubt that the commissioners were genuine in their dismay at what they heard about the invasion of Parihaka. They recognised the deep injustice inflicted on Māori in Taranaki (and elsewhere) by confiscation, and they tried to do something about it by establishing a trust fund. The problem was that the mechanisms behind confiscation (and limited return) of land remained.

Māori land was confiscated in 1865, and in 1880 the West coast Commission became the first of dozens of such inquiries established to investigate Māori complaints of injustice. The commission's findings led to the West coast Settlement (North Island) Act 1880, which awarded 201,395 acres to 5289 people. Management of these reserves, including land around Parihaka, was handed to the Public Trustee, a body that was required to 'act for the benefit of the natives to whom such reserves belong on the one hand and for the promotion of settlement on the other'.[49]

From the start, the system was a shambles, a mess that favoured settlers over Māori. The West coast Settlement Reserves Act 1881 was amended at least five times during the next ten years, because 'the legality of the leases became questionable due to administrative irregularities on the part of the Public Trustee'. The 20,000 acres of remaining Parihaka land was all leased to Europeans by the Public Trustee. Yet another bit of legislation, the West coast Settlement Reserves Act 1892, made these leases 'perpetually renewable for 21-year terms'.[50]

The word 'settlement' is embedded in the titles of all this legislation. It carries the echoes of many Pākehā desires: to 'settle' the west coast difficulty by replacing one settlement (Parihaka) with a series of other settlements (European farms and homesteads built on Māori land leased in perpetuity); to finish one thing and start another. Yet no matter how many acts of settlement were put in place, settlement was not achieved on the west coast, because Māori continued to protest at the lie embedded in the coupling of those two words: settlement and reserves. How could the same land do two things? How could it be reserved for Māori and also be a spot for white settlement?

Dion Tuuta, the general manager of Taranaki Māori land trust, Parininihi ki Waitotara Incorporated (PKW), has written that between 1892 and 1955, Māori owners called for government assistance so they could farm their own lands. These calls were ignored.

> *Instead the Government amended the legislation implementing more favourable terms to lessees and allowing Crown purchase. In 1920, the Native Trust took over control from the Public Trustee and during the 1920s, in particular, there was considerable freeholding by lessees where the beneficial owners wished to sell their interests in individual sections of land.*[51]

In 1931, Māori and Pākehā commemorated the fiftieth anniversary of the invasion of Parihaka. While Māori marked the plunder, Pākehā veterans in Masterton, Wellington and New Plymouth patted themselves on the back for the good job they had done in helping Māori progress from 'the aboriginal state to the present time when he was trying to adapt himself to modern life'.[52]

Students at Pungarehu School, the one closest to Parihaka, were encouraged to make a history of the area. The history opens with a hand-drawn map that puts the Cape Egmont dairy factory at the centre of a district that is still dominated, for Māori kids at least, by Māori places. The factory is across the road from a school and store, close to the site of the blockhouse constructed during the military campaign on Parihaka. Radiating out from this cluster are nine pā, including Parihaka, and right down on the Beach Road, the Cape Egmont Lighthouse.[53]

Before gas was discovered off the coast, it was dairy farming that made Taranaki. In 1953, Dick Scott met a local farmer at the Rahotu Hotel, a pub close to Parihaka. The farmer, who was waiting for a whisky, explained that it was good land. There were six or seven cheese factories within four miles of Rahotu and seven more between Rahotu and Okato – that was where Corbett the MP has his farm. '"Yes, it's good country," he repeated, giving the bell a long push "and we got it for next to nothing. It was thirty-year west coast leasehold," he began to explain … Over his shoulder he gave a short definition of easy wealth: "All Māori land, you know …"'[54]

Despite the commissions of inquiry and the small annual compensation payments, there was no hiding the fact that Māori Taranaki had been 'milked' for all it was worth. In New Plymouth on 5 November 1931, it was appropriate that Parihaka veterans charged their glasses not with beer, but with milk, and drank a toast in honour of commerce.

---

[1] Graham Butterworth, 'Pomare, Maui Wiremu Piti Naera 1875/76? – 1930', *DNZB*, URL: http://www.dnzb.govt.nz updated 22 June 2007.

[2] Buck, cited in C.F. Cody, *Man of Two Worlds: Sir Maui Pomare,* Wellington: A.H. and A.W. Reed, 1953, 81.

[3] Pomare, cited in Cody, *Two Worlds*, 68.

[4] Virginia Winder, 'Sir Maui Pomare's Life-long Quest', Puke Ariki Taranaki Stories Tangata Whenua. URL: http://www.pukeariki.com/en/stories/tangatawhenua/mauipomare accessed 19 January 2009.

[5] Buck, cited in Cody, *Two Worlds,* 61-62.

[6] Smith, 'Ko Tohu', 120.

[7] Miria Pomare interviewed by Virigina Winder for 'Sir Maui Pomare's Life-long Quest', PA.

[8] James Belich, *Paradise Reforged: A History of the New Zealanders From the 1880s to the Year 2000,* Auckland: Allen Lane Penguin, 2001, 193.

[9] Scott, *Writer's Life,* p. 292 and Scott, *Ask That Mountain,* 198. Scott relates that Taranaki Museum director Rigby Allan removed a long-handled plough that was the gravestone for one member of this community. In 1981, for the centenary commemorations, this plough stood at the entrance to Te Niho.

[10] See Belich, *Paradise,* 200. Carroll, who had fought as a kupapa soldier with government troops against East Coast leader Te Kooti, was Minister of Native Affairs in the Liberal government between 1899 and 1912.

[11] Pomare, cited in Cody, *Worlds,* 84-85.

The Parihaka Album

[12] Smith, 'Ko Tohu', 141.

[13] 'Māori Elder Momona Tamihana Death at New Plymouth', *Taranaki Herald*, 24 September 1948. Matarena (Marjorie) Rau-Kupa 'Te Kotahitanga Tautoru' scrapbook 1937-1952, ARC2002-985, PA.

[14] 'Māoris mourn respected leader at Parihaka Pa', *Taranaki Daily News*, 1 December 1951, in Rau-Kupa 'Te Kotahitanga Tautoru' clipping file.

[15] 'Parihaka today', undated clipping in *Pungarehu School: History of Pungarehu School and Parihaka District,* compiled by Māori students at the school, c. 1930, Manuscript Collection, ATL.

[16] 'Supreme Court Te Whiti Case', *Taranaki Herald*, 25 March 1926.

[17] *Taranaki Herald,* 18 and 20 March 1926.

[18] 'Te Whiti Case Plaintiffs' Action Succeeds', *Taranaki Herald* 15 April 1926. Pereni Te Whiti died in 1942, and by then divisions between herself and her brother appeared to have healed somewhat. Nohomairangi was one of the chief mourners at her funeral, which was attended by followers of Te Whiti and Tohu. See A.B. Whitten-Hannah, letter to the editor, *Taranaki Herald,* 29 April 1942, in Rau-Kupa, 'Kotahitanga Tautoru' scrapbook, p. 40, PA. Opinion is still divided about this judgment but Parihaka historian, Te Miringa Hohaia, has described Pereni as a leader and builder, someone who represented Parihaka at the Māori Land Court from 1915 onwards and fought to retain the remnants of Parihaka land that remained under the care of Parihaka elders. Hohaia said the court did not understand how much of their own money Pereni and her husband, Charlie Waitara, donated to the settlement. Further, the court ignored 'the fact that because she was appointed to her role, through traditional Māori processes, all funds given to her, by the people, were private not public monies'. See 'Ngaruaki Pereni Te Whiti', text panel, Parihaka: Struggle for peace, Puke Ariki, 2003.

[19] Memo for Cabinet, 10 September 1925, files of the Māori Affairs Department, 1925, MA 85 (b), ANZ.

[20] Michael Bassett, 'Coates, Joseph Gordon 1878-1947', DNZB, updated 16 December 2003, URL: http://www.dnzb.govt.nz/, accessed 16 March 2005. See also Belich, *Paradise Reforged,* 201-202. Bassett writes that Coates was said to have fathered two children with a Māori woman before he married his Pākehā wife and one of his five children from that marriage had a Māori name, Irirangi.

[21] Coates to Maui Pomare, 3 February 1925, MA 85 (b), ANZ.

[22] All quotes from Coates, Memo for Cabinet, 10 September 1925, MA 85 (b), ANZ.

[23] *Taranaki Daily News,* 11 February 1927, DS Smith Papers, ATL.

[24] *Evening Post,* 10 February 1927, clipping in David Smith's Papers, MS 3776-3/8, ATL.

[25] David Smith, Minutes of Evidence for the Sim Commission, 1927, MA 85, 1, ANZ, 140.

[26] Other petitioners who argued that land had been confiscated in 1881 to punish Māori for the Parihaka protests included Te Kapinga Makarati and others, petition No. 225/1925 (Hon. Sir Maui Pomare), MA 85 4, Petitions to Parliament by Māori; Pouwhareumutoi and 19 others, Petition No.44, 1925, MA 85 4; and Wiremu Te Kupenga Kahao and others, petition 19/1925, MA 85 4, all petitions at ANZ. Te Kupenga wrote that from 'the hinder part of Parihaka to the summit of Mount Egmont was confiscated for crimes committed by Tohu and Te Whiti. These men committed no crime. The crime they committed was Love, Peace and Goodwill.' Pouwhareumutoi asked: 'What offence had these persons [Te Whiti and Tohu] committed. What crime was committed to justify the confiscation of land as a reward for residing at their Pā at Parihaka?'

[27] Tamati Whanganui and others, petition 93/1925, 'To the Honourable speaker and Members in Parliament assembled at Wellington', MA 85, 4, ANZ.

[28] *Taranaki Herald,* 10 February 1927, clipping contained in DS Smith Papers, file 3776-3/8, ATL.

[29] *Taranaki Herald*, 11 February 1927, Smith Papers, ATL.

[30] *Taranaki Daily News*, 10 February 1927, Smith Papers, ATL.

[31] 'Ko Waitara' (Waitara), song performed before the Sim Commission, Ngāti Mutunga Deed of Settlement 2004, OTS, URL: www.ots.govt.nz

[32] *Daily News*, 10 February 1927, Smith Papers, ATL.

[33] *Taranaki Herald,* 10 February 1927, Smith Papers, ATL.

[34] *Dominion*, 12 February 1927.

[35] Rangi Matatoro Watene, Examined. Waitara, 16 February 1927, Minutes of Evidence, MA 85, 1, ANZ, 1.

[36] A spectacular huru huru kuri (dogskin cloak) 'acquired' at Parihaka by William Skinner in the 1890s is on display Puke Ariki. It is said to be the only surviving cloak made entirely from the skins of 'native dogs'. See William Skinner, 'The Ancient Māori Dog', *Journal of Polynesian Society*, vol. 23, 1914, 173-175. Puke Ariki also has a tokotoko, reportedly belonging to Te Whiti. When I saw this taonga on display, in 2003, the label said it had been 'given' to a police officer who participated in the raid on Parihaka. The small file connected with the tokotoko tells a fascinating story about Pākehā acquisition and guilt and restitution. The file contains a 1937 statutory declaration from retired police superintendant John Dwyer, a biography of Dwyer and an Appendix, written by Dwyer's grand-daughter in 1973, the year she gave the tokotoko to the Taranaki Museum. See Buchanan, 'Village of peace, village of war', 2005, 297-301 for a discussion about this object.

[37] In 1881, the *Lyttelton Times* reported that 217 guns were taken from Parihaka; *Lyttelton Times,* 9 November 1881.

[38] Kapinga, examined, Waitara, 16 February 1927, MA 85, 1, ANZ.

[39] Watene, examined. In his biography of Peter Buck, Condliffe also mentions children born as the result of 'fraternisation' between armed constabulary and Parihaka women. Of the protests of 1880 and 1881, Condliffe writes: 'When arrested for erecting fences to protect their cultivations, and incidentally block the roads, they [Parihaka residents] went cheerfully to jail in a righteous cause. Those who remained sent money and food to the prisoners. They also brought gifts of food – pigs and potatoes, fowls and peaches – to the constabulary when they began to make roads across disputed lands. There was considerable fraternisation and many children were born.' Condliffe, *Te Rangi Hiroa*, 37.

[40] Noho Mairangi Te Whiti, examined, Waitara 17 February 1927, MA 85, 1, ANZ.

[41] Scott, Writer's Life, 201-203.

[42] Kapinga and Watene, examined, MA 85, 1, ANZ.

[43] Nohomairangi Te Whiti, p. 2, MA 85, 1, ANZ.

[44] Report on Inquiry into Confiscated Native Lands and Other Grievances, AJHR, Vol II, G-7, 1928, 11.

[45] AJHR, 'Confiscated Native Lands', Vol II, G-7, 1928, 11.

[46] *Taranaki Herald*, 31 July 1946.

[47] *Taranaki Herald*, 31 July 1946. My family still receives tiny annual payments from the trust board. The complex and controversial impacts the board has had on concepts of 'Māori land' is discussed in the next chapter.

[47] James Cowan, *The New Zealand Wars*, vol II, Wellington, 1923, 476-491 and 517-518. Cowan's two-volume history was researched largely by collecting oral histories from Māori and Pākehā who fought in the wars. In 1918 he interviewed Colonel W.B. Messenger about the Parihaka expedition and Messenger said: 'Orders had been given that no property was to be touched, but I know there was a good deal of looting – in fact, robbery.' William Pember Reeves, *Land of the Long White Cloud* (1898), 225-226 and A.W. Shrimpton and Alan Mulgan, *Māori and Pākehā*, Christchurch: Whitcombe & Tombs, 1920?, 31-314. Shrimpton and Mulgan wrote of Te Whiti: 'He had evolved a religion of his own, based on the Bible, and had developed into a kind of Māori Tolstoi, or a Te Kooti without the blood lust,' 312.

[48] Confiscated Native Lands and Other Grievances, AJHR, 1928. p. 32.

[49] Dion Tuuta, 'Perpetual Leasing in Taranaki 1880-2008', unpublished paper presented at conference on 'Coming to Terms? Raupatu/Confiscation and New Zealand History', Victoria University, 27-28 June 2008.

[50] Riseborough, 'Te Pahuatanga o Parihaka', *Art of Passive Resistance*, 41.

[51] Dion Tuuta, 'Perpetual Leasing in Taranaki 1892-2008', 2008.

[52] Lieut. Colonel Bertrand in his toast to the Native race, *Taranaki Herald*, 6 November 1931.

[53] See *Pungarehu School: History of Pungarehu School and Parihaka District,* compiled by Māori students at the school, c. 1930, Manuscript Collection, ATL.

[54] Scott, *The Parihaka Story*, 151-52.

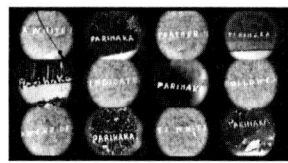

CHAPTER 8

Hearings

A great puzzle for any historian working on Parihaka is the way that the story of the invasion and its aftermath continues to be described as hidden or little known, despite plenty of evidence to the contrary. These claims of hidden-ness started in the 1950s and have continued, with increasing intensity, ever since. Before then, the invasion was an event in living memory, commemorated by Pākehā and Māori who had actually been there in 1881, as either soldiers or residents. Every year, ngā mōrehu (the survivors) gathered on 7 November at Parihaka to mark the plunder. In 1951, a local paper reported that giggling, gleeful kuia leapt over skipping ropes, mimicking the things they did as young girls when they and their ropes 'formed the major resistance to the advance of colonial troops marching on Parihaka'.[1]

By the time Dick Scott 'discovered' the place in the 1950s, few of the people who had been there in 1881 were still alive. Like many Communist comrades across the Tasman, Scott was quick to link workers' rights with indigenous rights. The communal non-violent resistance of the people of Parihaka offered exciting possibilities for contemporary radicals. The story of Parihaka that Scott had encountered in the transcript of the Bryce versus Rusden libel case seemed to have exciting parallels with the story of a more recently oppressed group in New Zealand, the 20,000 waterfront workers who had been locked out of every port in the country during the 1951 dispute. For example, Scott saw the West coast Settlements Act, which forbade Māori from assembling, as 'shades of '51', when repressive legislation restricted freedom of speech, banned gifts of food to watersiders' families and allowed the government to open personal mail.

In 1953, he got a bus to Parihaka to find out if the community still existed. He was surprised to find that it did. In the introduction to his self-published 1954 book, *The Parihaka Story*, Scott relates that he was welcomed, tentatively, by a 'big woman' who lived inside a substantial house of late-Victorian design. Things must have gone well enough because, the day after he arrived, Scott went along to a tangi at Oeo for a woman who had been at Parihaka, aged 10, when it was invaded. Among the mourners were some old women who had white feathers – 'immortal badge of Te Whiti's brave republic' – pinned to their black shawls.

At the tangi, Scott's guide was a young man, someone who Scott assumed was either a dairy factory worker or a teacher. The pair discussed how little most New Zealanders knew about Parihaka and how it was a story that had been 'killed by silence or distortion. "If it is mentioned at all in the histories," I said, "usually it's to tell a string of lies." "Yes", he added with a friendly smile, "white lies … it's a story the people have to carry in their hearts".'[2] Pākehā had forgotten the violence of the colonial past, Scott wrote, by 'blotting out' the memory of the cannon that had been trained down on Parihaka in November 1881.

The book – a modest tract peppered with blasts of Communist propaganda – reached a small but influential audience of activists, historians and artists. By the time Scott revised and expanded it, at the invitation of Parihaka people, in the early 1970s, the situation had changed greatly. The 1975 release of *Ask That Mountain: The Story of Parihaka* coincided with a time of national and international protest and change. A combination of decolonisation, the American civil rights movement, indigenous land rights protests and anti-apartheid protests challenged the status quo in New Zealand and many other settler nations.

The same year that the book came out, Dame Whina Cooper led the large land rights hīkoi from Cape Reinga to Wellington, and the Waitangi Tribunal was set up as a commission of inquiry to investigate Māori allegations of contemporary breaches of the 1840 Treaty of Waitangi. Ngā Tamatoa (the Young Warriors) were making headlines with their demands for Māori language to be taught in all schools; one of the founders, Syd Jackson, has since recalled how he was radicalised, in part, by reading Scott's first Parihaka book.

The new 1970s version had been stripped of the references to Communism. Instead, Scott put a greater emphasis on the non-violent nature of the 'commune' at Parihaka, implying comparisons between the peaceful prophets of Parihaka and the peaceful prophets of the hippy movement. New Zealanders, Scott wrote, would soon understand that Te Whiti was a figure of 'international significance' whose 'finely honed tactics anticipated those of Gandhi by a generation'.[3] The first book had suggested that the oppression suffered by people at Parihaka was an oppression that could be experienced by all working class people of any racial group; but the second book made it clear that Māori had been mistreated not because of what they did, but because of who they were. Parihaka was invaded and ransacked because its residents were Māori. The current divisions in New Zealand society, as Scott saw it, were caused by race, not class.

Although academic historians were critical of the book, the public loved it. *Ask That Mountain* became, and has remained, a bestseller. (At the 2000 Parihaka exhibition at Wellington's City Gallery, I brought the fourteenth edition.) Reviewers welcomed Scott's exposure of this hidden history, this 'dirt from the past'. 'New Zealand is at a painful stage of its historical development – the facing-of-facts stage', Kay Mooney wrote in a feature story in *The Hawke's Bay Herald-Tribune*.[4] New Zealanders had to acknowledge that the wars in the 1860s were not the result of 'bloodthirsty fanatics terrorising hapless and industrious settlers'.

The production of Parihaka stories escalated exponentially from 1975 onwards, but so did the claims of hidden-ness. This hidden-ness takes many forms. It can mean an absence, but it can also mean purposeful forgetting or misrepresentation or lack of sufficient interpretation, understanding or context.

Māori make this point, repeatedly, when they describe Parihaka as a hidden story in the context of settler-authored national histories. They have used the fate of the Parihaka story as an example of how Pākehā wanted to forget about the criminal acts involved in colonisation and, through this forgetting, to belittle or suppress Māori protest in the present. In 1981, documentary maker Merata Mita described the invasion of Parihaka as a repressed, little-known event. In her introduction to a centenary-of-invasion *Koha* special programme, Mita said: 'One of the least known episodes in our history is the story of Te Whiti-O-Rongomai and the sacking of the Māori village of Parihaka in Taranaki. That is not surprising because it tells of the dark side of British colonisation.'[5] In Mita's understanding, the phrase 'our history' appears to apply to a particular kind of 'white' national history, rather than collective or individual Māori knowledge about the past.

Mita made a powerful 1980 documentary, *Bastion Point: Day 507*, on the 1977 Ngāti Whatua occupation of Bastion Point, on Auckland's Waitemata Harbour. Māori occupied the site after the government announced it wanted to subdivide and sell twenty-four hectares on the picturesque point.[6] After seventeen months, protestors were forcibly evicted on 25 May 1978, a process captured by Mita in the film. As the documentary demonstrates, many Māori (and their Pākehā supporters) were well acquainted with the history of Parihaka and the 'dark side' of colonisation that it embodied. The occupation explicitly drew on the passive resistance strategies used at Parihaka a hundred years earlier, and the documentary includes many references to Parihaka.

As 600 members of the police and army encircled the occupation site, one of the leaders, Joe Hawke, yelled: 'At no time will we resort to violence, our stand is one of non-violence.'[7] He reiterates: 'This is a peaceful resistance …' During the occupation, Māori ploughed land at Bastion Point, re-enacting the Parihaka protests of a century earlier.[8] Speaking of the eviction in Parliament, Matiu Rata, Labour MP for Northern Māori, said: 'Very few actions have been taken [in New Zealand] about which I could truthfully say the country should be ashamed. Parihaka was one, and I believe today's events represent another.'[9]

More than a decade later, in a very different forum, the hidden-ness of Parihaka was restated. In its 1996 Taranaki Report, the Waitangi Tribunal wrote, in an overview of issues and events relating to Parihaka:

> *For decades, the shameful history [of Parihaka] lay largely buried in obscurity. Young Māori were schooled to believe that those of their forebears, whose images should have been carved with pride, were simply rebels, savages or fanatics. The Government's criminality was hidden. New Zealanders were not to know that forced removals, pass laws and other suspensions of civil liberties, so often criticised of governments elsewhere, had been applied here. We were not to know, when paying tribute to Gandhi and King, that their policies and practices had first been enunciated by Māori.*[10]

The story was said to have been hidden in a number of ways and from a number of different audiences. The tribunal observed that it had been hidden from young Māori, who had been deprived of a story that would have instilled cultural pride. Further, it had been hidden from 'New Zealanders' – meaning Pākehā – who had been deprived of a story that was a source of both shame (civil liberties had been suspended in New Zealand too) and nationalistic pride. (Māori had used passive resistance strategies long before world famous figures like Gandhi and Martin Luther King did so.)

The most spectacular claims of hidden-ness were made in connection with 'Parihaka: The Art of Passive Resistance', the City

Gallery exhibition in Wellington. The event took over the whole of the gallery's three large exhibition spaces and included significant new commissioned works of visual art and writing, as well as many older works of art inspired by the Parihaka story. Victoria University Press, the City Gallery and Parihaka Pā Trustees published a handsome exhibition catalogue and collection of new essays on Parihaka and its political, spiritual and artistic legacies.[11]

The care and attention accorded the project was so great that a special typeface, inspired by nineteenth century Māori manuscripts, was designed for the exhibition and the publication.

Again, Māori and Pākehā had different reasons for claiming that the story was hidden. For Pākehā, the moment of 'discovery' of Parihaka could be a time of personal catharsis, an intense encounter with what Australian historian and poet Robert Kenny has described as 'the moral aftershock' of settlement.[12]

Riseborough, author of tribunal research reports on Taranaki and the nineteenth century political history of the province, expressed this unusual but profound sentiment well. Writing about the rainy opening of the Parihaka exhibition, Riseborough said: 'There were other tears that day – tears of grief as well as tears of joy and release, and for some of the visitors who thronged the gallery, tears of anger over a history that until then had been hidden from them.'[13]

Some Māori saw the exhibition as a more open, pubic place for sharing Parihaka stories, outside the far more private spaces of the marae or the more adversarial zone of a tribunal hearing. As exhibition adviser and kaumātua Te Huirangi Waikerepuru said:

> At the moment most New Zealanders don't know anything about Parihaka, about the confiscated lands and what the people of Taranaki feel about it because there hasn't been a forum where these issues can be discussed openly. The exhibition is a wonderful forum to be able to share information about Parihaka. What has to follow is the process of addressing the grievance, the lack of resources and economic development.[14]

Waikerepuru suggested that the Parihaka story was still hidden because it was part of a broader event – the confiscation of land in Taranaki – that was not, in his opinion, well understood by 'New Zealanders'. His statement implicitly contrasts New Zealanders' lack of knowledge about confiscation with the painful and intense and profoundly contemporary (as opposed to historical) knowledge that Māori from Taranaki have about this event. The understanding of history that Māori from Taranaki have, in this statement, is outside the understanding of most 'New Zealanders'.

The tribunal hearings

New Zealand history is national history; the history of Māori from Taranaki is 'intra-national' or non-national or tribal history. It has, as cultural theorist Stephen Turner has pointed out, an anteriority or 'before-ness' to it, the result of a Māori experience of a long history and a deep identity that both precedes and exceeds the 'nation-based identity of Kiwi'.[15]

These different notions of history are revealed in the workings of the Waitangi Tribunal, in both its published reports and the large archives generated by tribunal hearings. The tribunal is a place where 'histories meet', a whirlpool of different kinds of stories governed by different kinds of rules.[16] It's a place where conventions of law butt against conventions of myth, where family history and national history collide, where the oral meets the written, where the subjective and the objective do battle (often within the one testimony). It is a testing site for historical authority and the nature of historical evidence. How successful is the tribunal as a historical storyteller? How has the tribunal aided understandings of difficult events, such as the invasion of Parihaka?

By early 2008, 1430 claims had been registered with the tribunal by individuals on behalf of themselves, whānau, hapū or iwi groups. Many commentators have argued that the Waitangi Tribunal is rewriting 'the entire history of European settlement'. It is a hybrid body that has affinities with the land claim commissions set up in the United States, Canada and Australia, but it also has similarities to international truth commissions.[17] The tribunal process is supposed to 'heal' the past and build a more settled future.

In Taranaki, this healing has been uneven, to say the least. Problems had emerged long before the Tribunal's report was released. In their submissions, many Taranaki claimants were angry about 'the charade' (and expense) of participating in yet another inquiry when previous inquiries, such as the 1927 Sim Commission and even the 1880 West coast Commission, had acknowledged the wrong done to Māori at Parihaka and elsewhere in Taranaki, but had still failed to settle grievances. The hearings, therefore, had created a new set of injustices, injustices that have become part of the history and living present of communities such as Parihaka.[18]

The Taranaki claims were heard in twelve sittings at various marae and motels in the province of Taranaki between 1990 and 1995. The tribunal sat twice at Parihaka, in 1991 and 1992. The Taranaki hearings grouped together twenty-one claims relating to the province of Taranaki. Claimants identified with one or more of ten 'Taranaki' iwi – Taranaki, Te Āti Awa, Ngāti Tama, Ngāti Mutunga, Ngāti Maru, Ngā Ruahine, Ngāti Ruanui, Ngā Rauru, Tangahoe and Pakakohi – and their grievances all resulted from the land confiscations of the 1860s.[19] It was the first time the tribunal had combined separate claims into pan-tribal hearings under the label 'Taranaki'. As Alan Ward has pointed out, the Taranaki district inquiry was 'defined only by the province created by Parliament in 1853 and by the confiscation itself'.[20]

At the time of writing, early in 2009, only four of the eight officially recognised Taranaki iwi had settled their claims.[21] Neither Te Āti Awa nor Taranaki, the two iwi most closely associated with Parihaka, were in active negotiations with the Crown. The claims process may have actually impeded the 'hearing' that is necessary for healing. Without 'hearing', no matter how many times it is told, the Parihaka story will remain 'hidden'.

What the report said

The Taranaki report was the first historical investigation into the confiscations enacted across the North Island in the 1860s. The tribunal commissioned no fewer than thirty-three research reports from Māori and Pākehā experts. This evidence is now described as 'technical' or 'historical' evidence. The tribunal also heard testimonies from dozens of claimants. This evidence is described as 'traditional', 'customary' or 'tangata whenua' evidence and may include waiata, whakapapa or kōrero. Although the Taranaki report gestures towards the feelings and emotions of claimants, its narrative draws mainly on the first kind of evidence, the professional research reports.

The Taranaki report was published in 1996, a year after Māori had occupied six sites around New Zealand to protest the National Government's 'fiscal envelope', a proposal to settle all historical Treaty claims from a common pool of one billion dollars. The tribunal found in the claimants' favour and argued, with considerable force, that the Taranaki claims could be the largest in the country because 'there may be no others where as many Treaty breaches had equivalent force and effect over a comparable time'. Armed conflict lasted for nine years in Taranaki – from 1860 until 1869 – the longest period of any district in New Zealand, the report found. If the definition of armed struggle was broadened to include the first signs of conflict in 1841 (the year after the first boat of white settlers arrived) and the 1881 invasion of Parihaka, then 'conflict over the use of arms was not spread over a few months, as in most places, or even over a decade, but over a staggering 40 years. In no other part of New Zealand did a contest of that nature continue for so long or Māori suffer so much the deprivations of strife after British sovereignty was proclaimed.'[22]

The report remains the tribunal's most controversial publication and the subject of academic, political and personal commentary because of the way it used the word 'holocaust'. In its conclusion, the report said: 'As to quantum, the gravamen of our report has been to say that the Taranaki claims are likely to be the largest in the country. The graphic muru of most of Taranaki and the raupatu without ending describe the holocaust of Taranaki history and the denigration of the founding peoples in a continuum from 1840 to the present.'[23]

A gravamen is Latin word connected with biblical history. It is 'the part of an accusation which weighs most heavily against the accused; the burden or substantial part of a charge or complaint.' Muru is plunder; raupatu is the word Māori use to describe the confiscation of land. In Taranaki, however, these words have slightly different meanings: muru describes land confiscated in war, and raupatu describes land 'confiscated' through perpetual leases.[24]

For Māori of Taranaki, the tribunal asserted, raupatu describes their 'marginalisation by the organs of the State, for on this view, they were never conquered by the sword but were taken by the pen'.[25] By using the word holocaust, the tribunal invited comparisons between the colonisation of Taranaki and the genocide of Jews in World War II.[26] This comparison followed earlier comments in the report about the similarities between events in New Zealand's past and present and the genocide in Rwanda and the war in Bosnia.

But are these comparisons appropriate or useful? The invasion of Parihaka – an event in which no one was killed – is compared, however indirectly, with the worst atrocities of the twentieth century, atrocities in which millions died. Rather than persuading Pākehā of the severity of Māori loss in Taranaki, the use of the word 'holocaust' in the Taranaki report is now often cited as a prime example of the tribunal's bias.[27] Many were outraged at the use of this word.

The report further inflamed some New Zealanders because it recommended that the government legislate to end the perpetual leases on west coast Māori land. In 1997, in response to the report, the government introduced the Māori Reserve Land Amendment Act, which aimed to move the leases from peppercorn rentals to market-based levels, and to give Māori owners the first right to buy back any leases that became available. A convoy of Taranaki farmers on tractors blocked roads to parliament in protest.

The report presented Parihaka as a site of extremes. Parihaka was the 'best' Māori settlement in New Zealand, the 'most' orderly and modern; the invasion, therefore, was the 'most' heinous act of colonisation, a site for the 'worst' excesses of colonisation. Parihaka was presented as an emblematic site of Māori agency as well as Māori loss, a place of collective, individual and intergenerational resistance. It was described as an almost utopian community whose aims of partnership, cooperation and indigenous autonomy could still be achieved after claims had been settled. Yet it was also a site of total destruction and annihilation, an atrocity that deserved to be recognised in a global context.

In the Taranaki report, Parihaka had at least two roles. It represented both an idealised Māori past and an idealised Māori future, the future that could be open to Māori should 'autonomy' be achieved, post-settlement.[28] The tribunal's focus on the 'destruction' of Parihaka creates a single, neat and dramatic moment of dispossession in Taranaki, a moment in which an ideal was lost.

If the story were less lopsided – only one page of forty-four is devoted to the post-1882 reconstruction of the pā – its message would be far more ambiguous. The tribunal's Parihaka story would look like far less of a 'holocaust' if it encompassed the Māori-financed rebuilding of the pā. If the restoration was given more space in its narrative, the 'moment' of colonisation would be muddied. Did the colonisation of Parihaka occur with the invasion? With the prophets' deaths in 1907? With any one of the sales of land from the Parihaka block throughout the twentieth century? These questions are difficult to answer and would involve exploring a story of loss far more recent and insidious and far less obvious than the invasion day story of Parihaka. It would be a story that included Māori who did not follow the teachings of Te Whiti and Tohu, the twentieth-century history of the community, the role of non-human actors in Taranaki histories and oral histories that cannot always be authenticated by written sources.

The Parihaka Album

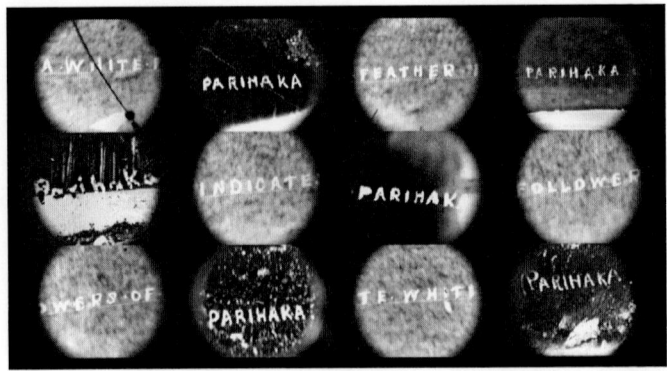

Figure 22 (a). Anne Noble, Parihaka ... From the Record. *2000. Reflections on the caption of a photograph by William Collis. Children of Parihaka with Taare Waitara, Parihaka, rephotographed with the permission of the National Library of New Zealand and the people of Parihaka ref.1/1-006430-G.*

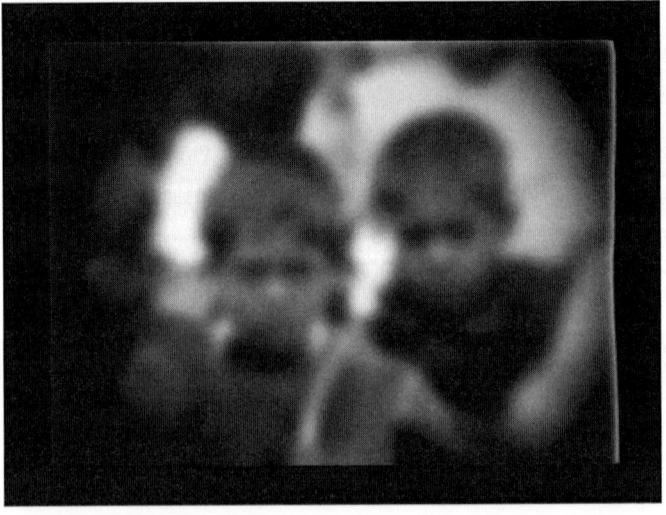

Figure 22 (b). Anne Noble, Parihaka ... seen and not heard. *2000. Reflections on a photograph by William Collis. Children of Parihaka with Taare Waitara, Parihaka, rephotographed with the permission of the National Library of New Zealand and the people of Parihaka ref. 1/1-006430-G.*

Hearings

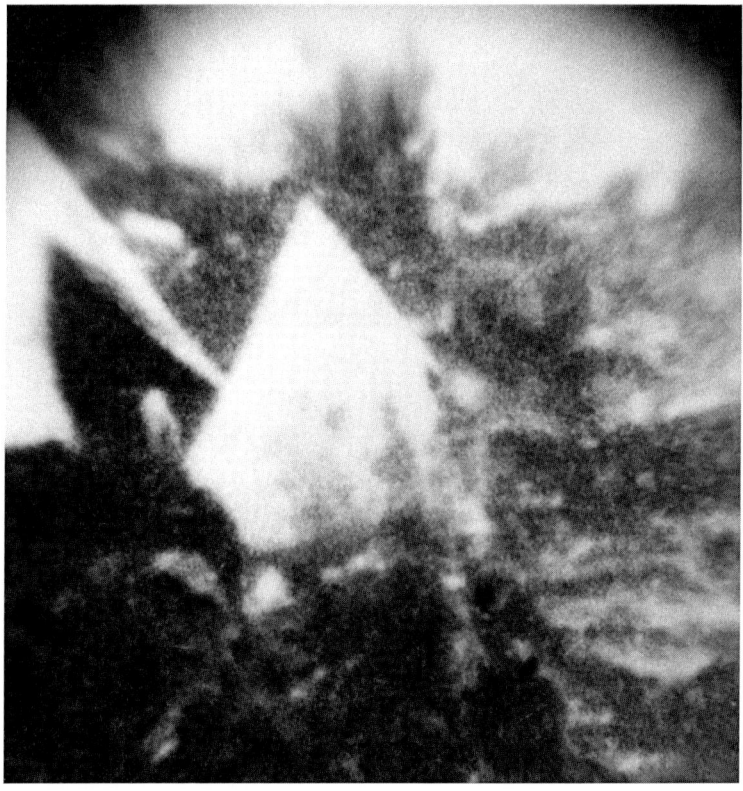

Figure 22 (c). Anne Noble, Parihaka, Tents of the Constabulary. *2000. Reflections on a photograph by William Collis. Tents of the Constabulary surrounding Parihaka. Egmont Co. 1881. Re-photographed with the permission of the National Library of New Zealand and the people of Parihaka.*

The grievance-based, conflict-ridden model of the tribunal process diminishes the ability of both the claimants and the Crown to make convincing, complex histories that provide some sort of window into the colonial past and present. As claimant counsel Richard Boast has argued, claims are essentially 'civil actions against the Crown', and hearings are similar to an adversarial court.[29] Allegiances and identities in nineteenth century New Zealand were multiple, complex and fluid. Yet the need to assess tribunal evidence within a legalistic framework often creates just two interpretations of events – a Māori one and a Pākehā one, a black or a white. One rather stark example of this division is the tribunal's practice of producing maps in which Māori land is marked in black, while everything else is shaded white. Once New Zealand was 'all black', then it was a patchwork of black and white, and now it is predominantly white, peppered with the tiniest specks of black.[30]

Māori and Pākehā identities and allegiances have never been this clear-cut. Indeed, the identity of Taranaki claimants before the tribunal was also the result of a mixture of forces, both 'black' and 'white'. The nineteenth century identity, affiliations and land holdings of Māori from Taranaki have been reshaped by twentieth century inquiries and bureaucratic decisions and judgments imposed on iwi. For instance, one of five bodies that launched general claims on behalf of all Taranaki tribes was the Taranaki Māori Trust Board, the body formed as a result of the 1927 Sim Commission.

Another umbrella claimant was the Parininihi-ki-Waitotara Incorporation (PKW). In 1963, the Māori Land Court amalgamated the interests of Māori in every revenue-producing reserve in Taranaki onto one title, which it called Parininihi-ki-Waitotara. PKW is a controversial body because it eroded hapū (sub-tribe) or iwi affiliations with tribal land by turning individual pockets of land into a single, generic Taranaki reserve and turning Māori into shareholders in this land. My whānau are among the 9000 shareholders in this group. PKW now looks after the paltry 20,000 hectares it still owns; 90 per cent of this land is subject to perpetual leases, until it can find the money to take up first rights of refusal in the future. So the farmers needn't have bothered taking their tractors to Wellington, because 'their' land is safe. The dairy boom has made 'our' land so valuable that we can't afford to buy it.

For a body that wants to tell a story that is as persuasive as possible – and so ensure that claimants win a 'full and final' settlement in negotiations with the Crown – the 'invasion day' Parihaka story is highly effective and easy to read. It is peopled with key actors who embody stereotypes of the evil coloniser and the good, non-violent but nevertheless still resistant colonised person. The tribunal sought to rewrite Taranaki history; but in regard to Parihaka, it found it necessary – and perhaps unavoidable, given its role as a 'court' – to reinscribe binaries around the words 'Māori' and 'settler'.

The report uses Parihaka as a central theme in its monumental story of loss and grievance; but the testimonies of Māori before the tribunal (and the stories Māori have recently begun to tell in other forums, such as museums and art galleries) suggest that although this story reflects one reality, there are other meanings that can be developed from 'the Parihaka story'.

What the claimants say

The lighthouse
In her careful and stimulating discussion of what she terms 'the paradox of Māori agency', Giselle Byrnes argues that Māori appear before the tribunal as 'obligatory victims'.[31] A booklet for claimants written by the tribunal's chief historian, Dr Grant Phillipson, explains the process. 'Claims to the Waitangi Tribunal are complaints,' the booklet begins. It goes on to explain that these complaints have two parts: first, that the Crown has breached the Treaty by its laws, policies, actions or inaction; and second, that Māori have been harmed by these breaches.[32]

In Taranaki, Māori carefully scripted their testimonies to demonstrate both the harm caused by Treaty breaches and the way they had resisted this harm and found creative ways to sidestep

Pākehā authority and maintain their authority over tribal land. Their testimonies are stories of victims and of people who refused to be victimised. They demonstrate what has been lost, but they also demonstrate how tenaciously Māori clung to what was theirs, and how local, informal agreements allowed Māori to continue to use and care for their land many decades after it had been 'colonised'.

At Parihaka, Taranaki claimant and tribal historian Te Miringa Hohaia and researcher Marlene Benson presented the tribunal with a history of the block of land on which the Cape Egmont Lighthouse stands. In Taranaki, settler politicians saw the construction of the lighthouse, the telegraph and the road as powerful symbols of their supremacy. The military installation of the lighthouse – the whitest of sentinels – was regarded as a particular triumph in the peaceful settlement of the so-called 'native difficulty' in Taranaki. But Hohaia and Benson's case study of the lighthouse reserve is a more complicated story in which settler triumph is deferred well into the twentieth century.[33]

The fate of this block of land challenges the tribunal report's hegemonic narrative of the 1881 invasion of Parihaka as the single, dramatic and stereotypical colonising moment in Taranaki. It also counters the more popular notion that colonisation occurred in the nineteenth century, and therefore it is not something that Pākehā now alive should be responsible for. What the lighthouse history reveals is that in one pocket of Taranaki at least, colonisation was resisted not by two charismatic Māori prophets, but by an elderly woman with a rent book. Conversely, the colonisation of this bit of land was achieved not by an evil government minister and his army, but by an anonymous bureaucrat. It was a slow, insidious, incremental and terribly ordinary thing achieved in an office rather than on a battlefield.

The long-standing Māori occupation of much of the lighthouse site suggests that the political effect of the construction of the lighthouse was perhaps not as great as the government might have hoped for in 1880. As documents collected by Hohaia and Benson tell it, six years after Parihaka was invaded, Te Whetu Moeahu, a Parihaka leader, negotiated an excellent deal with the government – approved by the Defence Minister, no less – to lease eighteen acres of the reserve from the Marine Department for a nominal annual rent. The deal was formalised when Te Whetu signed a warm letter from a Mr J. Pardy, an inspector of police in New Plymouth. It was conditional upon Te Whetu remaining 'of good behaviour'. And so Māori lived there by the lighthouse and grew kūmara, potatoes and pumpkin. When Te Whetu died in 1896, the lease was taken over by his widow, and Māori continued to live on the land and farm it, maintaining their presence through negotiations with the Marine Department.

After Te Whetu's death, the department had wanted to use all the reserve, but Māori objected. This objection was noted, Māori 'continued to occupy a portion of the reserve for the purpose of growing their crops, and the Department has never interfered with them'.[34] They also trapped eels in a 'good lamprey stream in the neighbourhood'.

By the early 1930s, this co-existence was being threatened. Pākehā farmers had made offers to buy the land. Māori should pay more for the lease, they argued. They should control the weeds – namely non-native introduced plants such as gorse and lupins – and fence the stock. The local council, the Egmont County Council, complained that Māori were squatters. 'It has been suggested that this land should be available to the public as a seaside reserve', the County Clerk wrote.

In the 1940s, when Mrs Te Whetu died, the lighthouse lease was taken over by Louie Okeroa. In 1951, Hohaia and Benson's account shows that Mrs Okeroa negotiated a new lease with the Marine Department. Again, neighbouring Pākehā farmers offered to buy or lease the land. The Commissioner of Crown Lands stepped in. A field officer was 'not very enthusiastic in respect of the proposed lease to a Māori'.[35] Mrs Okeroa went to the Lands and Survey office in New Plymouth to pay her new rent of nine pounds five shillings, but she was told to go to the Marine Department offices. Neither office would accept her money or let her sign the lease. The unsigned document, with Mrs Okeroa's personal details typed neatly at the top, is included in Hohaia's report. With the rent unpaid and the lease unsigned, the land was subsequently surveyed and sold to Pākehā farmers.

After seventy-four years, the Crown and settlers had finally possessed the lighthouse site. The documents that chart this loss reveal certain persistent Pākehā beliefs about Māori, most particularly the myth that Pākehā use of land is productive, while Māori use is unproductive. These beliefs connect with broader racist ideas that describe indigenous cultures as 'economies of waste'.[36] In 1952, for instance, a Marine Department field officer had inspected the lighthouse site and found 'that the land in question is a good piece of land but through neglect of the licensees has been allowed to almost revert to lupins etc; also it is not fenced in on the western boundary so that the control of stock is not possible'.[37]

In the nineteenth century, Māori of Taranaki had been described in terms of excess. There were too many of them, they had too much money, too much land and too much power. They were wasteful rather than provident and careless about the future. These statements overlooked the extensive, well-fenced and tended cultivations and herds of stock that Māori maintained around Parihaka. Settlers were blind to Māori farming. Instead, Māori farms were seen only as obstacles in the path of progress – the west coast road – so Crown troops repeatedly tore down fences and destroyed or plundered crops. In 1881, Māori fences and crops were criminal impediments to progress. Yet in 1952, it was the very absence of these things that was punished.

These are some of the contradictions of 'colonisation' illuminated by the study of the lighthouse site that Hohaia presented to the tribunal. The history of the lighthouse site reinforces the trajectory of colonisation – the site was eventually possessed by Europeans – but it leaves spaces for stories that challenge this trajectory too.

Hearings

The lighthouse report is an example of the way the tribunal process has allowed existing archives to be used in new ways. Hohaia's family history meant that he knew the lighthouse site had been used and cared for by Māori well into the twentieth century, a fact that runs counter to public narratives about Parihaka that situate dispossession in the nineteenth-century. The documentary record provided the evidence to support family stories. The documents, therefore, are no longer authored solely by Pākehā departmental and local government officials; their inclusion in the tribunal archive means they are 'authored' and 'author-ised' by Māori too. They become part of a story that extends far beyond one hazardous stretch of coastline into bigger debates about national historical narratives that locate colonisation in the nineteenth-century.

At tribunal hearings, Māori claimants steadfastly refused to place colonisation in the past, thus questioning the 'historical' nature of the tribunal's inquiries. In its report, the tribunal observed that the story of Parihaka was regularly retold at the pā, where 'striking photographs of the old village and invaded army are still maintained in the hall on the hill':

> *There was much pain and anger in the submissions of many who spoke of Parihaka. They challenged the Pākehā written record as inadequate and culturally biased and they would offset it with family accounts passed down orally. We have had regard to this evidence. We were constantly aware, from listening to the people, that the story of Parihaka is no past account but part of a living tradition.*[38]

A local whakataukī (saying) explains the way time unfolds in some Māori testimonies, signalling an understanding of time that is circular rather than linear, a 'living' history rather than a 'dead' one:

Koia kei a ia te wa aianei
Koia kei a ia te wa a muri

Koia kei a ia te wa a muri
Koia kei a ia te wa a mua
Wa muri ka oti a mua

He who holds the present holds the past
He who holds the past, holds the future
The past of our ancestors is our future

Rocky Hudson, whakataukī nā Aotea waka[39]

New futures are possible when the past is understood in new ways. For this to happen, the claimants appeared to insist that the boundaries between what is understood as past and what is seen as present be collapsed. Such a shift is not always easy to make.

A failed apology
Misunderstandings about the 'historical' nature of the grievances being aired at Parihaka in front of the tribunal are revealed in a tortuous exchange over an apology contained in the tribunal archives. Negotiated apologies have since become a powerful and significant part of 'Deeds of Settlement' between iwi and the Crown; but in the early 1990s, apology protocols had not been developed, and there was much space for misunderstanding.[40]

When the Waitangi Tribunal sat at Parihaka for the first time in 1991, a representative of the Crown offered an apology for the 1881 invasion and sacking of the village. Solicitor Tom Winitana, of Tūhoe, spoke on behalf of the Minister of Justice, Pākehā Doug Graham. Winitana said the Crown did not dispute Taranaki claimants' testimony about the sacking of the village at the 1927 Sim Commission, an earlier government inquiry into land confiscation, and it did not dispute claimants' version of events now. The Crown would listen respectfully if people chose to talk about the invasion; but it did not expect 'any one of you to come before this Tribunal and suffer the distress of re-telling those events'. Rather, Winitana concluded, the Crown was ready to enter into direct negotiations with Taranaki iwi to 'discuss any proposal whereby the mana (status) of Parihaka might be restored':

> *We are the descendants, the inheritors of that unhappy past. It is our duty to give it a proper burial. It is my duty, as one of Her Majesty's Ministers, to apologise to the ancestors of Parihaka and I now do so. In doing so I look now to the future. It beckons us all. Let us stand together as we face what is to come.*[41]

Parihaka leaders did not accept this well-meant but rather abrupt apology. It had come without warning, they explained, almost as an afterthought. It was addressed to the dead rather than the living, the descendants of those who had 'lived through the sacking and looting and destruction of Parihaka'. If an apology was to be offered to the living, it would have to be an event of national significance – rather than a local, low-key gesture – because Parihaka itself had been a gathering place for iwi from beyond Taranaki. It would have to be offered to a large audience that included Māori from around New Zealand, rather than the smaller group of Taranaki people assembled for a tribunal hearing.

As Parihaka leaders wrote: 'The hurt of Parihaka is therefore felt far beyond Taranaki. What happened there was something of an affront to nations. To the nations which embraced each other as Treaty partners in 1840.'[42] The timing and form of the apology would need to be negotiated between the Crown and the people of Parihaka. The bearer of the apology should have a status that matched the status accorded to the invasion of the village, an invasion that 'took place at the direction of the highest authorities'.

In response, Minister Graham wrote that he was 'deeply disturbed' his apology had been rejected. He had been acting in good faith and believed that his 'personal apology to your ancestors' would demonstrate to Parihaka people that 'as Her Majesty's

Minister responsible for Treaty claims I was listening to their grievances with sympathy and understanding'.[43]

The apology was undoubtedly well-meant, but it was not addressed to the right audience. In the fifteen years since the Parihaka hearings, negotiated apologies encompass the living, the dead and those yet to be born. Far from being a 'burial', an apology is supposed to signal the beginning of a new partnership between the Crown and the iwi in question. A recent settlement of 'historical claims' between the Crown and Ngāti Mutunga, one of the ten Taranaki claimant iwi, contains an apology 'to Ngāti Mutunga, to their ancestors, and to their descendants'.

Such apologies represent a radical upturning of the concepts of 'history' and 'historical grievance'. The personal testimonies of Taranaki claimants contained in tribunal archives reveal how the past 'vibrates' in their present and flow on into their future.

'The quiver on the bough'

Lindsay Rihari Waitara MacLeod, who opened the testimony for Taranaki iwi claimants at both Parihaka hearings, said that the words of nineteenth-century Parihaka leaders Te Whiti and Tohu continued to teach Māori not to be 'bitter and vindictive'.[44] MacLeod described nineteenth-century Parihaka by quoting 'E Rere Raa', a lament composed in the 1880s for Tohu by Muapoko people. MacLeod explained what the song was about: 'Everybody's on the move, they come from near and far to listen to the word of the Prophet, they highlight the climb to the Purepo where the Cannon stood (Mt Rolleston) to blast them out of existence thence down to Toroanui Marae to listen to the 'seething oratory and sweet talk''.'

MacLeod's translation of the song provided a commentary on the two histories embodied in many Taranaki landmarks. At Parihaka, for instance, locals call a hill overlooking the pā Purepo, 'the hill of cannons', whereas Pākehā know it as Mt Rolleston, the name of one of the government ministers involved in the raid on Parihaka. At the second Parihaka hearing, MacLeod reiterated this point about two kinds of history at work in New Zealand.

Further, he assumed that the present-day claimants who stood before the tribunal were not separated from the people who stood at Parihaka on the day it was invaded. MacLeod promised, at the end of the submissions, 'to describe events on that fateful dramatic day when we (our ancestors, Tupuna, Te Morehu) faced the threat of death itself by the dreaded Cannon strategically placed on the hill overlooking the Pa, the Purepo, now known in 'European history' as Mt Rolleston'.[45]

MacLeod used the term 'Te Morehu' (rather than 'ngaa morehu' a more generic phrase to describe a group of survivors) because he wanted to refer to the survivors who were gathered that day at Parihaka for the tribunal hearings.[46] Therefore, the 'we' in MacLeod's statement refers, very specifically, to the living and the dead.

MacLeod described nineteenth-century Parihaka as a home for hapū (large family groups) and iwi from around Aotearoa. It was like a miniature version of the nation, a spiritual and practical home. Waikato, Maniapoto, Whanganui, Muapoko, Te Āti Awa 'each had their own houses with Ancestral names such as Rangiatea, Koaiai ... each with their unique mode of Prayer chanting psalms while twirling their pois'. Kūmara and kamokamo (a kind of cucumber) was grown on beach reserves, and fish was gathered in open surf boats; people such as Te Rangiwakarurua distributed the fish at Parihaka, giving each family group what they needed. This harmony and cooperation was destroyed by 'the blitz', the invasion of the village.

> *For simply defending their 'house and home' they were declared REBELS, exiled and imprisoned without trial in Otago between 1869 and 1881. Housed and worked in caves like slaves and had large tracts of land confiscated. Some never returned but died in ignominy. The devastating breakup of their whole social structure*

> and peaceful lifestyle are seen in our kids of today, who are social and psychological misfits and refugees culturally in their own land with their economic base taken from underneath them.[47]

He concluded by naming the people – living and dead – who had provided him with his evidence. His informants included Tahuaroa Watson, the adopted son of Taare Waitara, the man who funded much of the post-invasion restoration of Parihaka. His testimony ended with a proverb and statement that reinforced the continuity between past and present generations at Parihaka, a continuity that was expressed through descendants' ongoing adherence to the teachings of Te Whiti and Tohu.

> A proverb of Te Whiti is translated as: 'The bird startled has flown, only the quiver of the bough remains.' We are the quiver – their descendants whom despite all their pain and hurt and feelings on injustice, never taught us to be bitter, vindictive or take revenge but on the contrary – Give Glory to God in the Highest, Peace on Earth and Goodwill to all Mankind. Thank you for your patience. 'Ka Aroha – Ka Tangi Au Kia Ratau.'

MacLeod's testimony reinforced the ongoing importance of Parihaka as both a place and a value system, a site of moral power for Māori. In his submission at Owae Marae, Donald Hugh McDonald makes a similar point. His testimony is a heart-wrenching story of a family who have been so damaged by the loss of Māori land that many 'feel more comfortable being Pākehā'. It was too difficult to take up the responsibilities of 'gathering the family together and enhancing iwi development'. McDonald, the fifth son in a family of fifteen, said it was traditionally the job of his four older brothers to lead and support, but the places where 'we used to gather food at certain times of the year are no longer places of sustenance and support'.

> *One is made to feel like an intruder when we have to ask Pākehā if we could have ready access to the places we used to go for generations, to gather watercress, preserve our corn, fish for eels, or dye harakeke in the black mud ... we used to have ample land to sustain all our families ... the resources have gone.*[48]

McDonald's submission ends in Māori, but his final comment in English is a plea to the Crown to put things right, followed by the statement: 'I firmly hold to the teachings of Tohu Kakahi and Te Whiti o Rongomai.' In this context, Parihaka is evoked as a signal of the speaker's forbearance in the face of remarkable adversity and as a pledge of ongoing resistance and protest.

Inherited struggles, often connected with nineteenth century events at Parihaka, were a common theme of the hearings. Between 1863 and 1947, Māori from Taranaki alone made 169 petitions to government pleading for the return of land.[49] One way that claimants demonstrated the continuity of their resistance, the 'living' nature of the history being shared, was by using their whakapapa to provide a genealogy of protest that preceded the speaker's life and would continue, if necessary, after the speaker's death.

One of the measures of a family member's life is the number of years they will be able to continue the struggle. Ngatata Love ended his submission by introducing the four generations of his family at the hearing:

> *Let there be no doubt in the minds of the Crown that this injustice will not die or disappear. Taking the lead from our kaumatua, Sir Ralph, who fights the case at 85, the next generations are selected and ready to continue the struggle until at least 2060.*
>
> *Makere 85*
>
> *Ngatata 53 31 years 2021*
>
> *Catherine Amohia 30 55 years 2045*
>
> *Sharmia 10 75 years 2060*[50]

A similar measure was used by Peter Moeahu, who introduced his first-born grandchild, Moeahu Edwards, as 'an offspring of Taranaki and Tainui, two iwi who suffer much from confiscation of their land. We recently gathered at our family marae to celebrate the christening of my mokopuna. The name of her marae in Taranaki is Muru Raupatu (confiscation and marginalisation).'[51] In Moeahu's testimony, various marae have been places for learning about injustices. At Muru Raupatu, for instance, he learnt how his great-grandfather, Tamati Whanganui, had been imprisoned for ploughing family land 'just north of Bell Block' as part of the Parihaka protests. At Te Niho on Parihaka, he had learned from his grandmother and other female relatives about 'the wonder and tragedy of Parihaka', how it had been a place of refuge and plenty, surrounded by 'land so fertile that it sustained all who gathered' there. Finally, at Te Aroha Marae, he learnt about the warrior Titokowaru and how Moeahu, an ancestor, had carried Te Whiti's words of peace to him, and how Titokowaru eventually 'turned to Parihaka for peace'. The destinies of these three marae were intertwined: like Te Raukura, the three feathers of Te Whiti, they stand as a reminder of 'the immeasurable beauty that could have been, and the desolation and suffering that is'.[52]

These testimonies, in which peaceful Māori resistance and protest are one way of continuing the traditions of Parihaka, are absent from the Taranaki report. So too are the non-human historical actors, which are a significant feature of some testimonies. But spiritual forces, including curses, have been important agents in Taranaki history well into the twentieth century. Two examples demonstrate this, giving a glimpse of a world in which Pākehā motivations, faiths and understandings are marginal, at best.

Hohaia said that in the 1890s, many of the tribunal claimants' great-grandparents were owners of blocks of land surveyed out of Crown grants. But this land was leased to Pākehā without the Māori owners being given details about the lease or rent. Hohaia said:

> *This situation steadily deteriorated so that by the 1920s our great grand parents had come to regard the situation imposed as a curse which caused families to disintegrate amidst suspicion and deceit. Many of our Tuupuna sold what land they had in order to break that curse. These are the effects of confiscation.*[53]

The second example of the power of spiritual forces relates to the comet Rauhoto Tapairu and ancient petroglyphs. Te Puniho, the sister pā of Parihaka, is the resting place for Rauhoto. The comet, Hohaia relates, was moved to the pā in 1948 by a famous tohunga (healer), Te Ao Maarama, 'who died two days later having said that this would be the outcome'.[54] She was helped by Mrs Wiki Hau, aged in her nineties and still living in Oakura at the time of the hearings. The comet was moved because other important mauri kōhatu (treasured stones) had been stolen, and other tribes had interfered with Rauhoto, 'hoping to remove her and therefore possibly [gain] the right to claim the mountain through the possession of Rauhoto'. 'Upward of seventy people had died attempting to interfere with Rauhoto Tapairu who was regarded as extremely tapu indeed', Hohaia related.

The lethal, sacred comet streaks across the tribunal archives, illuminating new possibilities for writing Taranaki histories, histories that pre-date the arrival of Pākehā and, indeed, Māori themselves. The absence of this kind of evidence in tribunal reports demonstrates the limits of that body's ability to 'rewrite' New Zealand history, but the inclusion of this evidence in the tribunal archives offers opportunities to push these historical limits, to create new histories that move beyond an impoverished grievance framework.

Parihaka in a deep past

In Australia, historians working for heritage bodies have started to record post-contact Aboriginal heritage sites in an effort to overcome an institutionalised bias towards 'prehistoric' Aboriginal sites. In New Zealand, the work of the tribunal, which can only report on things that happened after 1840, has created a bias towards post-contact sites and stories. 'Prehistoric' Māori sites and events are absent in the Taranaki report, despite the tribunal's insistence that all claimants present two types of evidence: 'traditional' and 'historical'.[55]

In the tribunal's framework, historic events are the grievances that relate to things that did or did not happen after settlers arrived in New Zealand, specifically the actions or omissions of the Crown post-1840. While the tribunal strives to tell a Māori side to the story of colonisation, it is unable to narrate a Māori view of history, a story that begins hundreds of years before white settlement.

Yet the tribunal still requires Māori to include traditional history reports in their claims. A traditional history report has to explain who an iwi is and how that group of people relate to particular pieces of land. Traditional history reports require a detailed history of genealogy, geography, customary practices, warfare, alliances, migrations and so on, both pre- and post-1840. Specific histories are required for every site of special significance, whether it be a wāhi tapu (sacred site) or a mahinga kai (place used to grow or gather food). Claimants should interview kaumātua and kuia (senior men and women) and consult whakapapa books or other written sources in tribal possession. If possible, a researcher would search Native Land Court records and other archives.

When traditions are shared, Tipene O'Regan cautions that this history is not tested by the empirical standards applied to academic history. Rather, it is either 'accepted or discounted on the basis of the manner in which it was presented'.[56] For instance, in a revealing and sensitive article, the tribunal's chief historian Grant Phillipson has described how the behaviour of Moriori claimants during hearings on the Chatham Islands, 'the content of what was said and done, though outside the official hearing of evidence, was crucial to the Tribunal's view of the Moriori claim'.[57]

Until the information contained in Māori traditional history reports – the ones that are performed before the tribunal and the ones that are written and deposited in the archive – is accorded the same status as information contained in historical reports, it is tempting to argue that these reports are nothing more than a necessary performance of Māoriness. This performance is undoubtedly deeply meaningful for the small audience at the hearings, but it has limited meaning beyond the marae or motel if it is not allowed to shape the history the tribunal writes. How might the story of Parihaka be altered by being placed in a context provided by one such traditional history report?

The tribunal history of Taranaki opens with illegal purchases of land at Ngamotu, a settler action that breached the 'good faith' shown by Māori. The report then provides information about war and confiscation that sets the scene for 'the holocaust of Taranaki history', a catastrophe in which the invasion of Parihaka is a central event. But when it is freed from the restrictive lens of Treaty breaches, Parihaka can occupy a different kind of time and space, one that is arguably more 'historical'.

In his submission, Danny Keenan commented on the absence of historical monuments in New Plymouth, the region's capital, where Ngāti Te Whiti people once lived and thrived. 'Today a complete townscape has replaced the historical landscape of Ngati Te Whiti', he said. Later he reflected, 'New Plymouth city reflects little of its past; in its physical and architectural design, and in its administrative and human emphasis which has the deeper resonance of Europe, not New Zealand, it is thoroughly reflective of its present, a very long present that began in 1841.'[58]

The 'present' that is dominated by the region's recent arrivals may be long, but the past that pre-dated white settlement is far longer.

In his traditional history, Hohaia located Parihaka in a history that began with Te Kaahui Maunga, a people who were in Taranaki 'before even the mountain when Rua Tawhito (the Pouakai) and Rua Tipua (the Kaitake Ranges) stood and were associated with the creation story beginning 'I noho a io I roto I te aha o te aao' wherein is told the development of life and knowledge through the interplay of past and future.'[59] Part of this story tells the history of Puke Te Whiti, a prominent hill in the Kaitake ranges that is visible from the coast, even as far south as Parihaka. Hohaia relates that this hill is a sentinel guiding the flight path of the comet Rauhoto Tapairu. As such, Puke Te Whiti is 'the guardian of the now and the crossing between the past and the future'. He said some people believe Te Whiti o Rongomai and his namesakes were named after the comet Rauhoto Tapairu and its flight path past Puke Te Whiti.[60]

Markers of the deep past depicted in this story were the ancient carved stones (petroglyphs) and tauranga waka ('monolithic statements carved into the landscape of the reefs') of Taranaki. The boulders were carved or pecked with eyebrow or spiral motifs and are believed to have been used to convey information about territory and relationships between groups. Hohaia uses these boulders to construct an interplay between past and future, a conversation that includes – but does not excessively dwell on – the invasion of Parihaka. He relates that some of these carved boulders were created by Kaahui Maunga people. One, Te Mapua, 'was in operation when Kupe circumnavigated the Island'. Te Mapua is at Te Ika Roa, one of the launching points for fishing boats that used to supply Parihaka maraes and families with food during the war. Hohaia relates that this launching point was used until the 1940s:

> *Mrs Louie Okeroa, who is 93 and still lives at Te Ika Roa, was the lighter of the fires at night to guide her husband's 13-oar clinker in from fishing expeditions to and from offshore grounds. Her eldest son James Okeroa remembers well how the fish was allocated to various families who at that time had no boats on the water.*

Hearings

During the war years these Parihaka fishing boats supplied the maraes and families with food which was otherwise difficult to come by. Boat sheds stood at many of the landings, complete with sleeping quarters for the crew.[61]

Another of the tauranga waka is Te Opu Opu, a launching place that is special for Parihaka and Ngāti Moeahu people. A mauri (carved rock, life force, guardian or protector) was taken from here to Otakou (Otago) in 1987 to commemorate the Taranaki men who died there during their imprisonment in the nineteenth century. Māori had authority over this place well into the twentieth century. Hohaia relates that in the 1950s, elders Tom Inia and Wharepouri let Pākehā start fishing from there, as long as they gave some of the catch to marae. No commercial fishing was allowed. By the 1960s, Pākehā boats started to outnumber Māori ones at Te Opu Opu, and 'today the Cape Egmont Boat Club enjoys almost exclusive use of the channel'. Many club members were not aware of the 1950s agreement, but senior Māori had suggested a kōhatu (stone) and plaque to explain the significance of the place to Māori. Hohaia further suggested that the 1950s agreement should be put in the boat club's charter.

The stories associated with these landmarks demonstrate how Parihaka can be positioned in a dynamic web of meanings and connections far broader than that provided by 'the holocaust of Taranaki history'. In this Parihaka history, the settlement is one of sixty wāhi tapu (sacred sites) around Taranaki. By drawing on the links between Parihaka and coastal fishing and garden settlements, Hohaia's testimony links Parihaka with the deep past (through the carved stones) and the near present (the agreement with the boat club). It encourages an understanding of Parihaka as a place that developed out of a complex history that includes the musket wars which predated white settlement in Taranaki, the work of Lutheran missionaries and the nineteenth-century land wars. The ongoing development and history of Parihaka includes twentieth-century events, such as local inter-cultural cooperation – and lack of cooperation – over fishing rights and farming and the hearings of the Waitangi Tribunal itself. The hearings are a part of Taranaki history now too. The tribunal archives are a 'historic site' that is waiting to be explored, a foundation for new pasts, presents and futures.

[1] '70-year Rites at Parihaka', *Taranaki Daily News,* 7 November 1951.

[2] Dick Scott, *The Parihaka Story,* Auckland: Southern Cross, 1954, 14.

[3] Scott, *Ask That Mountain,* 1975, 7.

[4] Kay Mooney, 'Book rubs NZ nose in some dirt from the past', *Hawke's Bay Herald-Tribune,* 24 May 1975. With thanks to Dick Scott for kindly supplying me with copies of reviews of both editions.

[5] Merata Mita, *Koha,* Television New Zealand, 1981, NZFA.

[6] For background on occupation, see Aroha Harris, *Hikoi,* Huia, 2004, 78-84, and Ranginui Walker, *Ka Whawhai Tonu Matou: Struggle Without End,* Auckland: Penguin, 1990, 215-219.

[7] Joe Hawke quoted in Merata Mita, director, *Bastion Point: Day 507,* Awatea Films, 1980, NZFA.

[8] See 'Bastion Point Campers Till the Soil and Wait', *New Zealand Herald,* 10 January 1977, 1, reproduced in Johnson, 'Land of the Wrong White Crowd', MA thesis, 2002, 154. In 2000, as part of the City Gallery show, this connection was made explicit when Joe Hawke gave a floor talk on how Parihaka strategies had inspired protestors at Bastion Point. In 1977, Hawke made the first Waitangi Tribunal claim, into allegations of Treaty breaches over fisheries.

[9] Matiu Rata, New Zealand Parliamentary Debates, 1978, 322. Cited in Johnson, 'Wrong white crowd', 17.

[10] *The Taranaki Report: Kaupapa Tuatahi,* Wellington: Waitangi Tribunal, 1996, 209.

[11] Te Miringa Hohaia, Gregory O'Brien and Lara Strongman (eds), *Parihaka: The Art of Passive Resistance,* Wellington: Victoria University Press, 2001, new edition 2005.

[12] Robert Kenny, *The Lamb Enters the Dreaming: Nathanael Pepper & the Ruptured World,* Melbourne: Scribe, 2008, 32.

[13] Riseborough, 'Introduction', *Days of Darkness,* 2002, 14.

[14] Te Huirangi Waikerepuru, 'The Living Legacy' in Te Miringa et al., eds, *Passive Resistance,* 75.

[15] Stephen Turner, 'Inclusive Exclusion': Managing Identity for the Nation's Sake, *Arena Journal* no. 28, 2007, 97.

[16] I am drawing here on the work of Maria Nugent, *Botany Bay: Where Histories Meet,* Sydney: Allen & Unwin, 2005.

[17] Richard Boast, 'Waitangi Tribunal Procedure' in J. Hayward & N.R. Wheen, eds, *The Waitangi Tribunal: Te Roopu Whakamana I te Tiriti o Waitangi,* Wellington: Bridget Williams Books, 2004, 54.

[18] On this point, see especially Hana Te Hemara, 'Statement by Te Atiawa women in support of Taranaki Raupatu claims', 9 April 1991, Documents to the end of the fourth hearing, D10, Waitangi Tribunal Archive (WTA).

[19] The claims were lodged by individual iwi, trust boards and other blanket organisations between 1987 and 1996.

[20] Ward, 'Settlements and Non-settlements', in An *Unsettled History: Treaty Claims in New Zealand Today,* Wellington: Bridget Williams Books, 1999, 65.

[21] When the tribunal released its report, it included Tangahoe and Pakakohi claims into those of Ngāti Ruanui. This was a controversial decision. For more information see 'The Pakakohi and Tangahoe Settlement Claims Report', Wellington: Waitangi Tribunal, 2000. Available online at: www.waitangitribunal.govt.nz, accessed 7 July 2009.

[22] 'Overview', *Taranaki Report,* 1-2.

[23] Taranaki Report, 312.

[24] H.M. Williams, *Dictionary of Māori Language,* 215 and 330. For Taranaki meanings see Belgrave, 'Something Borrowed' in Bronwyn Dalley and Jock Phillips, eds, *Going Public: The Changing Face of New Zealand History,* Auckland: Auckland University Press, 2001, 106.

[25] Taranaki Report, 7.

[26] For a discussion of the debates around the use of the word 'holocaust' in the report, see Byrnes, *Waitangi Tribunal,* 149-152; Laurence Simmons, 'Bearing Witness', *Landfall* 201, Autumn 2001, 167-172; Belgrave, 'The Tribunal and the Past' in Belgrave et al., eds, *Waitangi Revisited,* 36. For a broader discussion of the use of the word 'holocaust' within the Taranaki report and elsewhere to describe colonisation in New Zealand, see David B. Macdonald, 'Daring to compare: the debate about a Māori "holocaust" in New Zealand', in *Journal of Genocide Research,* vol 5, no 3, 2003, pp383-403. With thanks to Ann Curthoys for this reference.

[27] See editorial, 'Sour taste of protest', *Dominion Post*, 19 January 2005. The editorial noted: 'The Tribunal angered many Pākehā by its use of the term 'holocaust' in its report of the invasion of Taranaki. Many share the sentiment of former member Michael Bassett, who said in 2002 he believed the tribunal operated with an assumption that Māori were always right, and the early settlers were always wrong, a view he reiterated last year when he suggested the tribunal was the captive of crusading historians and was an organisation that had passed its use-by date.'

The Parihaka Album

[28] W. H. Oliver comments that the tribunal is concerned to provide redress 'not only in material ways by the award of compensation, but also through an eloquent story of indigenous loss told to underpin the campaign for a better indigenous future'. 'Future behind us', Sharp, ed *Histories, Power and Loss*, 10.

[29] Boast, 'Waitangi procedure' in *Waitangi Tribunal*, 57.

[30] For example, see 'Māori land loss mapped in the North Island', Waitangi Tribunal, National Overview: Rangahaua Whanui Series, 1997, cartography; G.M. Oulton, reproduced in *Histories, Power and Loss* (2001), viii-ix.

[31] Giselle Byrnes, *The Waitangi Tribunal and New Zealand History*, Auckland: Oxford University Press, 2004, 140.

[32] Dr Grant Phillipson, 'Preparing Claimant Evidence for the Waitangi Tribunal', Waitangi Tribunal, 1999, 1.

[33] Te Miringa Hohaia and Marlene Benson, 'Cape Egmont Lighthouse Reserve', case study presented at second Parihaka hearing, 22 October 1992, I11, WTA.

[34] 'Cape Egmont Reserve', report by Principal Keeper, Cape Egmont Lighthouse to G.C. Godfrey, (secretary of the Marine Department?), 4/11/1929, document included in Hohaia, I11, 2, WTA.

[35] Memorandum to Secretary for Marine from O.H.Burns, Commissioner of Crown Lands, 22 May 1952, in I11, WTA.

[36] See Deborah Bird-Rose, 'Decolonizing the discourse of environmental knowledge', in G. Hawkins and S. Muecke, eds, *Culture and Waste: The Creation and Destruction of Value,* Boston: Rowmann and Littlefield, 2003, 53-72.

[37] Memorandum for The Principal Keeper, from W.C. Smith, Secretary for Marine, 9 June 1952, 'Cape Egmont Lighthouse Reserve' case study, WTA.

[38] *Taranaki Report,* 212. The tribunal made similar observations about dealing 'not with a dry record or past habitations but with evidence that is lived' in its Whanganui report. Cited in Miranda Johnson, 'Honest acts and dangerous supplements: Indigenous oral history and historical practice in settler societies', *Postcolonial Studies,* vol 8, no 3, 2005, 264.

[39] Cited in the frontispiece of Tony Sole, *Ngati Ruanui: A History,* Wellington: Huia Publishing, 2005.

[40] For a discussion of the role of apologies in New Zealand, see Maureen Hickey, 'Negotiating History: Crown Apologies in New Zealand's Historical Treaty of Waitangi Settlements', *Public History Review,* vol 13, 2006, 108-124. An excellent, more general discussion on historical justice, including apologies, is Jana Thompson, *Taking Responsibility for the Past,* Cambridge: Polity Press, 2002.

[41] Doug Graham, 'Iwi o Taranaki', statement from Office of the Minister of Justice, delivered by Tom Winitana on 17 October 1991 at Parihaka, see Record of Inquiry, Taranaki report, F17 (a), p.3, WTA.

[42] Miringa Hohaia, letter to the Minister of Justice, re: Apology for Parihaka, 27 February 1992, Taranaki report, Record of Inquiry, F17 (b), WTA.

[43] Graham to Hohaia, 9 April 1992, F17c, WTA.

[44] Lindsay Rihari Waitara MacLeod, opening evidence for Taranaki iwi claim, Parihaka, 16 October 1991.

[45] For a full version of this song, in Māori and English, see Hohaia, *Passive Resistance,* 48-50.

[46] Personal communication, Te Miringa Hohaia, 7 July 2009. He wrote: 'The reason Lindsay uses the term "te morehu" is because it refers specifically to the survivors who were gathered that day, not any other generic group of survivors wherein "ngaa moorehu" is commonly used throughout the country.'

[47] MacLeod, first Parihaka hearing, F12, p3. Emphasis in original.

[48] 'My name is Donald Hugh McDonald – My Tribe is Ngati Mutunga', submission at Owae Marae, 3-6 September 1990, WTA.

[49] 'Muru Raupatu – Taranaki', Documents to the end of the first hearing, 7 September 1990, A17, WTA.

[50] Dr Ngatata Love, A17 (a), WTA.

[51] Peter Moeahu, 'Muru Raupatu', A17, WTA.

[52] Moeahu, 9. Moeahu's extraordinary submission is structured like an epic poem with a series of statements under various evocative headings.

[53] Hohaia, 'Opening for Taranaki iwi', A17, p8, WTA.

[54] Hohaia, 'Waahi Tapu', site 28, F14, WTA.

[55] Phillipson, *Claimant Evidence,* 3 and 16. A kaumātua (elder) sits on every tribunal and it is this person's job to assess traditional evidence. The historical evidence is assessed by a 'professional historian'.

[56] Tipene O'Regan, 'Old Myths' in Judith Binney, ed., *The Shaping of History: Essays from The New Zealand Journal of History,* Wellington: Bridget Williams Books, 2001, 22-23.

[57] Phillipson, 'Talking and Writing History: Evidence to the Waitangi Tribunal' in Hayward, ed., *Waitangi Tribunal,* 44-45.

[58] Danny Keenan, 'Ngati Te Whiti Muru me te Raupatu Waitangi Tribunal presentation', Documents to the end of the fourth hearing, 12 April 1991, D14, WTA. The emphasis is mine.

[59] Hohaia, 'Submission concerning traditional history presented by Hohaia on behalf of Taranaki iwi, Documents to the end of the sixth hearing, 17 October 1991', F12, WTA. For a further elaboration of Māori creation stories and an explanation of how they influenced the teachings of Te Whiti and Tohu see Hohaia, *Passive Resistance,* 43-44. For stories linked particularly to the history of Maunga Taranaki, see Hohaia, 'The Foundation Story' in *Te Maunga Taranaki,* 9-15.

[60] Hohaia says others believe the prophet was named after the comet 'Te-Auahi-Tu-Roa'. In the *Williams Māori* dictionary, 'whiti' has at least four meanings. The first set of meanings are all concerned with transformation: to cross over, to reach the opposite side, to change, to turn, to pass through, to return present. The second meaning is shine or shine upon, ra-whiti is sunrise. The third set of meanings are connected with alarm, surprising and awakenings. The fourth is to relate or recite a charm or verse, 497-98.

[61] Hohaia, 'Tauranga Waka', F15, WTA, 2.

CHAPTER 9

Dementia wing

When I was small, I loved to visit my grandparents in Wellington in the winter-time, because that meant I could go to the rugby at Athletic Park in Newtown. A test match was the best. There were so many people everywhere, great crowds streaming up Adelaide Road. Their trousers smelt like wet sheep. Scarves held their heads and shoulders together. The wind blew right through us. At half-time, Grandad brought me a battered sausage on a stick. The top was dipped in tomato sauce, the bottom was just plain batter over the red skin. I bit into it and looked across the field at the poor people swaying around in the open-topped Millard Stand. We sat in the members' stand.

The last game of rugby was played at the park in 1999, and in early 2000, the famous Millard Stand was demolished. A few years later, in the middle of 2004, my father Leo and his aunty Leah attended the opening of Village at the Park. This is a retirement complex on the park site that was built and is run by the Wellington Tenths Trust, a Māori organisation. Of particular interest to them was the Rawinia Buchanan Dementia wing, a thirty-bed facility built over the old heaving, sweating, scrummaging, liniment-infused twenty-five-yard line.

Rawinia was my dad's mother, Leah's sister. As the name Rawinia suggests, my grandmother had what is sometimes described as Māori heritage. The Dementia wing was named after Rawinia for two reasons. First, it recognised her influence at Athletic Park through her many decades of service as the assistant secretary of the Wellington Rugby Football Union. 'Ra' or 'Mrs B' (as she was known in rugby and business circles) allocated seats for test matches, a position that gave her unrivalled power and status.

Second, it acknowledged her identity as a descendent of Hemi Parai, a Taranaki chief who was one of the founding fathers of Te Aro, the pā that used to exist in the pocket of land in central Wellington, now occupied by a park, an opera house, a highway, a repurposed ambulance building and a glittering harbour foreshore.

It's highly appropriate that my grandmother's name has been coupled with a home for people suffering from memory loss. In my family, 'Māoriness', for want of a better term, is something that has been remembered and forgotten and remembered again, an ancestral push-me-pull-you influenced by private and public, local and national forces.

Memories are malleable possessions, things we can hoard or share or reshape. They are, as Susannah Radstone has put it, 'complex products shaped by diverse narratives and genres and replete with absences, silences, condensations and displacements', products that are 'related, in complex ways, to the dialogic moment of their telling.'[1] My moment of telling is now.

My grandmother had been given an obviously Māori first name, Rawinia. Her second name, the royal Queenie, is also popular in Māori communities (Kingi is the equivalent for boys), but it is normally spelt Kuini. Her names suggested Māoriness but she rarely, if ever, used them in full. I never heard her describe herself or my dad as Māori. I never even called her by her real name; she insisted her grandchildren address her as Flossie.

Dementia wing

Figure 23. Face to face. The Alexander Turnbull Library describes this photograph as 'Carte de visite of Hemi Parai, chief of Ngati Haumia, taken by E S Richards of Wellington between 1862 and 1872'. Black and white original photographic print, albumen print 92 x 52 mm, with rounded upper corners mounted on 104 x 59 mm, Alexander Turnbull Library, reference number PA2-2940.

Flossie's fair skin meant she could easily pass as Pākehā. In his recent memoir, Kim Scott has described how his Aunty Hazel and her brother, his Uncle Lomas, talk about 'the difference between being a Noongar with white skin and one with black skin. Not because of anything inherent, but because people treat you according to the degree to which you are recognisably "Aboriginal". That was true in the past, and it still is.'[2] In New Zealand, if you are not recognisably Māori, the default setting is Pākehā.

The Dementia wing is an unlikely monument to my family's Māori past and present, a place for remembering that cares for those who have forgotten. Like a headstone in a graveyard, the Dementia wing memorialises a dead individual; but it also serves to recall others who died before her, deaths that stretch back to the wars of colonisation in Aotearoa New Zealand – when one strand of my grandmother's family were the invaders, the other the invaded – and beyond that to the countless generations of family deaths that predate colonisation altogether, and go right back to the time of creation.

My grandmother was no soldier, but our Dementia wing is a kind of war memorial, one of the most flexible and surprising kind: it commemorates victory and defeat, assimilation and resistance to assimilation, white power and black power, war and peace. For my white-skinned family, the Dementia wing is a place where we can recall and foreground the brown-ness that lies beneath, behind or in front of us. It is a place that darkens our family name. More than this, the Dementia wing of our family history is a metaphor for the Dementia wing of national history that I've explored in this book, for the way separate and intertwined Māori and Pākehā histories have been remembered and forgotten and reinvented, in complex cycles, since settlement of Aotearoa began. The conflicting actions of members of my own family in New Zealand's wars of foundation provide a pathway towards increasing the complexity and richness of memorialising all wars, at home and abroad. Beyond military history, the Dementia wing also contains stories of peace, non-violence, cooperation and love.

Fractions

How is identity made?[3] When I was a child, being Māori was not part of my identity. It had not been an obvious part of my father's identity when he was young either. Māoriness was not hidden or secret–indeed, my father used to enjoy telling stories about our supposed connection to Te Rauparaha, a legendary six-toed nineteenth-century Māori warrior – but it was not significant either. It was an interesting, exotic add-on, rather than something inherent to who we were.

There were public and private reasons for this, I think. Until 1974, and the introduction of the Māori Affairs Amendment Act, my grandma and my great-grandma did not even qualify, officially, as 'Māori'. Before 1974, the law said that only people with 'half or more' Māori blood qualified as Māori. The 1974 Act changed that to say that anyone with Māori ancestry could be Māori; but the racist assumptions behind a fixation on rare and endangered indigenous purity and common but regrettable indigenous contamination cast a long shadow over many lives, including those of my dad Leo, his mum Flossie and Flossie's mum Hannah Bramley (nee Wallace), whom we knew as 'Gar'.

The law had changed, the 1975 land march had happened, the Waitangi Tribunal had been set up, but you can't wipe out 130-odd years of assimilationist policies and beliefs so easily, especially when those ideals (and the silence about all things Māori that accompanied them) are part of the inheritance you have received from your Māori forebears. Those ideas of percentages or portions, a genealogy of diminishing return, remained powerful in my 1970s childhood. I remember dad talking about fractions of Māori blood, quarter caste, eighth, sixteenth and onwards to some diminishing point of nothingness.[4] I thought of my body as a beaker. It contained layers of different blood types, just like one of those red-orange-and-green fizzy 'traffic light' drinks we used to get from Cobb and Co when it was Dad's birthday. The beaker was filled with Irish blood and Scottish blood and Māori blood and Jewish blood and English blood. The blood was a measure of the different stories I had heard about relatives, especially dead relatives. Aside from the tiny little fraction of Māori blood – a portion no deeper than the cream on top of the bottles of milk delivered to us each morning – all my other blood came from elsewhere.

The idea of Māoriness as fractional identity, something that could (and should) be bred out of a respectable, modern New Zealand family, was embedded in the 1960 *Report on Department of Māori Affairs* written by J.K. Hunn, acting secretary for Māori Affairs, and known as the Hunn Report. It explained that 'Māori today' could be grouped into three categories. These were:

> A. A completely detribalised minority whose Māoritanga is only vestigal.
>
> B. The main body of Māoris, pretty much at home in either society, who like to partake of both (an ambivalence, however, that causes psychological stress in some of them).
>
> C. Another minority complacently living a backward life in primitive conditions.[5]

My grandmother and great-grandmother were 'A-grade Māori,' a status earned by the faint traces of Māoritanga that clung to them, the echoes, ghosts, remnants of a lost wholeness. They lived in the city. Aside from distant Taranaki, there were no rural marae for them to return to, no 'C-grade' relatives keeping a paepae warm. They were inner-city people, and all the inner-city marae had been destroyed by the late nineteenth century. They did not become involved, as far as I know, in the pan-tribal group behind the establishment of Pipitea Marae in Thorndon.

It wasn't just blood that was fractional. It was land too. The Waitangi Tribunal's 2003 report on the Wellington District gives a detailed account of how Māori land was alienated in Wellington.[6]

Dementia wing

In 1839, Colonel Wakefield, the principal agent for the New Zealand Company, arrived in Whanganui-a-Tara on the survey ship *Tory*. He started to negotiate with Māori leaders to buy land. Before agreement had even been reached with Māori, the company had sold almost 100,000 acres of land to settlers. It held a lottery in London to allocate this land. On 27 September, Te Puni, Wi Tako Ngatata, Te Wharepouri and thirteen other chiefs signed a 'deed of purchase', which comprised 'the whole bay, harbour and district of Wanga Nui Atera, commonly called Port Nicholson, situated on the North-eastern side of Cook's Straits of New Zealand'.[7]

In return for this land, Māori were given, according the original deed of purchase:

100 red blankets
100 muskets
2 tierces of tobacco
48 iron pots
2 cases soap
15 fowling pieces
21 kegs gunpowder
1 cask ball cartridges
1 keg lead slabs
100 cartouche boxes
100 tomahawks
40 pipe tomahawks
1 case pipes
2 doz spades
50 steel axes
1200 fish hooks
12 bullet moulds
12 doz shirts
20 jackets
20 pairs trousers
60 red night caps

> 300 yards cotton duck
> 200 yards calico
> 100 yards check
> 20 doz pocket-handkerchiefs
> 2 doz slates and 200 pencils
> 1 doz pair shoes
> 1 doz umbrellas
> 1 doz hats
> 2 lbs beads
> 100 yards ribbon
> 1 gross jews harps
> 1 doz razors
> 10 doz dressing combs
> 6 doz novels
> 2 suits superfine clothes
> 1 doz shaving boxes and brushes
> 20 muskets
> 2 doz adzes
> and 1 doz sticks sealing wax.[8]

One interesting observation on the 'sale' is made by historian Angela Ballara in her work on Māori occupation of the harbour. Ballara argues that the 'sale' of the harbour allowed certain Taranaki iwi to cement their occupation rights. 'The sale of Te Whanganui-a-Tara by Te Wharepouri and Te Puni was itself an act designed to set the bounds of their mana over the harbour.'[9]

Te Aro leaders refused, at first, to sell their land to the New Zealand Company, and some residents pulled up survey pegs in protest. In 1844, however, Te Aro leaders, including Hemi Parai, signed a Deed of Release for the pā. The New Zealand Company paid each of the seven signatories 300 pounds in 'full payment and satisfaction for the absolute surrender of our title to all our claims in all our lands which are written in the document attached to this …

On the other hand, the pā, the cultivations, the sacred places and the places reserved will always remain all for us … the only lands left for us are the aforementioned.'[10] None of these promises were honoured. The 'sales' and 'releases' were a sham.

The New Zealand Company claimed to have bought most of what it called Port Nicholson before the British Crown had even declared sovereignty over New Zealand. The British government declared that pre-Treaty sales were invalid until they had been investigated by the Crown. Even so, the company sold sections that were occupied by pā and associated gardens. Two inquiries, by William Spain and later by Lieutenant-Colonel W. A. McCleverty, failed to protect Māori or to satisfy the claims of the company and its settlers.

As well as getting some money and the blankets, tobacco, umbrellas, beads and other things on the above list, Māori were also promised that a tenth of every bit of land sold should be reserved in trust for their heirs forever. This fraction, a tenth, is where the title of the Wellington Tenths Trust comes from. Trust beneficiaries are people descended from Te Āti Awa, Ngāti Tupaia, Taranaki and Ngāti Tama tupuna who were living around the harbour in 1840. In 1888, according to the Native Land Court, there were 301 beneficial owners. Now there are more than 4500, including me.

We, the 'beneficiaries', did not have any role in administering this land, including iconic sites such as Athletic Park, until 1985. Before that, the remnants of remaining Māori land were administered by various trusts. My father has a small archive of papers relating to these trusts, papers kept by his mother and grandmother, papers collected by family members, including Paul Walker and Raumahora Broughton, and papers collected from his own, more recent involvement in trust matters, including Village at the Park. In one 1994 letter, Paul Walker explained: 'I find the documents ask as many questions as the answers they provide.'

When I look at these papers now, with my researcher's eyes, I can see that what this trust system did was to further fracture Māori families, splitting land interests up into ever smaller portions, making them fractions of connection to a place. There is North Island Tenths and Wellington Tenths rent money. Fractions abound. Traditional owners become shareholders. Interest in land is divvied up: one third, one sixth, one twenty-fourth … As the fabric of the nation was being woven, Māori were left with the scraps, the offcuts and the remnants; then these remainders were divided up again and again and again until the portions were so small that it was hard to see them at all.

For example, my great-grandmother's father Taare Warahi (also known as Taare Rongouaroa and Charlie Wallace) died in 1932 with no will. On 17 January 1933, one of his childern, Gar, appeared before the Māori Land Court to determine who would inherit her father's shares in Māori land. Gar was one of seven children: William Wallace, Ella Simeon, James Wallace, Cyril Wallace, Doris Julia O'Connor, Hannah Bramley (Gar) and Isabel Wallace. The court order was made 'in favour of six children living for 1/7 share each and for children shown as succeeding to William Wallace for 1/35 share each'.[11] The land mentioned is Polhill Gully, Wellington, Sections 17 & 19, Blk. X Opunake S.D. (Part Orimupiko 22), Orimupiko No. 1, Oriumupiko Block 1892 Act Leases Grant 3924 4th Residue and Ngatihawe Block 1892 Act Leases Grant 3954 2nd Residue. Polhill Gully (also known as the Ohiro Block) is land with an exceptionally complicated history – like so much Māori land – but Wellington residents can find clues to the original, very large block by walking up Aro Street.[12]

The land was there, but Māori had to make polite requests to get any information about it. While Pākehā families could make their own decisions about land, who would inherit and who would not, Māori had to let someone else decide for them. The system kept Māori in a state of near total ignorance about their inheritances. In 1947, for example, Gar received a letter from the Native Department informing her that Oriumupiko 22, sections 18 and 19 Block X Opunake 'a block of 72 acres is leased to Isaac George Short of Opunake, farmer who transferred his lease to Hugh Joseph Mullin of Opunake, farmer. The lease is for 10 years from 1/12/45 at a yearly rent of 45 pounds and this amount is payable to the Native Trustee, Wellington.'[13] My great-grandmother had to ask for information about 'her' land, but the farmer, the tenant, could do as he pleased.

These papers provide valuable whakapapa and other information; but they are sad documents, soft little yellowing scraps of the past. When I hold them, it is like touching an uncanny identity card. Look! Proof! Māori Trust. Māori Land. Māori language. Māori person. This is what I think but what did my great-grandmother think? What did she feel when she got these letters from the Native Department, or the square payment slips, in envelopes marked with a blue cross and the letters O.H.M.S.?

> *From: Māori Trust Office, Private Bag Palmerston North.*
> *To: Hannah Bramley, 12 Fraser Ave, Johnsonville*
> *Date: 7 December 1960*
> *Period ending April 17. Rent, purchase money, etc., as Hereunder: Polhill Gully Rent, 85 shillings. North Island Tenths, £2 and 94 pence.*
> *Name of Account: Taranaki.*
> *Payment of the above money can be obtained at the Post Office shown above and should be collected within one month. Ma te Poutapeta e mau ake nei e utu mai te moni nei, me haere koe kit e tango mai I roto o te kotahi marama.*

With such small portions split between many descendants, interests in the skerricks of remaining trust land quickly became 'uneconomic'. The system created a mathematics of oblivion.

In 1963, the registrar of the Māori Land Court wrote to my great-grandmother about the Ohiro Block (also known as Polhill

Gully). The letter explained that 'one of the greatest problems in the administration of this reserve is the ever increasing number of beneficiaries with extremely small shares ... You own 108.623 shares out of a total of 34742 shares, and your shares are valued at £5-15-0. Your interest is therefore uneconomic in terms of the Act and at the next sitting of the Māori Land Court at Wellington ... I propose to ask the Court to vest all uneconomic interests in the Māori Trustee.'[14]

It must have been sad for Gar to get such letters because she had worked hard, over the years, to protect whānau interests. Another letter in Dad's archive relates to a hearing of the Māori Land Court in New Plymouth eight years earlier, in 1955. Gar attended because her sister, Ella Simeon, had died. The notice she received read, in part:

> *Tuunga o te Kooti Whenua Māori ki Niu Paremata a te 5 o nga ra o Hepetema 1955/Sitting of the Māori Land Court at New Plymouth on 5 September 1955 ... Ka te te Kooti kit e Māori Hostel, Morley Street, Niu Paremata/Court will sit in the Māori Hostel, Morely Street, New Plymouth.*
>
> *Tono Whakatu Kai-riiwhi ki nga paanga whenua I raro o te ture 1953*
>
> *Applications for succession under 1953 Act*
>
> *Kai-tono (Applicant): Hannah Bramley*
>
> *Te Ingo o te Wenua (Name of Land): Grant 3954 Ngatihawe and another*
>
> *Te Tangata Kua Mate (Name of Deceased): Ella Catherine Simeon.*

Her sister's surname, Simeon, raises questions. In 1881, Wellington tailor Frederick Simeon (husband of Agnes, 'a part-Māori descendant of an early New Plymouth family') paid advertising rates to have a letter published in the *New Zealand Times* calling for an inquiry into the brutal treatment of Parihaka men imprisoned down south.[15] Had Ella married one of the Simeon children?

When I first read this document, I could hardly believe that it was my great-grandmother who appeared in this court, that it was she who held and read this bilingual document; but the death of a sister required her to take action, to enter the Māori world and to look after whānau affairs. These bits of paper help me to imagine the woman who did this, a stranger.

When I was little, neither Hannah (Gar) nor her daughter Rawinia (Flossie) behaved in ways that I could recognise as 'Māori'. I remember Gar living in a dark house. The blinds were half-down and the furniture was heavy, but there was enough light for me to find the bowls of barley sugars and other boiled lollies she kept on a side-table and to enjoy the clickety-clack of a plastic red and blue horse that would trot down the tin side of a tilted kitchen tray.

Of my grandmother Flossie, I have a much fuller picture. I would say that, first and foremost, my grandmother was concerned with her version of good manners and good taste. She was someone who cared very much about appearances, someone who was secretive about her age and vain about her looks. When a person asked how old she was, Flossie would say, with a straight face, 'twenty-one and holding'. She kept fit by riding her three-wheeler bike had a large, sheepskin-covered seat – an oversized toddler with a bedazzled chiffon scarf knotted under her neck to keep her dyed hair neat. She played hymns on an organ imported from Germany. She also played popular twentieth century songs. A favourite went 'Beautiful, beautiful brown eyes …' She cooked with margarine instead of fattening butter. A cup of tea was sweetened with two sucrose pills shaken from the white canister she kept in her handbag.

At least once a year, Flossie would holiday in Rotorua with her girlfriends. They spent their afternoons immersed in the hottest pool at the mineral baths, winding down afterwards with a couple of gin and tonics mixed with devil swizzel sticks. When I attended rugby matches with my grandparents, I would hear Flossie's special 'lady' voice, a plummy, ornate voice that she used for conversations with important people she met at Athletic Park, such as ex-All Blacks or ex-All Black coaches. Former All Black Ivan Vodanovich was a special favourite of hers (and mine). He had dark black hair that swept back from his forehead, and he always wore beautiful suits from his menswear shop in Newtown.

Flossie was posh, but she could also be fierce when the occasion demanded it. One family legend is connected with the 1981 Springbok tour. Flossie and her husband Frank, rugby people to the core, were pro-tour. 'Sport and politics should not mix,' they said. Flossie worked at the Wellington rugby union offices near the corner of Lambton Quay and Willis Street. The office was up some stairs, and Flossie ruled it. The tickets to test matches at Athletic Park were issued there, and Flossie bundled them up with elastic bands. Apparently anti-tour protestors stormed in there one day and Flossie beat them off with a furled polka-dotted umbrella. The tickets were safe. The show would go on.

These are some of the things I remember about my grandmother and great-grandmother in life, but in death, people can become something quite different, as those who knew them imagine all sorts of other identities for them, or the masks they wore in life slip away, replaced by masks made by the living.

Gar became recognisably Māori for me only in death. After her funeral mass, we went back to her house in Johnsonville and watched a group of old Māori women with greenery in their hands and hair sing Māori songs outside and inside the house. My grandmother died in 1992, and a similar thing happened at her funeral. After everyone had received communion, an old man leaning on a tokotoko stick walked up the aisle, stood next to my grandmother's coffin and spoke to her in Māori. That old man was Ralph Love, the one who lodged the first Māori land claim in Wellington back in 1987. Sir Ralph has also passed away since then. Representatives of Taranaki Whānui ki Te Upoko o Te Ika (Port Nicholson Block Claim) and the Crown signed a Deed of Settlement in August 2008.[16]

Stephen Muecke has observed that death is central to the formation of the nation. 'A surplus of social significance or power is transferred to the dead so that their fixed and symbolic narrative can control us,' he writes.[17] Families also need the 'magical or spiritual agency' of death to create new foundation stories or reinforce old ones.

When Flossie was a girl, being Māori was something to play down or hide away. This was especially so for someone growing up in the city, as she did. A metaphor for this, perhaps, is the dozens of letters regarding various Māori land trusts – including Wellington Tenths, Polhill Gully and PKW Incorporation – that I've already mentioned. These documents were kept tucked away, and my dad discovered them only after she died.

Children were strapped for speaking Māori at school. Assimilation was the dominant ideology. But by the time Flossie reached old age, in the 1970s and 1980s, things had changed. Māori staged land rights protests, urban marae were built, Māori kindergartens were opened and Māori and Pākehā – including my dad and me – started to learn the Māori language. Rather than being something to hide, Māoriness became something to be proud of.

This cultural shift has changed the way I think of my grandmother. Of course she is still the eccentric 'Flossie' I knew, the character I have sketched here, but she has also become a link between me and two radically divergent pasts, one Māori, one Pākehā. After his mother's death, my father did a great deal of work to research the Māori side of our family. His labours in the archives and in conversation with Māori relatives, such as Aunty Agnes Broughton and her daughter, family-history researcher Raumahora, have restored our family's whakapapa, making possible the kinds of observations that opened this chapter. His work has also allowed our family to be registered members of the Port Nicholson Block Claim, a process that requires whakapapa verification.

This recovery has also led to my father becoming a member of the Māori Doctors Association, a role that has given him immense satisfaction personally and professionally. Moreover, he is now an active participant in the Wellington Tenths Trust and was on the board that helped develop Village at the Park, with its Rawinia Buchanan Dementia wing.

My doctoral research on history-making about Parihaka represents my most serious engagement with what I earlier described as the 'connections, privileges, responsibilities, silences, losses and gains' of an indigenous history. I knew our whakapapa linked our family with Taranaki and Te Āti Awa iwi, two of the tribes most closely associated with Parihaka. That was one of the reasons why I felt able to take on such a topic. Influenced by Linda Tuhiwai Smith's writing on decolonising history, I wanted to work on stories that were related to me through place, through genealogy and through life experience.[18]

At the start of my research, Aunty Agnes and Raumahora had told me that they believed that Gar's father had lived at Parihaka for a time. Even though I had been given this information, it did not occur to me until I was well into the archival research that what I was actually doing in my thesis was a kind of family history, a history I felt obligated to pursue.

I was startled and then thrilled to discover further unexpected links between my family and Parihaka through our ancestor Hemi Parai. For example, Parai was a regular actor in the Appendices to the Journals of the House of Representatives. Parai never fought against the Pākehā. Indeed, in 1860, he was one of 107 Māori leaders who signed a seven-point resolution that condemned the establishment of a Māori King, and appeared, in newspaper reports at least, to support the government's military action at Waitara. The document, signed after the so-called 'Native Conference at Kohimarama' in the Bay of Plenty, also condemned 'in the strongest manner the murders of unarmed Europeans, committed by the Natives now fighting at Taranaki', and thanked both the Governor, the Bishop of New Zealand and Native Secretary Donald McLean for their 'kindness' towards 'the Māori people'.[19] McLean was one of the convenors of the meeting.

In 1866, Parai was one of four absentee Taranaki chiefs awarded land under the Confiscated Lands Act. He was awarded '100 acres ... in consideration of his having remained in Wellington at the insistence of the government when he might have returned to Taranaki' during the wars of that decade.[20] The other awards were made to Te Puni, 200 acres 'in recognition of his long and faithful services'; to Wi Tako, 100 acres 'for recent services'; and to Mohi Ngaponga, 100 acres 'because the court had said he had a letter claiming them for the rest of the absentees'.

This land was not granted swiftly. In 1880, the West coast Commission into confiscated land wrote: 'The spectacle of these four chiefs trying in vain for 13 years to get the paltry dole of land which was promised in recognition of their loyal services is sad enough; but when it is remembered that one of these chiefs is Te Puni, the earliest and truest friend the English settlers ever had, the story ought to fill us all with shame.'[21]

It is impossible to know whether Hemi would have eventually joined the prophetic community at Parihaka because he died in about 1877, but two of his sons, Mohi and Te Awhi (from his marriage to Pirihira Matangi), took part in the non-violent ploughing and fencing protests and were there when the village was invaded. One of the Parai brothers was reportedly deaf and mute, but the other had been imprisoned in Lyttelton for taking part in the fencing protests. He had been released 'on the promise of not joining further Parihaka operations but had scarcely returned when he again quitted his proper home and went to the place where he was at the time of dispersion'.[22]

I could not find any evidence relating to the whereabouts of Charles Wallace in 1881, but our family is in possession of a photograph of Charles's mother, Arapera Ronguaroa, and in that photograph, Arapera wears a raukura in her hair.

For Parai and his immediate descendants, neither loyalty nor war nor non-violent protest had succeeded in regaining stolen family land. What did work was inter-marriage. Charles Wallace's marriage to a white woman, Margaret O'Toole, earned him respect in the eyes of a government-appointed commission and allowed him, in 1880, to claim the 100 acres that had been promised to his grandfather. The commission wrote that Wallace was 'educated, he speaks English perfectly, lives in a European fashion, has married an English-woman and was capable of using the land for himself and his family'. His uncles, Mohi and Te Awhi, were not considered capable because they were 'whole blood Māori and entirely habituated to Māori life'.[23] Charles was allowed to make his home in the new New Zealand because he 'lived in the European fashion'. His relatives were not nearly as welcome.

Within my family, the Dementia wing of our Māori history has been cracked open and the inhabitants are now free to wander around as they please. The slow-growing dementia about our Māori past (and present) has been halted. The knowledge lost or suppressed as each generation in my branch of the Wallace family became whiter and whiter by following Charles's lead, and marrying people who were not Māori, is being regained. Demented patients forget most of the things they once knew, whereas my family has started to slowly remember or relearn. As these small war stories I have shared demonstrate, we may be in a recovery ward for families leaving the Dementia wing of their own history, but nationally, quite a different process is at work.

Tomb of the unknown warrior

Only a few months after our modest, demented memorial was unveiled, tens of thousands of people attended the internment and unveiling ceremonies for the Tomb of the Unknown Warrior at the National War Memorial in Buckle Street, Wellington. The first memorial to an unknown World War I soldier was erected in England after that war, and Australia's unknown soldier was interred in Canberra in 1993. New Zealand's memorial also contains the remains of an unknown World War I soldier; but its extravagantly bicultural form and title – it contains a warrior, rather than a mere soldier – makes it different from other foreign tombs.

The dead New Zealand man is purposefully without ethnicity. While my family is exploring the deep connections, privileges, responsibilities, silences, losses and gains accorded to us by our indigenous history, the Tomb of the Unknown Warrior seeks to erase or collapse historical difference. It represents an escalation of the process by which non-Māori New Zealanders look to Māori culture for globally recognisable makers of national cultural difference, a process that might be described as a case of kiwi (both the flightless bird that is the national faunal emblem and a colloquial term usually associated with a white male New Zealander) robbing iwi (tribes) for a bright new set of feathers.

The haka performed by the All Blacks is the most obvious example of this. Just as the haka lends both fierceness and mystery to all the rugby players who perform it, the tomb adds a mythic, noble-Māori-warrior strand to the memory of dead Pākehā soldiers, enhancing and enriching the 'hard man' stereotype most often associated with the Pākehā at war, the image of a fighter who is a 'strong and versatile pioneer with gentlemanly morals'.[24] The wisdom or justice of this masculine enhancement can be debated; but what is clearly troubling about the memorial – to me at least – is the way this overtly bicultural tomb ignores New Zealand's wars of foundation, wars in which the supposedly superior fighting skills of the white male were radically undermined both by the superior military strategies and fighting skills of their Māori opponents and by the fierceness of their Māori allies, the 'kupapa' neutral or friendly troops, who were at the forefront of many Crown attacks against Māori.[25] Memories of these complicated foundational wars, including war stories associated with the site on which the tomb has been built, nibble away at this elegant new memorial, diminishing its mana and power.

What are the competing and overlapping desires at work in the Rawinia Buchanan Dementia wing and the Tomb of the

The Parihaka Album

Unknown Warrior? It has been argued that all memory work starts with the 'local' and the 'subjective'.[26] Stories connected with our family memorial – an almost private, local and very discreet site – challenge the stories embodied in a public, national and very prominent monument. Whakapapa recovered from the Dementia wing of my own family's Māori past offer new possibilities for memorialising national foundations in a settler nation such as New Zealand, possibilities that go beyond the 'us' and 'them' framework of tribunal histories.

Writing about the ever-growing cult of Anzac worship in Australia, Marilyn Lake has recently argued that 'national memory has been powerfully influenced by the militarisation of history through the construction of war memorials and the annual commemoration of Anzac and Remembrance days'.[27] In her work on public memory in post-apartheid South Africa, Annie Coombes has observed that monuments and memorials are 'animated and reanimated' by performance.[28] In Australia and New Zealand, the rituals associated with annual Anzac and Armistice Day commemorations enliven war memorials, making them potent sites for public memories of masculine sacrifice, in particular.

The internment and unveiling of the Tomb of the Unknown Warrior are believed to have been the largest commemorative project ever in New Zealand. It is now the site for annual commemorative ceremonies. On one level, the tomb continues New Zealand's long tradition of excessive war memorialisation. Every conflict that New Zealand has ever been involved in, including the nineteenth-century wars of foundation, has been documented in official histories commissioned by the state, paper monuments to the sacrifices of the dead. The memorialisation of foreign wars reached a stupendous apex with the forty-eight official war history volumes and twenty-four booklets produced on World War II.[29] The production of war stories about that war and the ones that have followed continues unabated. In 2001, for example, the then Prime Minister Helen Clark announced a major oral history project to gather the stories of New Zealanders who had been imprisoned by the Japanese in World War II.

More recently, as I have already argued, the work of the Waitangi Tribunal is another form of military history, a memorialisation of the many types of Crown violence against Māori. The tribunal's report on Taranaki tells a story of 'never-ending war' in that province, a war whose climax was the invasion of Parihaka.

As a researcher, I found the massive written archive generated by twelve hearings held over five years to be a painful memorial of the ongoing trauma caused by the wars of colonisation in Taranaki. But the tribunal archives are hidden inside storage boxes, accessed only by a few researchers. Tribunal reports make the news for a day or a week, then they too are relatively hidden from public view. Aside from the initial ceremonies to honour the publication of a tribunal report, and the Crown–iwi rituals that mark the settlement of a claim (should such a settlement be achieved), there are no ongoing, national annual rituals of commemoration to specifically mark New Zealand's wars of foundation. The fragility of national remembrance of foundational wars was demonstrated, perhaps, by the popularity of the conservative National Party's promise in the 2005 election campaign to govern for 'kiwis' rather than 'iwis', by ending all Treaty of Waitangi claims by 2010 and wiping out all 'special treatment' for Māori.[30] However, the National Party lost the 2005 election. It won in 2008 with a campaign that was, ostensibly, much less divisive. Its 'Māori' policy was far less prominent than three years earlier; but its tone was, perhaps, even more assimilationist. The party pledged to 'achieve just and durable settlements of all historic Treaty claims by 2014'. Once claims had been settled, National would begin a 'constitutional process to abolish the Māori seats. National wishes to see all New Zealanders on the same electoral roll'.[31]

The absence of any reference to New Zealand's first wars at the Tomb of the Unknown Warrior, or at the National War Memorial that looms up behind it, suggests that these wars are moving even further from the centre of national collective memory. The wars of foundation are certainly not forgotten, but they remain peripheral, problematic and contested, unable, somehow, to be integrated into popular, bicultural rituals of commemoration.

This ongoing marginality of foundational wars is particularly incongruous since New Zealand is often held up – at least in relation to Australia – as a place that has a superior record in remembering the wars of colonisation and in honouring the sacrifices made by indigenous and non-indigenous dead in the formation of the nation. For instance, Australian historian Ken Inglis has contrasted the absence of memorials to Australia's wars of foundation with the supposed proliferation of such memorials in New Zealand, a nation that was able, at least, 'to legitimate the racial wars by commemoration, and with ever more confidence as memories faded'.[32] Inglis, Henry Reynolds and artist Richard Franklin are among the many who have called for the Australian War Memorial to include some form of commemoration of people killed in wars fought on Australian soil. As many have pointed out, the absence of any acknowledgment of foundational wars in Australia is particularly cruel when the participation of white Australians in the wars against Māori is commemorated there. Inglis contrasts Australia's forgetting with New Zealand's superior remembering. His work suggests that the New Zealand countryside is awash with bicultural monuments to the wars of foundation and that brown and white war dead have equal significance. This has not been my experience, either as a historian or as a citizen.

The first Crown memorial to Māori war dead (rather than Pākehā soldiers killed by Māori or Māori who died fighting for the Crown) was not erected until 2002.[33] This unveiling, in a tiny coastal settlement close to Parihaka, attracted a few dozen spectators – nothing compared with the thousands who attended the preparation and internment ceremonies for the Unknown Warrior.

More than a year and a half of thick bicultural ritual accompanied the creation of the Tomb. For instance, Wellington Te Āti Awa kaumātua (elder), Sam Jackson, blessed the tomb site at the beginning and end of construction in May 2003 and November 2004 respectively. The warrior was accompanied from Longueval, France, to New Zealand by members of the New Zealand Defence

Forces Māori Cultural Group, an escort that was 'in keeping with Māori protocol' that the dead should never be left alone. In France and again in New Zealand, a piper played a special lament for the unknown warrior. The Tudor Consort performed a four-part choral composition at the 11 November internment. The ceremonies indicated a respectful blending of Māori and Pākehā tradition.

The title of the tomb is highly suggestive. While Australia's monument is the Tomb of the Unknown Soldier, New Zealand's commemorates a 'warrior', a word that evokes stereotypes about Māori as warrior resisters in the nineteenth century and warrior gang members in the twentieth.[34]

When I visited the tomb in January 2005, I was moved and repelled in equal measure. As I have reflected on this memorial, it has become clear that my repulsion was caused, at least in part, by the way it gestures towards difference on the surface while deep down – in its very bones – the monument seeks to erase historical specificity, to create, through the bones of one of 30,000 Māori and Pākehā soldiers who died in service in overseas wars, a nation founded on the sacrifices of a generic, non-threatening 'New Zealander'. The tomb contains the remains of one of the 9000 New Zealand soldiers who are buried in unmarked graves or whose remains could never be recovered. The bones, which belong to a man, were 'chosen by the Commission from the First World War Caterpillar Valley Cemetery in the Somme region of France as this was the area where the greatest number of various New Zealand regiments and battalions are known to have fought'.[35] The bones are purposefully bleached of all identifying markers, including race.

The absence of race in the unknown warrior is especially significant. On the War Memorial website, a list of answers is provided to frequently asked questions. One is: 'Why not pick one Māori and one non-Māori to return?' The answer reads:

Because the body is unknown, we will not know who he is except that he is a New Zealander. We will not know his name, rank, regiment, religion or any other detail of his life. The term 'Warrior' incorporates all these unknown details. He could be anyone and so represents everyone.

Being a 'New Zealander', by this definition, seems to involve an erasure of all markers of cultural or ethnic identity.

While the contents of the tomb are supposedly blank, the exterior is a gorgeous patchwork of extremely specific references to place, language, culture and race, references that are drawn almost exclusively from Māori culture. The tomb is embedded in the final flights of marble steps that lead to the National War Memorial carillon and hall of memories, an imposing singing tower that was opened on Anzac Day, 1932. Its design references the Southern Cross; 'the choice and treatment of materials, the use of symbols and language, strongly reflect the unique cultural identity of this land and its people'.[36]

The tomb is made from shiny black granite and its sides are etched with dozens of marks that could be crosses or stars. The internment booklet explains that: 'The Warrior will be guided by the stars of the Southern Cross on his journey back to New Zealand. The distance of the foreign land he leaves behind is represented on the base of the Tomb by a night sky of black granite inlaid with light grey Takaka marble crosses.'

The tomb is covered by a bronze 'mantle' or 'cloak' inlaid with four pounamu (greenstone) crosses. (The crosses were carved by my cousin Mary-Anne's husband, Steve Myhre). The crosses reference the Southern Cross on the national flag; but the use of the word 'cloak' to describe the bronze tomb top recalls tangi (funeral) rituals in which a feather cloak would be laid over the body of a dead person. 'Cloak' also suggests the precious ceremonial garments worn by Māori men and women of high standing. Further, the symbolism of a warrior's body being guided home by a compass of stars links the journey of this anonymous serviceman with the great foundational migrations of Māori from Hawaikinui to New Zealand about 800 years ago, epic journeys made by waka guided only by stars.[37] Chiefly mana, celestial guides, physical strength, tenacity and endurance, as well as ancient funeral rituals, not to mention the coveted title of warrior ... this unknown 'New Zealander' appears to have gained most of his 'unique cultural identity' from Māori history and tradition.

The karanga inscribed around the base of the tomb also gains its potency from the way it brings to mind the wailing karanga sung by kuia to call manuhiri on to a marae, a practice most New Zealanders would either have heard in person or seen on television at official events. I have heard many karanga, and these calls, sung in a single breath, often by a woman who is very elderly, never fail to send shivers through my whole body. The tomb's karanga says:

> *Te mamae nei a te pouri nui*
> *The great pain we feel*
> *Tenei ra e te tau*
> *Is for you who were our future*
> *Aue hoki mai ra ki te kainga tuturu*
> *Come back return home,*
> *E tatari atu nei ki a koutou*
> *We have waited for you*
> *Nga tau roa*
> *Through the long years*
> *I ngaro atu ai te aroha*
> *You were away. Sorrow*
> *E ngau kino nie i ahau aue taukuri e*
> *Aches within me.*

The Māori and English words, so perfectly chosen and composed, evoke the same ache contained in painter Ralph Hotere's Sangro paintings and the poetry of Cilla McQueen that is incorporated into these works. The art of Hotere and McQueen mourned the death of Hotere's brother who was killed on the Western Front in World War I and the pain his people continued to feel at his distant burial place, his far-ness from his place and his people.[38] This pain of distance is felt by all Māori and Pākehā whose loved ones died while serving in overseas wars; but it is especially acute in Māori communities where the two world wars claimed the lives of so many young men who had been ordained as future tribal leaders.[39]

It is appropriate that the distant deaths of so many young Māori and Pākehā people be commemorated through a beautiful and poetic monument such as the new Tomb. It would be an unfeeling visitor, indeed, who could fail to be moved by the sentiments expressed in the tomb's karanga. But my sadness was not so much for what was there as for what was not. There are many other bodies – brown and white – waiting to be called home to the centre of national remembrance, waiting to be tracked and treasured and honoured with a mantle of bronze and greenstone, a skirt of stars.

Naming the unknown warriors

The Tomb of the Unknown Warrior was unveiled in the very year when the linking of my grandmother's name with a Māori land trust development had shifted our family, quite irrevocably, from a state of uneasy kiwi-ness to one much closer to the more difficult but satisfying position of iwi-ness. My doctoral research on Parihaka has contributed, in small part, to this process.

Many of the men who lived at Parihaka had been famous military adversaries of the Crown. But at Parihaka, residents had rejected violence as a way of fighting colonisers. The community's non-violent strategy was partly pragmatic – by the 1870s, Māori were massively outnumbered by Pākehā, so military victory was unlikely; but it was also ideological, growing from a sophisticated pacifist culture developed by Parihaka leaders.

The men and women and children expressed resistance in a firm but gentle manner, through actions that are the opposite of the

Māori warrior mystique embedded in phrases such as 'The Tomb of the Unknown Warrior'. In the twentieth century, there has been a noble tradition of non-warrior behaviour among both Māori and Pākehā. For instance, poet James K. Baxter's father Archibald was a conscientious objector who was tortured for refusing to join up in World War I. *Sedition*, Russell Campbell's film about pacifists during World War II, documents the suffering and beliefs of those men who refused to fight a generation later. In 1977, Ngāti Whātua and their Māori and Pākehā supporters invoked the non-violent legacy of Parihaka during their 507-day-occupation of Bastion Point, Auckland. The tradition has continued. Under the leadership of Helen Clark, New Zealand shifted its military spending from war to peacekeeping operations.

It has occurred to me that New Zealand could express its cultural difference in a radical way now – before a local and global audience – by erecting a bicultural 'Tomb of the Known Non-Warrior' at its national war memorial. My ancestors, Mohi and Awhi Parai, could be named on such a memorial. Like hundreds of others, Mohi and Awhi were arrested for ploughing and fencing land around Parihaka and sent, without trial, to prison-exile in the South Island. Prisoners en route from Taranaki to the South Island were held in Wellington while they waited for their transport ship to arrive. The men were locked up in the barracks built by Governor Hobson in the 1840s on Te Āti Awa land at Pukeahau (which he called Mt Cook).[40]

The barracks, which could house 200 troops, were built to withstand a Māori attack that never came. The barracks were demolished in 1882 and replaced with a prison built by prisoners with bricks made from clay taken from Pukeahau. In 1894, another smaller red-brick barracks was built. This building still stands, an office for a kitchen design firm. Five cells, with grille doors and prison bell, remain intact but disused at the rear.

This building is at the corner of a large pōhutukawa-covered rectangle of land between Tasman and Taranaki Streets. The site, fronted by Buckle Street, is a palimpsest of competing histories and uses. Most of it is occupied by the National War Memorial, an enormous carillon housing fifty-two inscribed bells of varying shape and weight, built atop a 'hall of memories', and by the former National Art Gallery and Museum, which is now leased by Massey University from the Wellington Tenths Trust and used as a design and art school.

The Tomb of the Unknown Warrior is on the steps in front of the carillon. After lying in state at Parliament, the remains of the unknown soldier were put in the tomb in a bicultural ceremony that began with the carillon's largest bell, Peace Rangimārie, being tolled eleven times (to mark the eleventh hour of the eleventh day of November, Armistice Day). Peace Rangimārie is the heaviest of the four new bells cast to mark fifty years since the end of World War II. Indeed, at three metres wide and weighing 12.25 tonnes, it is the heaviest bell to be cast anywhere in the world since 1934. It was hung, in 1995, along with Grace Aroha, Hope Tūmanako and Remembrance Whakamaharatanga. Peace, Hope, Grace and Remembrance toll for all the newly unknown warriors of New Zealand's foreign wars, but for the participants in the wars of colonisation, they remain silent.

There are many other war stories connected with the site on which the unknown warrior is buried. In my family, those stories concern 'warriors' or 'non-warriors' called Awhi and Mohi and their father Hemi. They concern Hemi's daughter Arapera, who married a Pākehā settler, William Ellerslie Wallace. They concern Charles (Tare) and his European wife Margaret. They concern my great-grandmother Hannah and her daughter Rawinia. They concern my dad and me. In 1987, I learnt to do the karanga in a prefab polytech building on Buckle Street, opposite the war memorial. The kaumātua of Kuratini, as the school was known, was Te Huirangi Waikerepuru.

Even so, I can't argue that Hemi and Mohi and Te Awhi and their descendants are totally forgotten at the National War Memorial. Up at the back of the site, far from the magnificent and ostentatious tomb, is a modest memorial erected in 2001 by the Wellington Tenths Trust. The memorial depicts a prisoner standing with his head bowed, wrapped in a blanket. It is made from grey stones and white pebbles. The grey stones, gathered from Taranaki streams, represent each of the prisoners who passed through Wellington in the late nineteenth century on their way to prisons in the South Island. The pebbles refer to the 'lost genealogy' of the men taken who 'died in prisons'.

My family's 'hall of memories' shows that what was lost can be found, what was foreign can become familiar. New Zealand's unknown warriors have names, ranks, regiments, religions and race. They died in the back paddock, not some foreign field. They do not need pipes and stars to guide them home. They are already there, waiting to be released from the Dementia wing of history, the bony archive beneath our feet.

---

[1] Susannah Radstone, 'Working with Memory: An Introduction' in Susannah Radstone, ed., *Memory and Methodology,* Oxford and New York: Berg, 2000, 11.

[2] Kim Scott and Hazel Brown, *Kayang & Me,* Fremantle: Fremantle Arts Centre Press, 2005, 19.

[3] For interesting recent work on hybrid Māori/Pākehā identities, see Melinda Webber, *Walking the Space Between Identity and Māori/Pākehā,* Wellington: NZCER Press, 2008. See also Avril Bell, '"Half-castes" and "White Natives": The politics of Māori-Pākehā hybrid identities' in C. Bell and S. Matthewman, eds, *Cultural Studies in Aotearoa New Zealand,* Australia: Oxford, 2004, 121-138.

[4] The title of a fascinating paper on demography explains this feeling well. See Len Smith, Janet McCalman, Ian Anderson, Sandra Smith, Joanne Evans, Gavan McCarthy and Jane Beer, 'Fractional Identities: The Political Arithmetic of Aboriginal Victorians', *Journal of Interdisciplinary History;* XXXVIII:4 (Spring 2008), 533-551.

[5] J. K. Hunn, *Report on Department of Māori Affairs: With Statistical Supplement,* 24 August 1960, Wellington: Government Printer, 1961, 16.

[6] See *Te Whanganui a Tara Me Ona Takiwa: Report on the Wellington District,* Wellington: Waitangi Tribunal, 2003.

[7] 'Purchase of Port Nicholson from the Maories' in Walter K Bishop, *Guide to Wellington & District,* second edition, 1883, 90.

[8] For a copy of the 'Port Nicholson Deed of Purchase' see Appendix 1, *Te Whanganui a Tara,* Waitangi Tribunal, 495-498.

[9] Angela Ballara, 'Te Whanganui-a-Tara: Phases of Māori Occupation of Wellington Harbour c. 1800-1840', in D Hamer and R Nicholls, eds, *The Making of Wellington*, 1990, 33.

[10] 'Deeds of Release Port Nicholson (Te Aro pa) 6 February 1844', National Archives, Wellington.

[11] Extract from Wellington Minute Book 27/281 and 282, Tuesday 17 January 1933, Wellington. Well. Tenths – Taare Warahi dec'd.

[12] In 1873, the Māori Land Court gave the name Polhill Gully to sections 19 and 21 of Ohiro Block. In 1902, the Māori Land Court decided who the 38 rightful owners of this land were – all people with clear links to Te Aro Pā. It is unclear when part of this land was first used as a tip (Ohiro tip) but this was done without the owners' (our) consent. My father has pointed out that there is a sign near the top of Aro Street that says 'Polhill Gully'. This sign is, perhaps, a remnant of the earlier days when the original area termed Polhill Gully was much more extensive than the 100 acres down near the present tip. It included a swathe of land from Ohiro Bay right through to the area of Kelburn where Victoria University now stands. Wellington residents will note that the first street off to the left from Aro Street is Ohiro Road.

[13] Registrar to Hannah Bramley, 'Re Orimupiko 22, secitons 18 & 19 Block X Opunake S.D' 21 July 1947, MW/12 (d).

[14] K Laurence, registrar to Hannah Bramley, 'Ohiro Block 10 Sections 19 and 20 (Polhill Gully)', 1 July 1963, Māori Land Court, File: 14/1/92.

[15] Scott, *Ask That Mountain*, 85.

[16] See 'Taranaki Whanui ki Te Upoko o Te Ika Deed of Settlement' signed on 19 August 2008, available online at Office of Treaty Settlements, http://www.ots.govt.nz, accessed 8 December 2008.

[17] Stephen Muecke, *Ancient & Modern: Time, Culture and Indigenous Philosophy*, Sydney: UNSW Press, 2004, 65.

[18] Linda Tuhiwai Smith, *Declononizing Methodologies: Research and Indigenous Peoples*, London, New York and Dunedin: Zed Books and University of Otago Press, 1999.

[19] See *Daily Southern Cross,* 24 August 1860.

[20] 'The Government Awards', AJHR, vol II, 1880, G-2, xxxviii.

[21] 'The Government Awards', AJHR, vol II, 1880, G-2, p. xxxviii.

[22] 'Special Grants – West Coast Land District', No 7, (2) Charles Wallace, AJHR, vol II, 1882, G-5, 30.

[23] 'Special Grants – West Coast Land District', No 7, (2) Charles Wallace, AJHR, vol II, 1882, G-5, 30.

[24] Jock Phillips, *A Man's Country? The Image of the Pākehā Male,* Auckland: Penguin, 1987, 151.

[25] Phillips, *Man's Country,* 134–35. See also James Belich, *The New Zealand Wars and the Victorian Interpretation of Racial Conflict,* Auckland: Auckland University Press, 1986, and Belich, *Titokowaru's War,* 1989.

[26] Radstone, 'Working with memory', 12.

[27] Marilyn Lake, *'Introduction', Memory, Monuments and Museums,* Melbourne: Melbourne University Press, 2006, 5.

[28] Annie Coombes, *Visual Culture and Public Memory in a Democratic South Africa,* Durham and London: Duke University Press, 2003, 12.

[29] Roberto Rabel, 'War History as Public History: Past and Future' in Bronwyn Dalley and Jock Phillips, eds, *Going Public: The Changing Face of New Zealand History,* Auckland: Auckland University Press, 2001, 155-173.

[30] The National Party website at that time described New Zealand as a nation drifting to 'racial separatism'. This process would be halted by, among other things, 'returning the seabed and foreshore to clear Crown ownership on behalf of all New Zealanders' and 'abolishing the separate Māori seats in Parliament'.

[31] National Party, 'Māori Affairs, Treaty & Electoral Law policies released', 28 September 2008, see http://national.org.nz/Article.aspx?Articled= 28602, accessed 5 January 2009.

[32] Ken Inglis, *Sacred Places: War Memorials in the Australian Landscape,* Melbourne: Miegunyah Press, 1998, 23.

[33] The first memorial erected by the Crown in honor of Māori who fought against it in the New Zealand wars was unveiled at Oakura, Taranaki, in 2002. The rather ugly concrete slab honored twenty Māori killed at Fort St George in an assault by 873 colonial troops backed up by artillery from HMS *Eclipse.* This slaughter was enacted in revenge for the death of one white soldier who had been ambushed by Māori some days earlier. At the unveiling, one kaumātua (elder), Te Ru Wharehoka, said the fact that it had taken 139 years for the Crown to acknowledge the wrong it had done was a sign that there was no genuine partnership between Crown and Māori. 'Why did it take so long? It's not historical, it's hysterical', Wharehoka was reported as saying. See *Daily News,* 17 June 2002, p. 3. The same day this Taranaki newspaper carried a story (on page 2) and photograph of the blessing of a stone to commemorate the death of Private Richard Absolon, a local man who was killed in 1982 in the Falklands War. The stone would be sent to England where it would be placed in a cairn for all those killed in the war. A memorial to Absolon was built in 1988 in New Plymouth.

[34] Aside from the pre-match haka, the most potent contemporary Māori warrior imagery has been produced by Alan Duff in his novel O*nce Were Warriors,* Tandem Press, Auckland 1990, and in director Lee Tamahori's 1993 film of the same name.

[35] Tomb of the Unknown Warrior, Background Information, National War Memorial URL: http://www.nationalwarmemorial.govt.nz/unknown/index.html accessed 30 September 2005.

[36] 'Tomb design', Tomb of the Unknown Soldier souvenir interment booklet, 14.

[37] For a discussion of how the 'great voyage' myth works in New Zealand, Australia and the United States, see Davison, 'Great Voyage' in *Use and Abuse of Australian History*, 56–79.

[38] Gregory O'Brien, *Out the Black Window: Ralph Hotere and New Zealand Poets*, Wellington: Godwit in association with City Gallery, 1987, 108.

[39] For a Te Ati Āwa example relating to WWII, see Susan Love de Miguel, 'Eruera Te Whiti O Rongomai Love 1905-1942', DNZB, URL: http://www.dnzb.govt.nz/ updated 22 June 2007. Love was the first Māori to command the Māori battalion. He was killed at El Alamein. 'The loss of Eruera was a tremendous blow to his family, and the ramifications were to be felt for generations ...', Miguel writes.

[40] Chris MacLean, *For Whom the Bells Toll: A History of the National War Memorial*, Wellington: Heritage Group, Department of Internal Affairs, 1999.

CHAPTER 10

Pioneers

The rain pelted down in thick icy drops. By the time we had rushed from the railway station to the little chapel on Bolton Street, we were soaked. My dad and I were going to meet Nick Perrin, a member of the Friends of Bolton Street Cemetery. Perrin had offered to give us a tour of the old graveyard. We were both hoping that Perrin might be able to give us some clues that would help us find the burial place of our tupuna, Te Aro Pā rangatira Hemi Parai, a man who died in 1877 and was buried, according to later newspaper reports, at 'Waipiro'.

Waipiro is the name of a stream that used to run from the Dell in the Botanic Gardens, through the Lady Norwood Rose Garden, down between Sydney and Bowen Streets, on through the middle of the land now occupied by the national parliament and then out to sea. Waipiro was also the name of an urupā (graveyard) that included the land on which parliament House is now built. Only the headwaters of the stream remain, a little bubbling bog south of the Dell, just below the Meteorological Office. Of the other Waipiro, there is nothing to be seen.

The city dripped. The rain was so heavy that my coat was useless against the onslaught. Water trickled down my back. I wrapped my notebook in a plastic bag and put it in my backpack. Nick Perrin arrived, and we slipped around the corner to the oldest remaining part of the remembered cemetery.

Headstones listed between ancient pōhutukawa roots. Broken chains sagged onto the grass. A sad angel bowed her head towards a streaky tomb. A massive oak, sprouting tender new growth, spread its branches over the ruins. Across the road, less than fifty metres away, is the wooden house where the Prime Minister lives; a little further down the hill is the bustle of The Terrace, one of Wellington's busiest streets. The cemetery, though, was quiet. Maybe the rain dulled the city noise.

Dead babies have nourished the soil here. Perrin estimates that about half of all the 8500 recorded burials at Bolton Street between 1840 and 1900 were children under the age of ten. Their deaths are 'not of much interest to genealogists'. They represent a lopped limb in a family tree, a terminal identity. Most of their graves were unmarked. The birth and death of stillborn babies was often not recorded at all. Their short lives remained a secret grief. A mother's body was their headstone.

Perrin was careful where he stepped. 'There's a grave there,' he said of a muddy rise. Time and weather have destroyed many of the headstones; of the ones that remain, many have long since been washed clear of names, dates and inscriptions, leaving nothing but moss and mould. On others, though, the writing is still clear:

> *Died of wounds murderously inflicted by rebel Natives early in the Evening of April 2nd on the banks of the Hutt River.*
>
> *Sacred to the memory of ...*
>
> *In loving memory of ...*
>
> *There is a reaper whose name is death/And with his sickle keen,/ He reaps the bearded grain at a breath/and the flowers that grow between ...*

This last, from a poem by Longfellow, is the inscription on a restored marble headstone: 'Sacred to the memory of the beloved children of John Howard Wallace and Sarah Ann Wallace carried off by scarlet fever in 1865.' Five of their children – William, Marian, John, George, Alice – died of the throat infection in May. Another child, a son, died three months later.

The rain muffled the traffic on the nearby motorway too. The motorway, opened in 1978, cut the cemetery in two. Thousands of bodies were disinterred, and many of the old headstones you can see today were relocated from their original spots, separated from the human remains they commemorate.

The curved, concrete Denis McGrath footbridge, streaked with water, circles the edge of the oldest part of the remembered cemetery. Many graves butt against it. The Wallace graves, the resting place of the children and those of their parents, form a border between the tiny, undisturbed remnant of the old cemetery and the rest of Bolton Street.

When officials looked at the cemetery almost fifty years ago, they saw an area that was rundown and weed-infested. They saw a site of decay, a waste of valuable inner-city space. Photographs taken in the late 1960s by the sexton, P. J. (Ted) Shotter, support this assessment.[1] Although the viewer can glimpse some of the splendid trees, especially very old cabbage trees, that grew there, the four albums are, overwhelmingly, a record of neglect. They contain page after page of black and white images of graves thatched with supplejack and broken railings. One grave has on old mattress on top of it. The images are contained in red folders at the Alexander Turnbull Library. The folders are marked with a message for researchers: 'This is part of our national heritage. Please handle it with care …' White gloves are required to examine the photos. The image of the object is handled far more lovingly than the object itself was.

The Parihaka Album

Figure 24. Resting place. The Wallace family grave, plot 2209, Bolton Street Cemetery, between 1965 and 1969, black and white original negative, individual frame on 35 mm strip, cellulose triacetate negative. The Alexander Turnbull Library says it was 'taken in the late 1960s by City Sexton, P J E Shotter prior to its being dismantled to make way for the Wellington motorway'. The graves belonged to Robert Douglas Wallace, H R Wallace, Walter James R Wallace and Marion Wallace, Shotter Collection, Alexander Turnbull Library, reference number 25510-21A-F.

In the mid 1960s, the National Roads Board and the Wellington City Council agreed that 3.7 acres of the remaining 8.2 acres of cemetery could be taken for the motorway, but the government acquired more land than it really needed. Perrin was still angry at the waste. He pointed out a tarsealed footpath bordered by two strips of green – The Chapel Walk – at the foot of the road. Graves were dug up there, but the planned off-ramp was never built. Now the area 'incorporates memorial tree plantings for eminent environmentalists'.

The authorities had expected to unearth about 2000 bodies. Council contractors started the distinernments in November 1968; but only ten months later, according to a notebook kept by the Wellington City Council's engineer's department, 3528 bodies had been unearthed. Of these, 1005 were categorised as 'unknown burials'. At the request of relatives, a few of these bodies were cremated or reburied at Karori Cemetery, but most went into a mass grave on the city-side of the motorway.[2]

The vault is beneath a surprisingly small patch of soft green grass. It is smaller than half a tennis court, a tiny space, it seems, for so many bodies. Cabbage trees stand to the left, and large stone steps, a small ampitheatre above a bone yard, to the right. A wall built from different-shaped round stones is in the background. A narrow, grass-less border surrounds the place where the bodies are buried.

The cemetery section of the motorway opened in 1978. As so often happens, the site became historic only after it had been destroyed. The new Te Aro 'historic precinct' around upper Cuba Street, which consists of renovated, repainted, relocated and now empty Victorian houses displaced by the new bypass, is another example of this trend. After the motorway opened, the remaining part of the Bolton Street Cemetery was declared a historic reserve, a place to be cared for and maintained as an addition to the nearby Botanic Gardens.[3] The cemetery would become a park, dedicated to the memory of the pioneer dead of the city and the nation.

On the steps above the Memorial Lawn in the Bolton Street Memorial Park, a modest memorial has been erected. A bronze book is mounted on a black and grey marble plinth. It is open at a page that says: 'To the memory of the Early Settlers whose remains are reinterred in the mass grave below.'

Like 'heritage', the words 'settlers' and 'pioneers' are linked with European people and their history in New Zealand. Māori were not early settlers. Māori were not pioneers. Māori places and things are not normally considered to be part of the national heritage in the same self-evident and uncomplicated way that this cemetery is. Heritage itself is a word defined as 'the culture, traditions and national assets preserved from one generation to the next' or 'that which comes to one by reason of birth, an inherited lot or portion'. These lots are not distributed evenly.

In *Wellington: Biography of a City*, Redmer Yska explains that the Wellington City Council first considered putting a motorway through the cemetery in 1959. In 1960, it paid American consultants De Leuw Cuther and Co the huge sum of $220,000 to do a feasibility study. Wellington people learnt of the plan only in 1964, when mayor Frank Kitts revealed that 'settler graves and monuments' would be affected by a motorway. 'The way I look at it,' Kitts told a crowd at a memorial service by Wakefield family graves, 'it seems that these men of great stature would not want to stand in the way of progress'.[4]

Immediately, the Bolton Street Preservation Society was set up to preserve the cemetery as open space and 'as a memorial to the early settlers of Wellington'. It was headed by historian John Salmon and enjoyed the support of a diverse range of groups, including the National Council of Women, the New Zealand Founders Society, the Registered Nurses Association, the Wellington Women's Christian Temperance Union, the Women's Division of Federated Farmers, the Greater Wellington and Hutt Valley Retailers Association and even the New Zealand Ice Cream Manufacturers Association.[5]

At its first meeting in November 1964, the society decided that its opposition to the motorway was twofold: it would destroy one of the few open spaces in the central city, and it would damage a site associated with the settlement of New Zealand and, in particular, Wellington. The society's first letter was especially concerned to protect the cemetery's magnificent trees. 'Some of these trees reputedly were planted by Bishop Selwyn and any of them if destroyed will take another hundred years to replace,' Salmon wrote.[6]

In public and in private, protestors were distressed at the destruction of the city's and the nation's heritage. In arguments that would be echoed in the other anti-motorway protests of the 1990s and early 2000s, they questioned the need for such a 'grandiose motorway', a road that would displace thousands of people from their Thorndon homes. Hundreds signed a petition opposing the plan. They said the road would not solve the city's traffic problems, and it would 'pour thousands of cars and vehicles into the City each day where they will have nowhere to park'. Further, 'the Motorway is going directly through the Bolton Street Cemetery in an open cut. This offends many people's feelings and is unnecessary.'[7]

The destruction of the cemetery stirred strong feelings. *The Dominion* said the cemetery was 'our Westminster Abbey', and councillor Olive Smuts-Kennedy railed against the 'sacrilege' of putting a motorway through it: 'We have no ancient buildings and few early relics of a lasting character – the more reason to preserve what we have,' she said.

Descendants petitioned Kitts, imploring him to respect the resting place of 'our pioneer forebears'. Arthur Seed's father, William, arrived on 8 July 1840 on the *Martha Ridgway*. William was fourteen, and he had come from Liverpool with his parents. 'I claim to be still a first generation Wellingtonian and perhaps one of the very few surviving individuals whose actual pioneer parents (and kin) are buried in the Bolton Street Cemetery in the vicinity of the venerated "Wakefield" plot,' Seed wrote. He was horrified by the planned desecration 'in that hallowed spot and remnant of open space within the city bounds and imagined "last resting place" of our pioneer forebears'.[8]

Elizabeth Orr, president of the Wellington branch of the New Zealand Federation of University Women, said she deplored the plan. 'Members pointed out that the Cemetery is a unique memorial of the first years of our city's life, besides being one of the few well-treed green spaces in the inner city area.'[9] Irma O'Connor, a great-granddaughter of New Zealand Company director Edward Gibbon Wakefield, wrote from her home in Kohimarama, Auckland, a city where residents 'are supposed to have less sense of history than Wellington or the South Island; but even Auckland bestirred itself when Captain Hobson's grave was threatened by a new motorway'.

The Parihaka Album

Figure 25. Aerial view of Wellington motorway under construction, ca 26 August 1969, by an unidentified Evening Post *staff photographer, black and white original negative, individual image on a 35 mm strip, Alexander Turnbull Library, reference number EP/1969/3580/33-F.*

O'Connor's letter said the cemetery was so much more than a 'lovely oasis', a 'green sanctuary beloved by many … for the beauty of its old trees and its atmosphere of peace and quietness'. It was also 'a spot hallowed for all time by reason of its wealth of historical associations – a sort of national shrine, a guardian of the very roots of systematic colonisation in New Zealand and the bones of the pioneers who shared in the great adventure so many years ago'.[10] A short but eloquent letter from P.J. Leahy declared: 'On behalf of those early pioneers of this city who can no longer speak for themselves I ask that you give consideration to doing all in your power to prevent the desecration of their last resting place.'[11]

Dad's grandmother, Hannah Bramley (nee Wallace), known to us as Gar, helped raise him. When I started talking about the first Wellington motorway, my dad said, 'Gar was one of those protestors. That was the only time I remember her protesting.' As a kid, Dad liked to muck around at the fishpond in parliament grounds. He remembers Gar telling him: 'Our people had their gardens here. They grew vegetables here.' I did not find any protest letters from her in the Wellington City Archives, but it seems likely that Gar, like all the others, wanted to protect the sanctity of her people's final resting place.

Unlike the other protestors, however, Gar was thinking about two kinds of Wellington pioneers: the Māori and the Pākehā. As Stephen (Tipene) O'Regan wrote in 1990 in a collection on *The Politics of the Past*: 'Burials tend to be Māoris' principal concern. A deep reverence for the remains of tribal ancestors marks Māori thinking.'[12] Gar wanted to protect two different places on the same site: Bolton Street and Waipiro, the remembered cemetery and the forgotten one. Through her grandfather William Ellerslie Wallace, brother of John Howard Wallace and uncle to the six little children who died from scarlet fever, she was connected with both.

John Howard Wallace arrived in Port Nicholson in January 1840 on the *Aurora*, the first New Zealand Company settler ship to come to New Zealand. Howard's older brother, William Ellerslie Wallace, came a few months later on the *Glenbervie*. William had originally been booked to sail with John. But in his narrative of 'The voyage out on the *Aurora*', John writes that on 18 September 'My brother William Ellerslie left the vessel in disgust, did not at the last minute like the appearance of things and returned to Birmingham.'[13] The *Aurora*, the *Oriental*, the *Adelaide* and the *Duke of Roxburgh* were all docked at Gravesend, and on 15 September 1839, the brothers took part in a 'public demonstration' to bid 'adieu to friends' before leaving 'to found an Empire in the Southern Ocean'. One other ship left from Glasgow. Altogether, 1500 pioneers departed.

Their father, John Wallace, a watercolourist and art critic for Birmingham newspapers, was on the *Ameila Thompson*, the first New Zealand Company Ship to sail into New Plymouth. He arrived in September 1841, moved to Nelson, then landed in Wellington in 1843. Wallace senior died in 1880, and his grave was one of those dug up for the motorway. The inscription on his headstone was: 'In the midst of life we are in death.'

One of John Wallace senior's beautifully delicate watercolours is in the Turnbull collection. *View of Wellington Harbour from Thorndon Beach 12 July 1845* is a panorama of a busy world dominated by the beach, the crowded sea and an unusually big, pale blue sky softened by great skuds of white cloud. There are 'regular rib-shaped hills', but the perspective of the picture flattens them to almost nothing, small grey bolsters around an endless horizon. Wallace has sketched five whaling boats, including the *Falco*, an American brig, the cutter *Catherine Johnston* and the brig *Bree*.

There are also five waka, filled with a dozen men each. 'Canoes leave Te Aro pah', reads part of the caption. On the far right, there is a male observer, a European in a white suit and a cap, a figure Wallace describes as Robinson. To his left is a group of 'Māori girls', and further left again is a whaling boat raft, a jetty and stacks of wood. The picture seems to say: see, there is plenty here for everyone, Māori and Pākehā. Just help yourself!

Pioneers

Figure 26. A second ancestral view. John Wallace, 1788–1880. View of Wellington Harbour from Thorndon Beach, 12 July 1845, *watercolour and pencil, 253 x 422 mm, drawings and prints collection, Alexander Turnbull Library, reference number B-079-007.*

At the time Wallace created his picture, Te Aro Pā covered about five acres of waterfront, stretching from what is now Cambridge Terrace through Taranaki Street, right down to the southern end of what is now Frank Kitts Park. Te Aro itself was a fertile swamp bisected by the Waitangi stream, a rich source of seafood and eels, and a good place to grow flax to trade with Pākehā settlers. Te Aro people grew potatoes, corn, flax and other crops over another eighty acres, including cultivations that bordered the land Victoria University is built on. As Wallace's drawing demonstrates, the pā was in the thick of things, an ideal place for Māori to participate in the trade flowing into the fast-growing settlement. The pā was divided in two: about thirty-five Ngāti Ruanui lived at the eastern end, and about ninety-three Taranaki people (from the Ngāti Haumia and Ngāti Te Whiti hapū) lived in the west. Our whānau lived in the west.

Like the Taranaki people who already lived there, Wallace's sons were certainly busy on these shores and in these seas. 'Howard &

Ellerslie are now in a very extensive way as merchants and have made considerable shipments to various parts of the islands, have shipped about seven hundred pounds worth of whalebone home, and have now engaged to supply one of the whale fisheries in cloudy bay for the coming season, binding the parties down to ship the whole of the oil and bone caught for them', Wallace wrote to William Lort in 1842, after he had visited Wellington Port Nicholson on business.[14]

The family was entrepreneurial, and in his letter home, Wallace senior was careful to emphasise that the islands of New Zealand were 'worth cherishing' because of the business opportunities they offered 'commercial men'. Howard and Ellerslie had sent Lort specimens of native plants, especially the trees. Their father described them as the 'finest imaginable timber'. At present, this timber could be cut down only 'for the colony', but Howard predicted it would soon be available for export and 'will rival all other timbers in the world for texture grain and beauty'. Ellerslie shipped his whalebone to England on the *Bully*. Howard also reported that Ellerslie returned 'yesterday in "The Jem" from the Chathams of which he brings us very favourable reports. The Jem brought a full cargo from there of pigs and potatoes'. Wallace was about to return to Taranaki, on the Sydney brig *Vanguard*, with supplies of 'flour tea sugar etc' for the colony of New Plymouth.

There were so many things to acquire. William Ellerslie became a shopkeeper on Te Aro beach, in the area where Manners Mall is now. One of his surviving shopping lists shows the diversity of his stock: spikes, giblets, 1 saw file, 1 pair hooks and hinges, 1 Banbury lock, 1 door bolt, 27 dozen screws, 23 lots spikes and nails, 3 tinder boxes, 3 dozen pipes, 2 oz negro-head tobacco, half a dozen bottles of ink, 1 pair of pincers, 1 small hand saw, 3 tomahawks, half a dozen boxes of Epsom salts, 1 box Seidlitz powders, 3 dozen pipes, 2 hats, 1 pair shoes.[15]

He also took a wife, Te Aro Pā resident Arapera Rongouaroa, but this fact is not mentioned in any of his brother's eight manuscript books, books that include everything from news cuttings to a recipe for orange marmalade and notes for Wallace's planned *Early History of New Zealand*, a monumental work that was eventually incorporated into Brett's 1889 *Historical Series Early History of New Zealand*.[16] William Ellerslie does not mention his marriage or his Māori father-in-law in any of his surviving letters either. Nor does Wallace senior.

The only evidence I could find of William's different sympathies is a fragment in a letter he wrote to John in November 1844. He begins by telling his brother about the goods he has aquired ('the three pots and three frying pans as you directed also gillies, yokes and bows and some yokes and bows for Bidwell'). Then he moves on:

> *There is a report now that the Governor has settled the question about the Heretaunga in fact that he has purchased all the land from here to Otaki many of the news vendors are full of it I think very little of it myself even if it were true but to suppose that the Aborigines would agree to give up all claim to the land from here to Otaki from the Governor talking to them for one or two days and giving the two head men three Hundred Pounds is quite absurd – do not forget to send the clothes I mentioned …*[17]

In these few lines, it is possible to see at least some insight into a Māori way of thinking. William's wife, Arapera, the daughter of Hemi Parai and Tawhirikura Karopihia, would have understood well the complexities of Māori connections with land up and down the west coast.[18] She was Taranaki (Ngāti Haumia) on her father's side and Te Āti Awa through her mother. Her whānau had not long been in Te Whanganui-a-Tara when New Zealand Company settlers started to arrive. The harbour was occupied by waves of different iwi – including Ngāti Toa from Kawhia, Ngāti Rangatahi from around Taumarunui and Taranaki iwi – in the decades that preceded white settlement. Historian Angela Ballara writes that between 1819 and 1836, the harbour 'was invaded by potentially hostile forces at least six times. It changed hands twice in that time, the last occasion occurring in the month of November 1835'.[19]

The story of how Taranaki iwi came to hold customary rights around the harbour is complex. It happened bit by bit, as more and more people fled south from Taranaki, gradually displacing the Māori who lived there, mainly Ngāti Ira and their kin. Following the lead of Mohi Ngaponga, in 1834 Arapera's father led a group of Taranaki people south from Waikanae to live first at Ngauranga and then Te Aro.[20] This was the last of many Taranaki iwi migrations south. The first heke was in about 1824, journeys made to escape Waikato retaliation during the musket wars. This migration was known as the Nihoputa. A further migration south, of more than 2000 people, happened in late 1832. In revenge for losses in a battle at Motonui, Taranaki, in 1822, Waikato people invaded Taranaki again. After a long siege, they took Pukerangiora, the pā above the Waitara River. Te Āti Awa refugees fled to Ngamotu (site of modern-day New Plymouth) and helped Te Wharepouri defend another pā, Otaka, against Waikato invaders. With the help of whalers and traders, such as John Love and Dicky Barrett, Taranaki beat Waikato, but so many people were killed that they knew revenge would follow. Ballara writes that Te Wharepouri, Te Puni and Wi Tako Ngatata and Raua-ki-tua then led the Tama-te-uaua migration south.[21]

Taranaki people fled their homes almost a decade before systematic, large-scale white settlement had begun; but when they were able to return north, they found that much of their land had been occupied by white settlers. Te Whangaui-a-Tara and Taranaki, therefore, had many Māori settlers and unsettlers before the Wallaces started to arrive on their first ships, ensuring that both Wellington and New Plymouth have streets named after them.

John Howard Wallace wrote two histories, and in both he doggedly positioned 22 January 1840, the day the *Aurora* sailed into Port Nicholson, as the 'birthday of the colony'. His first book, *The Manual of New Zealand History*, was published in 1886. The 70-page book was intended for school students. It was dot-point, anti-narrative history, a series of news bites, '480 short sections or paragraphs, all numbered and carefully indexed'. Reading it is like looking at a series of PowerPoint slides.

A contemporary *Sydney Morning Herald* review of the book noted that would-be historians of 'young countries' such as New Zealand had a difficult task for two reasons. First, the youth of these nations meant there was 'scant material' for historians to work with. Second, 'pioneer colonists took it as their work rather to make a history for these new lands than to record it'.[22]

Wallace was a self-promoter. He served as long-time secretary of the Early Colonists Association, and he remembered his status as a first-ship settler in numerous letters to editors, in his diaries, in newspaper reports written by 'an early settler' and in the jubilee celebrations he was so deeply involved with. In 1889, he led the settler parade through Wellington to commemorate 'the foundation of the colony', a parade in which Māori took a 'deep interest'.[23]

But Wallace's commemorative activity was about more than cementing his own place as old-colonist, early-settler New Zealander. While Wallace's histories ignore or repress Māori and their stories, the feverish nature of his work suggests that he was also frightened of how tenacious and powerful Māori claims on this place might be and how feeble settler claims were in comparison.

The first Māori to visit Whanganui-a-Tara was the explorer Kupe, in about AD 950, and he named many of the landmarks, including the islands Matiu and Makaro (later called Somes and Ward islands) and Te Tangihanga-a-Kupe (later known as Barrett's Reef).[24] The Wallace manuscripts express a kind of terror of forgetting, an anxiety that settlers' names-dates-events-lives-origins would not stick in this new place, that they could be washed away as easily as a child's drawing on a beach.

The Wallace papers contain dozens of near identical letters written to other settlers, including Edward Wakefield himself, asking them for information, especially for lists of names. Every foundational member of this new nation would be recorded, and Wallace would be the man to do it. One example gives a flavour of the requests. In March 1884, Wallace wrote to Samuel Revans in Greytown. Revans arrived in Port Nicholson in 1840 on the *Adelaide*; he was New Zealand's first newspaper owner and commercial printer. According to the *Dictionary of New Zealand Biography*, Revans published the *New Zealand Gazette* in April 1840, a month after he arrived at Petone. Wallace wrote:

> *I am preparing for the press an Early History of New Zealand – a narrative of events up to 1850 arranged in chronological order: not in chapters: events only, not opinions, neither political nor religious … I have kept a record of events since I arrived here … and with reference to what has already been published and what I have on hand, I shall be able to compile a very useful, and I believe, valuable book … of the work done by the early Pioneer settlers, all of whom, however humble they may have been, took a part in what is termed the 'historic work of colonization'. No book I am aware of contains a list of the Pioneers and I want to have their names down for <u>future generations</u>. I am endeavouring to get as complete a list as possible.*[25]

As cultural theorist Stephen Turner has noted: 'For the settler the Western notion of history is perhaps the deepest form of forgetting, a self-constructing form of repression.'[26] Wallace spent decades trying to create a settler whakapapa, a foundational moment for 'future generations' of white New Zealanders, a history that denied what Turner calls 'the experience of contact'. But contact, of course, gives birth to new lineages and new relationships. One such relationship would be that of John Howard to his Māori-Pākehā nephew, known as Taare Warahi, Taare Rongouaroa and Charles Wallace, and his niece, Turia Warahi, the son and daughter of William and Arapera.

Why was Wallace so determined to remember one group of people, the pioneer settlers, but to forget another, Māori? Why was he so fixated on starting points and beginnings? Perhaps Wallace suspected that other families shared a legacy as uncertain as his own. Maybe recording foundational moments – names of people and ships and dates of arrival – was safer than writing about what happened next. Failure does not fit a progressive historical narrative, where the present is supposed to be better than the past and the future is supposed to be brighter still. In his study of the Victorian country town of Beechworth, Tom Griffiths has argued that histories of Australian towns tend to focus on the early years of settlement – often involving the excitement of a gold rush – and ignore the retreat of money and people that followed. 'The processes of growth and progress have been frequently studied, but the experience of decline has been largely ignored. History, like memory, often erases the painful and negative things,' he writes.[27]

The problem was that the Wallaces had been prominent enough in their new country, but they had not really prospered. There is a sense, in John Howard Wallace's papers, of a promise not fulfilled, a feeling of deprivation, disappointment and loss. Wallace was a general merchant on Lambton Quay. In partnership with James Smith, who had married his sister, he also had a shop in Nelson. Later on, Wallace also became an auctioneer and a commissioning agent, businesses he ran from Hunter Street.[28]

From the mid-1870s, he lobbied the government to introduce a scheme so that all 'pioneer settlers and their families, now in the Colony, and who arrived prior to 1st January 1848, be entitled to free grants of land'.[29] A petition on this theme was presented to parliament on 30 July 1875. Despite being mocked in some newspaper reports, Wallace continued this battle until at least 1880, arguing that early settlers had done the 'heroic work' of colonisation – work that would, in Bishop Selwyn's words, make New Zealand 'the brightest gem in Britain's crown' – and should be compensated for their efforts.³⁰ His campaign was urgent. He retired in 1885 and by 1886 he was bankrupt, a bankruptcy caused, according to Wallace, by his son John 'who had charge of the business'.³¹ By 1888, he was living with his wife and his sister Helen in 'a cottage on Wellington Terrace a few doors south of the Synagogue'. His two surviving sons, John and Robert, lived in England and Sydney, and the one surviving daughter, Harriet, lived in Tinakori Road.

John Howard Wallace appears to have had no contact with his brother William. Despite the busy trading of the 1840s, newspaper reports suggest that by 1853, William was bankrupt. His business failed and so did his marriage to Arapera. He left her for another Māori woman – Kura, one of Te Rauparaha's wives no less. Apparently he had other affairs too. William's philandering offended everyone, both Māori and Pākehā. It is believed that William is buried in an unmarked grave at Otaki. Nevertheless, his marriages resulted in the two Māori Wallace lines: Taranaki iwi and Ngāti Toa.

One of the chapters Howard Wallace contributed to the Brett's history was called 'Māori Affairs'; it gives no indication that 'Māori Affairs' might also be 'family affairs' for many white settlers. Instead, Wallace wants to make Māori as separate from settlers as possible. He quotes, at length, a report written by a Mr Halswell, the New Zealand Company appointed Protector of Aborigines and Commissioner for the Management of Native Reserves in Wellington. Halswell's 1848 report said that for Māori in Wellington, the 'principal want is medical care. The native pahs – the crying evil – being a mass of filth and vermin, disease in various shapes always prevails.'³²

In those early days of Wellington, both Māori and Pākehā feared for their health. In 1854, both communities joined together at the Wellington Athenaeum to farewell surgeon J. P. Fitzgerald, who was returning to England. Ngāti Toa and Te Āti Awa leaders (including Mohi Ngaponga and Parai) gave speeches thanking Fitzgerald, 'our great physician', 'our makao taniwha' (shark's tooth). Hemi Parai's speech concluded with a passage translated as:

> *Go! O Guardian (or Father) our precious stone our good treasure, Go, who knows whether you will ever return to us: nevertheless, it is with the Council of our Queen to say the word to you, because you have been a kind guardian to us. The Queen is the nursing mother, and the Governor makes known her laws: the Missionaries are the heralds to proclaim the laws of Heaven, thus has this island of New Zealand been crowned with peace.*[33]

Wallace was, understandably, obsessed with dirt and disease. Nine years after the departure of Fitzgerald, he lost six children (and the future generations they represented) to scarlet fever, a disease associated, in part, with crowded houses and the dirt and poor hygiene that was common in nineteenth-century cities. Reporting on the epidemics of diptheria and scarlet fever in Melbourne in 1861, one doctor noted that 'unwholesome dwellings, imperfect drainage, marsh and other miasmas' contributed to the disease's spread.[34]

The death of his children meant that Wallace devoted considerable time to campaigning for a cleaner city. In 1873, he researched and wrote a drainage report for the Wellington City Council. This award-winning plan condemned Wellington's cesspools. According to one newspaper report, it proposed that all the existing main drains be flushed out 'on Te Aro. The flushing of these drains in wet weather from the surrounding high lands would not be a matter of any difficulty. The Lambton Ward and Thorndon Ward drains are then fully described – all with outlets to the harbour.'[35]

It is interesting that Wallace nominated Te Aro as a site for dumping the city's waste. By the 1870s, when Wallace wrote his report, Te Aro Pā was in decline. To some settlers, it was already a waste of space, and therefore a good space for waste. The pā was on a Te Aro flat crowded with poor settlers of many cultural backgrounds, including Chinese market gardeners. It was considered 'a slum within a slum', and Native Reserves Act commissioner Charles Heaphy wanted to see it and Pipitea Pā removed from the city.

In its 2003 report, the Waitangi Tribunal found that Heaphy supported the alienation of Māori reserve land and described Te Aro as 'a nest of immorality'. The tribunal noted that Heaphy argued 'that "for moral and sanitary reasons" it was desirable for the sake of Māori and Pākehā alike that Māori should leave the town and the pā should pass into Pākehā hands'.[36]

The population of Te Aro fluctuated depending on what was happening in Taranaki. In 1861, for example, there were only nine people living there – most of the other residents had gone to Taranaki 'to assist in the war efforts of that region'. By 1874, there were fifty-nine residents, including Hemi Parai. The word 'parai' means to repel or push away, and Hemi's actions involved a subtle push and pull, a mixture of friendship, cooperation, protest and resistance that bewilders me.

In 1866, the government promised to give him back some confiscated land in reward for his 'loyalty', but that never happened. Sometimes, it appears, he got fed up. In 1871, for instance, Parai wrote to McLean explaining his intention to travel 'to Taranaki, to Te Whiti' with 'Parete', who is likely to have been former whaler and publican Dicky Barrett.[37] In 1872, Hemi was in Taranaki again, this time with Wi Parata, the member for Western Māori, and Wi Tako. The men held a large public meeting in Opunake 'with the object of inducing the government to give back the township there of 1400 acres as well as the rest of the confiscated territory'.[38] Hemi also worked to keep Te Āti Awa land in what is now central Wellington. In 1874, for instance, government reports record that two petitions were received from Hemi: one was described as 'relating to Te Aro lands' the other as 'against the sale of barracks at Te Aro'.[39]

That same year, he was back in Taranaki again, this time to attend what the *Taranaki Herald* called the 'half-yearly' session of the 'Parihaka Native Parliament' on 17 March. The newspaper reported that about 400 'natives' attended. Te Whiti spoke, giving a 'most sensible address, which was devoid of that usual prophetic lore so customary in his speeches. Everything appeared to be going satisfactorily until Hemi Parai introduced the question of the extension of the telegraph wire across the Parihaka district. This was violently opposed by Ngatirakaunui [sic], who denounced it in strong language.'[40]

At Parihaka, Parai was certainly pushing a line favoured by the government. He was considered a 'friendly', but it was a lopsided friendship. His 'loyalty' was not repaid. The government did not return confiscated territory in Taranaki, even though Parai had never fought against the Crown, and it continued to take Māori reserve land in Wellington.

Te Aro land was communally owned, but between 1866 and 1868, under the provisions of the Native Land Act 1865, it was surveyed into twenty-eight allotments, which the Crown granted to individuals or small groups. An 1871 map lists Parai as sole or joint owner of seven of these lots, including three right on the foreshore. Once the pā had been divided up like this, the government encouraged Māori to sell. From then on, many lots were sold.

This carve-up further sped a decline that began with two earthquakes. In 1848, the city quivered for three days. The water rose 'suddenly, several feet, and then fell as quickly'. Houses shook. Chimneys collapsed and 'many parts of the flat rose a few inches'. Witnesses saw cracks in the flat, between high and low water mark, that were 'five or six feet wide and 100 yards long'.[41] The 1855 quake was less severe, but still 'there was a tidal wave at 9 o'clock and where the Star Hotel stands, water came up to a man's knees'.[42] New beaches and rock platforms were created along the coast, but the upheaval destroyed Waitangi Stream and drained Te Aro swamp, thus depriving Te Aro Māori of much of their livelihood.

Both the tribunal and the Tenths Trust say the loss of the stream 'was a key contributor to the decline in the Pa'.[43] With no source of food on their doorstep, and with settlers taking land all around them and the land reserved for them being brutally whittled away, Māori had to travel long distances – up to fifteen miles in one account – to get to their cultivations. Tenths Trust land was taken for schools, churches, hospitals, pubs, the Governor's stables and part of the Te Aro barracks up at Mt Cook, acquisitions that Māori, including Parai, vigorously opposed.[44]

Te Aro Pā homes were destroyed in the 'Opera House fire' of 1879, a blaze that burnt out three blocks of inner city Wellington. The 1881 census showed only twenty-eight people still living at the pā. The remaining homes were destroyed when Taranaki Street was extended down to the water. The new road bisected the degraded and besieged pā, separating the whare where Parai and his whānau had lived from the homes of his neighbours, including Mohi Ngaponga, Ahipane Marangi, Raniera Erihana, his son Tame Rangiwahia Erihana (Tom Ellison), solicitor and captain of the first official New Zealand Rugby Team and well-known statesman and politician Wi Tako Ngatata.

The new road quite literally buried the last physical traces of Māori occupation of inner-city Wellington – the pā at Pipitea, Kumutoto and Te Aro, as well as other settlements at Pakuao, Tiakiwai and Kaiwharawhara. Until very recently, there was nothing to show the existence of these communities, although remnants of earlier settler beliefs about Te Aro Pā and its residents and of Wallace's drainage plan itself were echoed in contemporary uses of Te Aro land.

The one strip of pā land that remained undeveloped, a handkerchief of green between Dixon Street and Manners Street, became Pigeon Park, a place for pests and a nice big toilet block. In 1992, in a belated, much-maligned and expensive ($825,759) commemorative gesture, the place was renamed Te Aro Park. A piece of greenstone was buried there, and a waka-shaped sculpture and water feature, built by Dunedin artist Shona Rapira Davies, was unveiled.

In Australia, Aboriginal people are rarely acknowledged in memorials to the colonial past. Yet Paul Ashton has argued that 'the Sydney landscape is replete with traces of Aboriginal presence and agency despite conservative paradigms that frame Aboriginal heritage as pre-historic and non-urban'.[45] In New Zealand, Māori connections with cities were all but forgotten. The depth of this forgetting is measured by popular and historical narratives of the massive Māori urban migrations in the 1950s and 1960s, stories that seemed to overlook earlier Māori migrations – either forced or voluntary – in the other direction, from city centres to rural towns and hinterlands.[46]

Yet as recent events in Wellington show, these lost histories have not disappeared. Rather, they are waiting, just below the surface. Often it is roadworks or some other kind of development that reveals what lies beneath.

In Wellington, roads connect the communities of the living and the dead, providing uncanny connections across time zones, places and peoples. In the nineteenth century, a new road blanketed the last few whare in Wellington's last remaining inner-city marae. In 2005, about forty buildings in the Aro Valley, including '19 of historical value had to be moved, demolished or reconstructed' to make way for an extension of the motorway that bisected Bolton Street cemetery thirty years earlier. Of these buildings, nineteen on Tonks Avenue, Willis Street, Vivian Street and Cuba Street were selected for preservation.

For the past twenty years, these buildings had served a variety of marginalised Māori and Pākehā inner-city communities. When I was a journalism student at Wellington Polytech in the mid-1980s, Tonks Ave was a secret, semi-private world at the top end of the city. It was a home for the homeless, where enormous trees engulfed peeling facades. Earmarked for long-delayed demolition, many of these buildings were squats, drop-in centres for people with mental illnesses, radical bookshops, student flats and bars.

This history was erased when Transit New Zealand stripped graffiti from wooden walls and replaced it with fresh paint in a range of heritage hues: gull grey, buff, earth green, pearl, dark crimson, butter, gooseberry and Nelson red.[47] Newly clad and emptied of any troublesome, disadvantaged or activist contemporary residents, the houses could serve as an empty shell waiting to be filled with the imagined, far-off histories of settler families, such as the Tonks.

In December 2005, as these settler buildings were being restored, the remnants of an older 'Te Aro precinct' were uncovered beneath the ruins of a recently demolished 1906 building at 39-43 Taranaki Street (just next to Molly Malone's Irish bar, and diagonally across from the spew-inducing reverse bungy jump ride on Courtenay Place). The Tenths Trust had urged developers to do an archaeological dig at the site because 'it was close to the original foreshore and may still hold some of its past under the current building'.[48]

Against all expectations, archaeologists found the remains of three ponga whare, surviving remnants of Te Aro Pā. They also found shell middens, a cannonball, fire-cracked rocks, rubbish pits, tobacco pipes, a toilet and associated postholes and alignments. The ponga whare are the only ones known to have survived anywhere from the early nineteenth century.

Construction stopped and developers, the trust, the city council and the Historic Places Trust met to decide what to do about the find. In what is considered a best practice example of cooperation between such diverse groups, the developer changed the design of its apartment building so the whare could be preserved on site. Instead of basement carparks, the building now floats on a 700-millimetre thick, 1500-tonne slab of concrete with anchors on each corner. Last year the New Zealand Archaeological Association gave project manager David Dowsett its Public Archaeology Award in recognition of his work on the pā site.[49]

Te Aro Pā, in the basement of the eight-story Bellagio Ataahua Apartments, is now listed as a Category 1 Historic Place. In its application for this to become a historic place, the Tenths Trust described the whare as being 'of outstanding archaeological, architectural, cultural, historical, social and traditional significance due to their association with early Wellington and North Island iwi, the archaeological rarity of the site, the educational value of the place as an example of early Māori residential architecture, and their strong associations with figures of cultural and social importance to Māori and Pākehā New Zealanders'. More than 200 people, including two busloads from Taranaki, came to the dawn unveiling of the site on 11 October 2008.

As soon as I heard about this discovery, I felt a surge of excitement. Looking at old maps, such as the one published in the Appendices to the Journals of the House of Representatives in 1871, only increased this feeling. I could see that sections 24 to 26 of the pā had been unearthed and section 26, associated with Ngatata-i-te-rangi's son, Wiremu Tako Ngatata, was very close to section 1, which was allocated to Parai. I would be able to see where my family had lived more than 180 years ago.

In October 2008, just before the unveiling, I finally managed to see the whare. I had a few days in Wellington. I was digging around in graveyards, archives and streets. My morning had been spent at Bolton Street cemetery in the rain, then I had an appointment at the council archives. Finally, late in the afternoon, I met Tenths Trust CEO Liz Mellish on Taranaki Street.

By the time I got there, the rain had stopped. When I put my nose against the window, I could see two glass lids rising up slightly from a pebbled floor. During the nine-day dig in 2005, archaeologists found evidence of three phases of settlement on the site. The top layer, discovered just below the surface, contained remains associated with the 1906 building, a bakery and the stables and cart shed that were associated with it. The second layer provided evidence of drains, postholes and rubbish pits associated with late nineteenth century European occupation of the site. The third layer held the whare, built in beach gravel, on the former shoreline of the city.

Liz Mellish arrived and we went in. Archaeologists use the metaphor of a bridge or a window to describe how unearthed material objects can link 'the now' and 'the then'. Mellish said the trust believed our ancestors slept in these whare, and it was likely that there were more of these structures preserved underneath Taranaki Street.

When I looked down at the first whare, I could see a corner of a blue and white Willow plate and a broken terracotta pipe. The ponga trunks traced a black outline of a very small building in the beach gravel. They looked like burnt tree stumps. Hundreds of shells – mussels, oysters, pipis, limpets – were embedded in the pale sand and dirt. Along the bottom, I could see the fringes of a flax mat.

Time drained away. In this tiny place, my relatives slept on a mattress made from flax in a house that is now insulated with shells, the remnants of the seafood they ate. The sea lapped at their doors. Their home was named Te Aro. The wind-whipped face of the pā turned north towards Taranaki and the mountain its people had left behind. It had been washed away on the tide of history, and now that tide had washed it back.

The words I had read on white settler graves at Bolton Street came back to me. 'In loving memory of …' 'Sacred to the memory of …' 'There is a reaper whose name is death/And with his sickle keen, He reaps the bearded grain at a breath/and the flowers that grow between …'

I dedicate Te Aro Pā, this historic site, a 'relic of lasting character', 'a spot hallowed for all time by reason of its wealth of historical associations', a 'resting place', to the memory of the pioneers and early settlers of Wellington.

Figure 27. A home by the sea. The author at the Te Aro Pā site, Taranaki Street, October 2008. Image: Liz Mellish.

The tour of the cemetery with Perrin had been fascinating. The geologist and former president of the Friends of Bolton Street Cemetery cares for the city's dead, but there is a limit to his knowledge too. Perrin has compiled a list of all the known burials at Bolton Street, but Parai was not on it. When I reflect on the tour of the cemetery and the things associated with it – the signs, the memorial trail booklet, the academic historical work that Perrin supplied – I can see that the discourse about Bolton Street as a resting place, primarily, for white pioneers and white early settlers, remains incredibly strong. Despite the best intentions of the Friends group, Māori remain excluded from this memorial place. The Bolton Street Memorial Park Memorial Trail pamphlet lists forty notable graves, including the Wallace one memorialising the dead children, but only one of these is obviously Māori. Site 34, in the northern section of the cemetery, is the burial place for Rira Porutu, 'a chief of Pipitea Pā who died in 1866. He was a signatory to the Treaty of Waitangi and uncle of the prophet Te Whiti.'[50]

When I looked through the Shotter photographs of graves that would be dug up for the motorway, I found some other Māori names. Mohi Ngaponga, whom Parai had followed south from Waikanae to Te Aro, had been buried in a plot in the cemetery's Sydney Street section. Ropia Motorua and Miriam Teira were buried nearby. The Tonks family were in this part of the cemetery, too.

A photograph of plot 96 lists it as the burial place of 'Te Awhe Parai 1930'. The spelling is so tantalisingly close that it seems possible this could have been the burial place of one of Parai's children, Te Awhi, a half brother to Arapera and a Parihaka ploughman protestor. But I'm not sure. On the red marbled wall, 'In Memory of Those Disinterred', listing the names of those who could be identified, there is no Parai. The closest name to the one referred to in the Shotter photographs is 'Te Awheoara'.

The memorial wall says about 3700 people were eventually disinterred. My research in the council archives suggests that about a third of these people could not be identified. The dairy kept by H. Johnson, who headed the disinternment team, reveals a man determined to be level-headed and pragmatic about his horrible task. He notes that he is determined to treat all the remains with respect. After the first grave was disinterred on 1 5 November 1968, Johnson decided 'it's just a job that has to be done so let's get on with it'.[51] A few weeks later, Johnson noted that he and the sexton, Ted Shotter, were 'feeling the long hours are very tiring'.

On 28 April 1969, around plot number 1414, Johnson noted that six unknown Māori burials were found next to the five known graves. 'During the opening of this UKN grave a very fine Greenstone mere was found and we are now classing this as a Māori grave and the boxes will be kept in the memorial grave but will be available if needed, hand over to Māori Affairs Dept, the mere will be placed in one of the boxes,' he wrote.

On 1 May, Johnson's diary shows that sixteen known graves and seventeen unknown ones were dug up. These statistics are followed by the note: 'During the opening of a large Unknown grave a Greenstone mere was found, have been in contact with Māori Affairs Department and they are interested and state that it should stay in the memorial grave and they do not want any publicity made about the mere. So we have it in there but not put directly away in case any of them would like to see it.'

On 9 May he noted: 'We are finding lots of UKN in this section of Bolton Street.' On 19 May he said: 'We are still working in an area near where the old Chapel was and we are locating a lot of UKN remains.'

These few sentences are a memorial to the disruption of an urupā. It is difficult to know whether the disinterment team found one mere – a short flat weapon of stone used in hand-to-hand fighting – or two; but what is clear is that Johnson was affected by the discovery, and was aware that there might be people, Māori, who would like to see this taonga. It was sad to read that the department that was supposed to care for 'Māori Affairs' advised Johnson to rebury this treasure, thus hiding, yet again, the evidence that Māori pioneers and leaders are buried in this historic site too.

Johnson's diary is terse and brief. All feeling is edited from it. Complaints and comments are few. He notes the weather — often wet — as well as the condition of the ground and the remains. 'Boggy' and 'messy' are often used. Yet he chose to write two long paragraphs about the mere, and his attempts to find someone to take care of it. When I told my father about this, he said quietly: 'That could be our man.'

From a distance, from a wide angle, the reality of colonisation is quite clear: 'Sometimes by negotiation and sometimes by warfare, the natives lost ground and the invaders gained it.'[52] This is what happened at Parihaka and elsewhere in Taranaki. It happened in Wellington and in many other places too. The cruel, insidious and mostly invisible mechanisations of perpetual leases and other systems to control the pathetic amount of Māori land remaining in Māori hands means that this past injustice continues in the present.

The big picture of colonisation is important; it needs to be examined, acknowledged and rectified. But zoom in and this reality blurs, dissolves, fractures and explodes. Spin the lens to close up on any corner of your family, your neighbourhood, your city, your nation, and different picture emerges, one that is more complex, one that cannot deny 'the experience of contact'[53], one in which forgetting is replaced by a rich, complicated and binding experience of entanglement. A more ethical future starts with a more ethical past, the sort that might be found in intimate histories, in crooked little family portraits.

Just as I was completing the final corrections on this manuscript, I read *The Anatomist*. It tells the story of the little-known Henry Carter, the doctor who illustrated the famous nineteenth-century medical text book, *Gray's Anatomy*. Henry Carter was a tortured man, and so was his brother Joe. In an 1855 letter to their sister, Lily, Joe wrote:

> *It often surprises me to find how intimately the past becomes interwoven with the present, and the apparent future. And I have,*

at times, immensely wondered to find that what is past – the past – does not, nor will it, detach itself and remain where it was (or where it might have been intended to remain) but it must bring itself forward, smilingly, or otherwise present itself as an old friend, and will not be denied.[54]

As the unearthing of Te Aro Pā demonstrates, the past does not remain where it was. Whether we like it or not, it will return and will not be denied. The dead will be heard.

The dead are buried all over Wellington: in archives, in cemeteries, under city streets. It is bittersweet to touch them, to feel the unusual textures of their lives and to consider how unearthing what is hidden can provide insights that counter older narratives of settlement as nothing more than a story of erasure, subtraction and domination; how it can suggest, rather, that settlement might also be (and become) a story of enrichment, addition and partnership.

What stories do your dead tell you? How do you see the past?

[1] P.J.E. Shotter, sexton from 1939-1975, photographs, PAColl-1406, ATL.

[2] Notebook from City Engineer's Department containing daily statistics of disinternments, reinternments, cremations, provision of new caskets, ashes carried out from Nov 15, 1968 to August 1969, 00244:1:6., Wellington City Council Archives (WCCA).

[3] Margaret Alington, 'Life After Death: An Old Cemetery Becomes a Memorial Park' in David Hamer and Roberta Nichols, eds, *The Making of Wellington 1800-1914*, 1990, 148.

[4] Redmer Yska, *Wellington: Biography of a City*, Auckland: Reed, 2006, 191.

[5] John Salmon to Frank Kitts, 3 June 1965, re Bolton Street Cemetery Preservation Society, 00009:571:35/1376/11 Pt1, WCCA.

[6] John Salmon to Frank Kitts, 'Bolton Street Cemetery', 2 November 1964, 00009:571:35/1376/11 Pt1, WCCA.

[7] Petition to 'the mayor and councillors of the city of Wellington and the Commissioner of Works and The Chairman and members of the National Roads Board', undated, 1965?, WCCA.

[8] Arthur Seed to Frank Kitts, 'Bolton Street Cemetery Desecration', 4 November 1965. WCCA.

[9] Elizabeth Orr to Frank Kitts, undated letter, Wellington Urban Motorway, Bolton Street Cemetery Section file, 00009:571:35/1376/11 Pt1, WCCA.

[10] Irma O'Connor to mayor Frank Kitts, 29 November 1964, 00009:571:35/1376/11 Pt1, WCCA.

[11] P.J. Leahy to Frank Kitts, 'Bolton Street Cemetery', 20 November 1964, 00009:571:35/1376/11 Pt 1, WCCA.

[12] Stephen O'Regan, 'Māori Control of the Māori Heritage' in P. Gathercole and D. Lowenthal, eds, *The Politics of the Past,* London: Unwin Hyman, 1990, 100.

[13] John Howard Wallace 1816-1891, 'The Voyage out in the Aurora' written ca 1890, typed transcript of part of MS Papers 0108-7, ATL.

[14] John Wallace to Wm. Lort Esquire, Birmingham, 4 January 1842. Lort William, MS Papers 5513, ATL.

[15] William Ellerslie Wallace, trading list contained in Vallance Papers, MS Papers 1347-5/17/2, ATL.

[16] Thomson W. Leys, ed., *Early History of New Zealand,* Auckland: Brett Printer and Publisher, 1889. From earliest times to 1840 by R.A.A. Sherrin, from 1840 to 1845 by J. H. Wallace.

[17] William Ellerslie Wallace to J Howard Wallace, 10 November 1844, letter contained in Charles Vallance Papers, ATL, MS Papers 1347-5/17/2.

[18] See Sandra Clarke and Neville Gilmour, 'Arapera Ronguaroa' in *Nga Tupuna o Te Whanganui-a-Tara,* vol 4, Wellington: Wellington City Council and Wellington Tenths Trust, 2007, 27. For a brief biography of Hemi Parai, see *Nga Tupuna o Te Whanagnui-a-Tara,* vol 1, 2001, 23.

[19] Angela Ballara, 'Te Whanganui-a-Tara: Phases of Māori Occupation of Wellington Harbour c. 1800-1840, in *The Making of Wellington,* 1990, 25.

[20] Mohi Ngaponga, *Nga Tupuna,* 2001, 15.

[21] Ballara, 'Te Whanganui-a-Tara', 22.

[22] 'Manual of New Zealand History, by J. Howard Wallace', *Sydney Morning Herald,* 14 December 1886. Clipping contained in Wallace Papers, MS-Papers-0108-2.

[23] Thomas McKenzie, secretary, 'The Jubilee', report contained in Wallace Papers, MS 0108-6.

[24] Cultural Impact Report 39-43 Taranaki Street Te Aro Pa', Wellington Tenths Trust, January 2004, 7.

[25] Wallace to Sam Revans, March 1884, Wallace Papers, MS Papers 107, Folder 1, ATL. The emphasis is from the original.

[26] Stephen Turner, 'Settlement as Forgetting' in Klaus Neumann, Nicholas Thomas and Hilary Ericksen, eds, *Quicksands: Foundational Histories in Australia & Aotearoa New Zealand,* Sydney: UNSW Press, 1999, 35.

[27] Tom Griffiths, *Beechworth: An Australian Country Town and Its Past,* Richmond: Greenhouse Publications, 1987, 2.

[28] 'John Howard Wallace', in G. H. Scholefield, ed, *Dictionary of New Zealand Biography,* Wellington: Department of Internal Affairs, 1940, vol II, 454.

[29] 'The Claims of Early Settlers', 18 June 1875, copy of advertisement in Wallace Papers, MS – 0108-8, ATL.

[30] Wallace uses a quote from Bishop Selwyn on the title page of his 'Manual of New Zealand History'. '… New Zealand would one day be the brightest gem in Britain's crown – her noblest effort at colonization.'

[31] Wallace Papers, folder 2.

[32] Wallace, 'Māori Affairs', *Brett's Historical Series Early New Zealand,* 590.

[33] Hemi Parai, Te Aro, August 14, 1854, *New Zealand Spectator and Cook's Strait Guardian,* 16 August 1854.

[34] J.H.L. Cumpston, *The History of Diptheria, Scarlet Fever, Measles and Whooping Cough in Australia,* Canberra: Government Printer, 1927, 26.

[35] J H Wallace Prize Drainage Report, sent to the City Council on May 21, 1873. Untitled newspaper clipping in Wallace Papers, MS Papers – 0108 -8, ATL.

[36] *Te Whanganui a Tara Me Ona Takiwa Report on the Wellington District,* 2003, 341.

[37] Hemi Parai to McLean, 19 April 1871, McLean Papers, Folder 695B, ATL. Holden Hohaia translated this letter for me. Hohaia said that the wording of the letter was very ambiguous and that Hemi may have been informing McLean of his intention to travel to Parihaka and explain the government's position to Te Whiti.

[38] Reports of the Royal Commission into Confiscated Land, AJHR, vol II, 1880, G-2

[39] See indexes to AJHR 1854-1890. Hemi Parai (Parae), 'Petition relating to Te Aro lands' and 'Petition against sale of barracks at Te Aro', 95 and 111.

[40] 'The Parihaka Native Parliament', *Taranaki Herald,* 8 April 1874.

[41] Walter K. Bishop, *Guide to Wellington & District* with complete map of city, 2nd edition, Wellington: Robert Burrett, 1883, 5.

[42] Bishop, *Guide to Wellington & District,* 5-6.

[43] Te Aro Pa, Registration Proposal for Historic Places Trust, September 2007, 7.

[44] For more details on Māori land taken at this time, see 'Report on Native Reserves in the Province of Wellington', Appendixes to the Journals of the House of Representatives (AJHR), Native Reserves F, no.4.

[45] Paul Ashton, 'The Past in the Present: Public History and the City of Sydney', in Tim Murray, ed., *Exploring the Modern City,* 2003, 18.

46 An excellent oral history of migration to the city, including the story of my aunty, Agnes ('Bubs') Broughton, is Patricia Grace, Irihapeti Ramsden and Jonathan Dennis, eds, *The Silent Migration: Ngati Poneke Young Māori Club 1937-1948,* Wellington: Huia, 2001.

47 See 'Wellington Inner City Bypass Project Heritage Buildings', undated booklet, Fulton Hogan and Transit New Zealand. For a detailed history of many of the buildings and the bypass, see Gary H. Tonks, *Tonks and the Bypass: 1847-2007 160 years,* Wellington: Wellington City Council, 2007.

48 Wellington Tenths Trust, 'Cultural Impact Report 39-43 Taranaki Street Te Aro Pa', January 2004, 3.

49 See Peter Ker, 'Downtown Discovery', *Heritage New Zealand,* Autumn 2008, available online at http://www.historic.org.nz/magazinefeatures/2008Autumn/2008_autumn_tearo.htm, accessed 20 October 2008.

50 'Step Back in Time', Bolton Street Memorial Park Memorial Trail, Wellington City Council.

51 H. Johnson, Bolton Street Cemetery Contract Disinternment of Human Remains Diary, WCA, file 00244:1:7.

52 Limerick, 'Haunted America', 33.

53 Turner, 'Settlement as Forgetting', 35.

54 Joe Carter to Lily Carter, cited in Bill Hayes, *The Anatomist,* Melbourne: Scribe, 2008, 154.

Select Bibliography

Unpublished Material

Alpers Sir O.J., Papers. Manuscript Collection, Alexander Turnbull Library (ATL).

City Engineer's Department notebook, containing daily statistics of disinterments, reinterments, cremations, provision of new caskets, ashes carried out from Nov 15 1968 to Aug 1969, Wellington City Council Archives (WCCA).

Bramley, Hannah, papers relating to Māori Land Court and land in Taranaki and Wellington, private collection of Leo Buchanan.

Bryce v. Rusden, Queen's Bench Division, High Court of Justice, London, 1886.

Deeds of Release, Port Nicholson 6 February 1844, Archives New Zealand Te Whare Tohu Tuhituhinga O Aotearoa (ANZ), Head Office, Wellington.

Duigan, J. Letters. Manuscript Collection, ATL.

Dwyer, J. File for Te Whiti's tokotoko, Collection of Puke Ariki Museum and Library, New Plymouth, Taranaki (PA).

Fromm, A., Diary, PA.

Gapes, G., Letter, PA.

Goodbehere, E., Letters, PA.

Gordon, W.F., Notebook and Papers, PA.

Hursthouse, C.W., Telegraph Books 1881, PA.

Hursthouse, C.W., Diary, PA.

Hutchinson, V. and Rau-Kupa, M., Script for 'Parihaka: A Photographic Survey', 1981, PA.

Māori Affairs Department, Petitions to Parliament by Māori 1925, Minutes of Evidence to Royal Commission into Confiscated Land, February 1927, ANZ.

McLean, D., Papers, letters from Māori, Manuscript Collection, ATL.

Motorway: Foothills motorway (general file) 1964-1965, WCCA.

Newall, S., Surveyors Notebooks 1880, PA.

Parker, W., Diary, October-November 1881, Manuscript Collection, ATL.

Rau-Kupa, M., 'Te Kotahitanga Tautoru' scrapbook, 1937-1952, PA.

Rolleston, W., Correspondence 1831-1903, Manuscript Collection, ATL.

Rolleston, W., Diary 1881, Manuscript Collection, ATL.

Skinner, T. K., Diaries 1872-1881, Manuscript Collection, ATL.

Smith, D. S., Papers. Manuscript Collection, ATL.

Smith, R., Account-keeping book, Manuscript Collection, ATL.

The Taranaki Report Kaupapa Tuatahi, Record of Inquiry, Documents to the end of the first hearing, 7 September 1990; Documents to the end of the second hearing, 26 November 1990; Documents to the end of the fourth hearing, 12 April 1991; Documents to the end of the fifth hearing, 11 June 1991; Documents to the end of the sixth hearing, 17 October 1991; Documents to the end of the ninth hearing, 22 October 1992; Documents to the end of the twelfth hearing, 15 June 1995, Waitangi Tribunal Archives (WTA), Wellington.

Vallance, Charles Augustus, Papers 1844-1860, ATL.

Wallace, John Howard, Papers 1841-1891, Manuscript Collection, ATL.

William, Lort, 1842, Letter from John Wallace, ATL.

Wellington Urban Motorway, Bolton Street Cemetery Section 1964-1968, WCCA.

Parliamentary Papers, Reports and Guides

Appendices to the Journals of the House of Representatives (AJHR), 1878-1928.

British Parliamentary Papers, Colonies, New Zealand, Irish University Press series (IUP).

'Cultural Impact Report 39-43 Taranaki Street Te Aro Pa', Wellington Tenths Trust, January 2004.

Healing the Past, Building a Future: a guide to Treaty of Waitangi claims and direct negotiations with the Crown, Wellington: Office of Treaty Settlements, 1999, revised 2002.

Melvin, G. *The Claims Process of the Waitangi Tribunal*, Wellington: Waitangi Tribunal, 2000.

Ngāti Mutunga and Her Majesty the Queen in right of New Zealand, 'Deed of Settlement of the Historical Claims of Ngati Mutunga: Initialled Deed of Settlement for Presentation to Ngati Mutunga' 14 December 2004, Wellington: Office of Treaty Settlements, 2004.

Phillipson, G. *Preparing Claimant Evidence for the Waitangi Tribunal,* Waitangi Tribunal, 1999.

The Taranaki Report: Kaupapa Tuatahi, Wellington: Waitangi Tribunal, 1996.

Taranaki Māori, Dairy Industry Changes and the Crown, Wellington: Waitangi Tribunal, 2001.

Te Whanganui a Tara Me Ona Takiwa: Report on the Wellington District, Wellington: Waitangi Tribunal, 2003.

Tomb of the Unknown Warrior, internment ceremony commemorative booklet, November 2004.

Waitangi Tribunal Practice Notes, Guide to the Practices and Procedures of the Waitangi Tribunal, Wellington: Waitangi Tribunal, 2000.

Unpublished Theses and Manuscripts

Buchanan, R. 'Village of Peace, Village of War: Parihaka Stories 1881-2004', PhD thesis, Monash University, 2005.

Johnson, M. '"Land of the Wrong White Crowd": Pākehā Anti-racist Organisations and Identity Politics in Auckland, 1964–1981', MA thesis, University of Auckland, 2002.

Pungarehu School: History of Pungarehu School and Parihaka District, compiled by Māori students at the school, c. 1930, Manuscript Collection, ATL.

Sargeson, P. *Bibliography of printed material on the Parihaka affair*, compiled at the request of the Alexander Turnbull Library in 1978.

Smith, Ailsa. 'Ko Tohu Te Matua: The Story of Tohu Kakahi of Parihaka', MA thesis, University of Canterbury, 1990.

'The Treaty of Waitangi: Its Origins and Significance', papers from a seminar 19-20 February 1972, under the auspices of Department of University Extension, Victoria University, Wellington, University Extension Publications, no. 7, 1972.

Ward, A. 'Towards One New Zealand: the Government and the Māori people, 1861-93', PhD thesis, Australian National University, 1967.

Film and Photographic Collections

Burton Brothers, C.P. Cottier, Trevor Ulyatt and James Bragge collections, Te Papa Tongarewa Museum of New Zealand (TP).

Collis, W. William Collis Collection, ATL.

Mita, M. *Bastion Point – Day 507,* Awatea Films, 1980, New Zealand Film Archive (NZFA).

Mita, M. (host), *Koha: Parihaka 1981*, NZFA.

'Māori Portraits' Album, PA.

'North Island' Album, TP.

'The Parihaka Album' and 'The Parihaka Album (2)', Album of Sydney and New Zealand Colonies, Soldiers and Towns, ATL.

Schaef, A.W., A.W. Schaef Collection, ATL.

Shotter, P.J.E., P.J.E. Shotter Collection, ATL.

Strange Album, Parihaka/Opunake, c. 1910, PA.

Gallery and Museum Catalogues

Bonyhady, T. *Burke & Wills: From Melbourne to Myth,* Canberra: National Library of Australia, 2002.

Hohaia, Te M., O'Brien, G. and Strongman, L. eds. *Parihaka: The Art of Passive Resistance,* Wellington: City Gallery, Victoria University Press and Parihaka Pā Trustees, 2000.

Kelly Culture: Reconstructing Ned Kelly, Melbourne: State Library of Victoria, 2003.

Mack, J. *Te Whiti o Rongomai of Parihaka as Seen by his Contemporaries,* produced to accompany the exhibition 'Taranaki Saw It All', Waikato Museum, March-May 1973, Taranaki Museum, June-July 1973.

O'Brien, G. ed. *Hotere: Out the Black Window,* Wellington: Godwit and City Gallery, 1997.

Paton, J. ed., with Kennedy, A. and Wevers, L. *Anne Noble States of Grace,* Otago and Wellington: Dunedin Public Art Gallery and Victoria University Press, 2001.

Te Maunga Taranaki Views of a Mountain, New Plymouth: Govett Brewster Art Gallery Publications, 2001.

Exhibitions

'Parihaka: The Art of Passive Resistance', City Gallery, Wellington 2000-2001.

'Parihaka: The Art of Passive Resistance and Te Iwi Herehere: the story of Māori prisoners from Taranaki in Otago 1869-1882', Dunedin Public Art Gallery, Dunedin 2002.

'Parihaka: The Struggle for Peace', Puke Ariki Museum and Library, New Plymouth 2003.

Select Bibliography

Newspapers and Magazines

Age; Argus; Auckland Star; Australasian Sketcher; Christian Pacifist; Daily Southern Cross; The Dominion; The Dominion Post; Education Journal; Graphic; Hawke's Bay Herald-Tribune; Illustrated Australian News; Listener; Lyttelton Times; New Zealand Building Worker; New Zealand Herald; North & South; Otago Daily Times; People's Voice; The Press; Sunday Star-Times; Sydney Morning Herald; Taranaki Daily News; Taranaki Herald; The Times (London)*; Waikato Times.*

Books and Journal Articles

Amin, S. *Event, Metaphor, Memory: Chauri Chaura 1922-1992,* Delhi: Oxford University Press, 1995.

Anderson, B. *Imagined Communities: Reflections on the Origin and Spread of Nationalism,* London: Verso, 1983.

Appadurai, A. *The Social Life of Things: Commodities in Cultural Perspective,* Cambridge: Cambridge University Press, 1986.

--- *Modernity at Large: Cultural Dimensions of Globalization,* Minneapolis: University of Minnesota Press, 1996.

Ashplant, T.G, Dawson, G. and Roper, M. eds. *The Politics of War and Commemoration,* London and New York: Routledge, 2000.

Ashton, P. 'The Past in the Present: Public History and the City of Sydney' in Tim Murray ed. *Exploring the Modern City,* Sydney: Historic Houses Trust New South Wales, 2003, 1-23.

Attwood, B. and Mogowan, F. *Telling Stories: Indigenous History and Memory in Australia and New Zealand,* Sydney: Allen & Unwin, 2001.

Attwood, B., Mogowan, F and Foster, S.G. eds. *Frontier Conflict: The Australian Experience,* Canberra; National Museum of Australia, 2003.

Ballara, A. 'Te Whanganui-a-Tara: phases of Māori occupation of Wellington Harbour c. 1800-1840' in D. Hamer and R. Nicholls eds, *The Making of Wellington, 1990,* 9-34.

--- 'I riro I te hoko' Problems in Cross-Cultural Historical Scholarship', *New Zealand Journal of History,* 'Millennium Issue', vol. 34, no. 1, 2000, 20-33.

Barthes, R. *Camera Lucida,* New York: Farrar, Straus & Giroux, 1981.

Beaglehole, J.C. *New Zealand: A Short History,* London: Allen & Unwin, 1936.

Belgrave, M., Kawharu, M. and Williams, D. eds. *Waitangi Revisited: Perspectives on the Treaty of Waitangi,* Melbourne: Oxford University Press, 2005.

Belich, J. *The New Zealand Wars and the Victorian Interpretation of Racial Conflict,* Auckland: Auckland University Press, 1986.

--- *I Shall Not Die: Titokowaru's War New Zealand 1868-1869,* Wellington: Allen & Unwin/Port Nicholson Press, 1989.

--- *Making Peoples: A History of the New Zealanders From Polynesian Settlement to the End of the Nineteenth Century,* Auckland: Allen Lane Penguin, 1996.

--- *Paradise Reforged: A History of the New Zealanders From the 1880s to the Year 2000,* Auckland: Allen Lane Penguin, 2001.

Bell, C. and Matthewman, St. eds. *Cultural Studies in Aotearoa New Zealand: Identity, Space and Place,* Melbourne: Oxford, 2004.

Bhabha, H. ed. *Nation and Narration,* London: Routledge, 1990.

--- *The Location of Culture,* London: Routledge, 1994.

Binney, J., Chaplin, G. and Wallace, C. *Mihaia: The Prophet Rua Kenana and his Community at Maugapohatu,* Wellington: Oxford University Press, 1979.

Binney, J. and Chaplin, G. *Nga Morehu: The Survivors,* Auckland: Oxford University Press, 1986.

Binney, J. and Chaplin, G. 'Taking the Photos Home: The Recovery of a Māori History', *Visual Anthropology* 4, 1991, pp. 431-442.

Binney, J. *Redemption Songs: The Life of Te Kooti Arikirangi Te Turuki,* Auckland: Auckland University Press and Bridget Williams Books, 1995.

Binney, J. ed. *The Shaping of History: Essays from The New Zealand Journal of History,* Wellington: Bridget Williams Books, 2001.

Bishop, W. *Guide to Wellington & District: With a Complete Map of the City,* second edition, Wellington: Robert Burrett, 1883.

Bornholdt, J. 'The Legacy of Parihaka', *New Zealand Historic Places Trust,* no. 78, August 2000, 8-10.

Briggs, A. *Victorian Things,* London: BT Batsford, 1998.

Brookes, B. ed. *At Home in New Zealand: History, Houses, People,* Wellington: Bridget Williams Books, 2000.

Buchanan, R. 'The Powder Room', *Meanjin,* vol. 63, no. 1, 2004, 54-59.

--- 'The Dementia wing of History', *Cultural Studies Review,* vol. 13, no. 1, March 2007, 173-186.

---'Decolonizing the Archives: The Work of New Zealand's Waitangi Tribunal', *Public History Review,* vol. 14, 2007, 44-63.

Buchanan, R. and James, P. 'Lest We Forget', *Arena,* no. 38, December-January 1998/9, 25-30.

Select Bibliography

Buck, P. 'The Taranaki Māoris: Te Whiti and Parihaka', Te Aute College Students' Association Conference, Papers and Addresses, December 1897, in J.B. Condliffe, *Te Rangi Hiroa: The Life of Sir Peter Buck,* Christchurch: Whitcombe & Tombs, 1971, 40-45.

Burdon, R.M. *New Zealand Notables: Henry Williams, Te Whiti, Johnny Jones,* Christchurch: Caxton Press, 1941.

Burton, A. *Dwelling in the Archive: Women Writing House, Home and History in Late Colonial India,* New York: Oxford University Press, 2003.

Byrne, D. and Nugent, M. *Mapping Attachment: A Spatial Approach to Aboriginal Post-contact Heritage,* Sydney: Department of Environment and Conservation New South Wales, 2004.

Byrnes, G. *Boundary Markers: Land Surveying and the Colonisation of New Zealand,* Wellington: Bridget Williams Books, 2001.

Byrnes, G. *The Waitangi Tribunal and New Zealand History,* Auckland: Oxford University Press, 2004.

Caselberg, J. ed. *Māori Is My Name: Historical Māori Writings in Translation,* Dunedin: John McIndoe, 1975.

Chakrabarty, D. *Provincializing Europe: Postcolonial Thought and Historical Difference,* Princeton and Oxford: Princeton University Press, 2000.

---'Reconciliation and its Historiography: some preliminary thoughts.' *UTS Review*: subaltern/indigenous/multicultural, vol.1, no. 1, May 2001, 6-14.

Clifford, J. *The Predicament of Culture,* Cambridge, Mass: Harvard University Press, 1988.

Cody, J.F. *Man of Two Worlds: Sir Maui Pomare,* Wellington: AH and AW Reed, 1953.

Cohen, P. *History in Three Keys: The Boxers as Event, Experience and Myth,* New York: Columbia University Press, 1997.

Cohn, B.S. *Colonialism and Its Forms of Knowledge: The British in India,* New Jersey: Princeton University Press, 1996.

Condliffe, J.B. and Airey, W. T. G. *Short History of New Zealand,* Christchurch and London: Whitcombe & Tombs/Allen & Unwin, 1935.

Consedine, R. and Consedine, J. *Healing our History: The Challenge of the Treaty of Waitangi,* Auckland: Penguin, 2001.

Coombes, A. *History after Apartheid: Visual Culture and Public Memory in a Democratic South Africa,* Durham and London: Duke University Press, 2003.

Cowan, J. *Hero Stories of New Zealand,* Wellington: Harry H. Tombs, 1935.

Cowan, J. *The New Zealand Wars: A History of the Māori Campaigns and the Pioneering Period* [1922-23] vol. II, Wellington: Government Printer, 1955-56.

Crosby, D. *The Musket Wars: A History of Inter-iwi Conflict 1806-1845*, Auckland: Reed, 1999.

Cumpston, J.H.L. *The History of Diptheria, Scarlet Fever, Measles and Whooping Cough in Australia*, Canberra: Government Printer 1927.

Curthoys, A. and McGrath, A. eds. *Writing Histories: Imagination and Narration*, Melbourne: Monash University Publications in History and Australian National University, 2000.

---'Immigration and Colonisation: New Histories', *UTS Review*, vol. 7, no. 1, May 2001, 170-179.

---'Constructing National Histories' in B. Attwood and S. G. Foster eds, *Frontier Conflict* (2003), 185-200.

Dalley, B. and Labrum, B. eds. *Fragments: New Zealand Social and Cultural History*, Auckland: Auckland University Press, 2000.

Dalley, B. and Phillips, J. eds. *Going Public: The Changing Face of New Zealand History*, Auckland: Auckland University Press, 2001.

Dansey, H. *Te Raukura: The Feathers of the Albatross*, Auckland: Longman Paul, 1974.

Darian-Smith, K. and Hamilton, P. eds. *History and Memory in Twentieth Century Australia*, Melbourne: Oxford University Press, 1994.

Davison, G. *The Use and Abuse of Australian History*, Sydney: Allen & Unwin, 2000.

Dening, G. *Performances*, Melbourne: Melbourne University Press, 1996.

Dudding, J. 'Photographs of Māori as Cultural Artefacts', *Journal of Museum Ethnography* 2003, 8-18.

Duff, A. *Once Were Warriors*, Auckland: Tandem Press, 1990.

Dyer, R. *White*, London and New York: Routledge, 1997.

Edwards, E. *Raw Histories: Photographs, Anthropology and Museums*, Oxford: Bergmann, 2001.

Edwards, E. and Hart, J. eds. *Photographs Objects Histories*, London: Routledge, 2004.

Elsmore, B. *Mana From Heaven: A Century of Māori Prophets in New Zealand*, Tauranga: Moana Press, 1989.

Fielding, K. and Vincent, E. eds. *Cover Your Tracks: Creative Histories by Young Victorians*, Fitzroy: Express Media, 2001.

Gandhi, L. *Postcolonial Theory: A Critical Introduction*, Sydney: Allen & Unwin, 1998.

Gibson, R. *Seven Versions of an Australian Badland*, Brisbane: University of Queensland Press, 2002.

Goodall, H. 'Too Early or Not Soon Enough? Reflections on Sharing Histories as Process', in Kate Darian-Smith ed., *Australian Historical Studies Special issue: Challenging Histories: Reflections on Australian History*, vol. 33, no. 118, 2002, 7-24.

Gooder, H. and Jacobs, J.M. '"On the Border of the Unsayable": The Apology in Postcolonizing Australia', *interventions* (special issue) vol. 2, no. 2, 2000, 229-247.

Gourevitch, P. and Morris, E. *Standard Operating Procedure: A War Story*, London: Picador, 2008.

Grace, P., Ramsden, I. and Dennis, J. eds. *The Silent Migration: Ngati Poneke Young Māori Club 1937-1948*, Wellington: Huia, 2001.

Grenville, K. *Searching for the Secret River: A Writing Memoir*, Melbourne: Text, 2006.

Griffith, P., Hughes, P. and Loney, A. eds. *A Book in the Hand: Essays on the History of the Book in New Zealand*, Auckland: Auckland University Press, 2000.

Griffiths, T. *Beechworth: An Australian Country Town and Its Past*, Melbourne: Greenhouse, 1987.

Hamer, D. and Nicholls, R. eds. *The Making of Wellington, 1800-1914*, Wellington: Victoria University Press, 1990.

Hamilton, P. and Ashton, P. eds. 'Australians and the Past, special issue', *Australian Cultural History*, Perth: Curtain University of Technology, 2003.

Harris, A. *Hikoi: Forty Years of Māori Protest*, Wellington: Huia, 2004.

Hawkins, G. and Muecke, S. eds. *Culture and Waste: The Creation and Destruction of Value*, Boston: Rowman & Littlefield, 2003.

Hayward, J. and Wheen, N.R. eds. *The Waitangi Tribunal: Te Roopu Whakamana i te Tiriti o Waitangi*, Wellington: Bridget Williams Books, 2004.

Healy, C. *From the Ruins of Colonisation: History as Social Memory*, Melbourne: Cambridge University Press, 1997.

--- *Forgetting Aborigines*, Sydney: UNSW Press, 2008.

Hickey, Maureen, 'Negotiating History: Crown Apologies in New Zealand's Historical Treaty of Waitangi Settlements', *Public History Review* vol 13, 2006, 108-124.

Hinchcliff, J. *Parihaka: A Novel*, Wellington: Steele Roberts, 2004.

Hirsch, M. *Family Frames: Photography, Narrative and Postmemory*, Cambridge, Mass: Harvard University Press, 1997.

Hunn, J.K. *Report on Department of Māori Affairs: With Statistical Supplement*, 24 August 1960, Wellington: Government Printer, 1961.

Inglis, K. *Sacred Places: War Memorials in the Australian Landscape*, Melbourne: Melbourne University Press, 1998.

Ingram, C.W.N. and Wheatley, P.O. *New Zealand Shipwrecks 1795-1960,* Wellington: Reed, 1961.

Irvine, R.F. and Alpers, O.T.J. *The Progress of New Zealand in the Century,* Philadelphia: Linscott and London: W. R. Chambers, 1902.

Jones, K. *The Penguin Field Guide to New Zealand Archaeology,* Auckland: Penguin, 2007.

Kawharu, I.H. ed. *Waitangi: Māori and Pākehā Perspectives on the Treaty of Waitangi,* Auckland: Oxford University Press, 1989.

Kenny, R. *The Lamb Enters the Dreaming: Nathanael Pepper & the Ruptured World,* Melbourne: Scribe, 2008.

Kidman, F. *The Captive Wife,* Auckland: Random House, 2005.

King, M. *Being Pākehā Now,* Auckland: Penguin, 1999.

King, M. *The Penguin History of New Zealand,* Auckland: Penguin, 2003.

Klein, K.L. 'On the Emergence of Memory in Historical Discourse', *Representations 69,* Grounds for Remembering, Winter 2000, 127-143.

Knight, H. *Photography in New Zealand: A Social and Technical History,* Dunedin: John McIndoe, 1971.

Knight, H. *New Zealand Photographers: A Selection,* Dunedin: Allied Press, 1981.

Lake, M. ed. *Memory, Monuments and Museums,* Melbourne: Melbourne University Press, 2006.

Langford, M. *Suspended Conversations: The Afterlife of Memory in Photographic Albums,* Montreal and London: McGill/Queen's University Press, 2001.

Ledger, Private J. *Pen and Ink Sketches of Parihaka and Neighbourhood with Scenes of Māori Life,* Dunedin: Fergusson & Mitchell, 1883.

Leys, T.W. ed. 'From Earliest Times to 1840 by R.A.A. Sherrin', 'From 1840 to 1845 by J.H.Wallace', *Early History of New Zealand,* Auckland: Brett Printer and Publisher, 1889.

Limerick, P. *Something in the Soil: Legacies and Reckonings in the New West,* New York and London: W.W. Norton & Company, 2000.

Lloyd, D. 'Colonial Trauma/Postcolonial Recovery?' *Interventions* (special issue), vol. 2, no. 2, 2000, 212-228.

MacLean, C. *For Whom the Bells Toll: A History of the National War Memorial,* Wellington: Heritage Group, Department of Internal Affairs, 1998.

Mead, H.M. and Grove, N. *Nga Pepeha a Nga Tipuna,* Wellington: Victoria University Press, 2001.

Moeahu, P. 'Hikoi Ki Te Waipounamu', *New Zealand Historic Places,* no. 78, August 2000, 12-13.

Select Bibliography

Muecke, S. *Ancient & Modern: Time, Culture and Indigenous Philosophy*, Sydney: UNSW Press, 2004.

Murray, T. ed. *Exploring the Modern City: Recent Approaches to Urban Archaeology*, Sydney: Historic Houses Trust New South Wales, 2003.

Neich, R. *Painted Histories: Early Māori Figurative Painting,* Auckland: Auckland University Press, 1993.

Neumann, K., Thomans, N. and Ericksen, H. *Quicksands: Foundational Histories in Australia and Aotearoa New Zealand,* Sydney: UNSW Press, 1999.

Ngata, H.M. *English-Māori Dictionary,* Whanganui-a-Tara: Learning Media, Ministry of Education, 1993.

Nga Tupuna O Te Whanganui-a-Tara, volumes 1, 2, 3 and 4, with contributions by Sandra Clarke, Neville Gilmour and others, Wellington: Wellington City Council and Wellington Tenths Trust, 2001, 2003, 2005, 2007.

Nora, P. 'General Introduction: Between Memory and History', in P. Nora, ed. *Realms of Memory: The Construction of the French Past*, vol. 1, New York: Columbia University Press, 1997, 1-20.

Novick, P. *The Holocaust in American Life*, Boston and New York: Houghton Mifflin, 2000.

Nugent, M. 'Aboriginal Family History: Some Reflections', *Australian Cultural History* (special issue), vol. 22, 2003, pp. 143-153.

--- *Botany Bay: Where Histories Meet*, Sydney: Allen & Unwin, 2005.

O'Brien, G. *After Bathing at Baxters: Essays and Notebooks,* Wellington: Victoria University Press, 2002.

Oliver, W.H. *The Story of New Zealand,* London: Faber and Faber, 1960.

Oliver, W.H. and Orange, C. eds. *Dictionary of New Zealand Biography*, vols I and II, Wellington: Allen & Unwin/Department of Internal Affairs, 1990 and 1993.

Oliver, W.H. *Looking for the Phoenix: A Memoir,* Wellington: Bridget Williams Books, 2002.

Orange, C. *The Treaty of Waitangi,* Wellington: Allen & Unwin/Port Nicholson Press, 1987.

Orsman, H.W. ed. *Oxford Dictionary of New Zealand English,* Auckland: Oxford University Press, 1997.

Our Nation's Story: A Course of British History, std III, std VI, Christchurch: Whitcombe's Primary History Series, [undated c. 1920s].

Pandey, G. *Remembering Partition,* Cambridge: Cambridge University Press, 2001.

Phillips, J. *A Man's Country? The Image of the Pākehā Male*, Auckland: Penguin, 1987.

Pound, F. *Frames on the Land: Early Landscape Painting in New Zealand,* Auckland: Collins, 1983.

Prickett, N. *Excavations at Warea Redoubt January-February 1978,* Auckland: University of Auckland Archaeology Society, 1979.

Prickett, N. *Historic Taranaki: An Archaeological Guide,* Wellington: Government Printer, 1990.

Prickett, N. *Landscapes of Conflict: A Field Guide to the New Zealand Wars,* Auckland: Random House, 2000.

Radstone, S. ed. *Memory and Methodology,* Oxford and New York: Berg, 2000.

Rajan, R.S. 'Righting Wrongs, Rewriting History?' *Interventions* (Special issue), vol. 2, no. 2, 2000, 159-170.

Reeves, W.P. *The Long White Cloud,* London: Horace Marshall & Son, 1898.

Reilly M. and Thomson, J. *When the Waves Rolled In Upon Us: Essays in Nineteenth-Century Māori History,* Dunedin: Otago University Press, 1999.

Riseborough, H. *Parihaka and the Historians,* Parihaka: Te Niho o Te Ati Awa Parihaka Seminars no.1, 1993.

Riseborough, H. *Days of Darkness: The Government and Parihaka Taranaki 1878-1884*, revised edition (first published 1989), Auckland: Penguin 2002.

Ross, J. *The Lighthouses of New Zealand,* Palmerston North: Dunmore Press, 1975.

Royal, A.C. *Te Haurapa: An Introduction to Researching Tribal Histories and Traditions,* Wellington: Bridget Williams Books/Historical Branch, Department of Internal Affairs, 1992.

Royal, T. A. C. 'Some Notes on Oral and Indigenous Thought and Knowledge', *Oral History in New Zealand,* 2002, 7-10.

Rusden, G.W. *History of New Zealand,* vols I, II, III, London: Chapman & Hall, 1883 and Melbourne and Sydney: George Robertson, 1883.

--- *Aureretanga: Groans of the Māoris,* London: William Ridgway, 1888.

--- *Tragedies in New Zealand in 1868 and 1881. Discussed in England in 1886 and 1887* (London: Richard Clay & Sons, 1888).

Salmond, A. *Between Worlds: Early Exchanges Between Māori and Europeans 1773-1815,* Auckland: Viking Penguin, 1997.

Samuel, R. *Theatres of Memory: Past and Present in Contemporary Culture,* London: Verso, 1994.

Scanlan, B. *Taranaki People and Places,* New Plymouth: distributed by Thomas Avery and Sons, 1985.

Select Bibliography

Schwartz, R. *The Curse of Cain: The Violent Legacy of Monotheism,* Chicago and London: University of Chicago Press, 1997.

Scott, D. *151 Days: The Great Waterfront Lockout and Supporting Strikes February 15- July 15, 1951* (50th anniversary facsimile edition of 1952 first edition published by New Zealand Waterside Workers Union), Auckland: Reed/Southern Cross 2001

--- *The Parihaka Story,* Auckland: Southern Cross, 1954.

--- *Ask That Mountain: The Story of Parihaka,* Auckland: Reed/Southern Cross, 1975.

--- *A Radical Writer's Life,* Auckland: Reed, 2004.

Scott, K. and Brown, H. *Kayang & Me,* Freemantle: Freemantle Arts Centre Press, 2005.

Sekula, A. 'Reading an Archive', in B. Wallis and M. Tucker eds. *Blasted Allegories,* Cambridge, Mass: MIT Press, 1987.

Sharp, A. and McHugh, P. eds. *Histories, Power and Loss: Uses of the Past – a New Zealand Commentary,* Wellington: Bridget Williams Books, 2001.

Shrimpton, A.W. and Mulgan, A. *Māori and Pākehā: A History of New Zealand,* Christchurch: Whitcombe & Tombs [undated, c. 1930s].

Simmons, L. 'Bearing Witness: Parihaka and the Art of Passive Resistance' in *Landfall 201*, Autumn, 2001, 167-172.

Simpson, P. 'A Very Real Symbol' [review of 'Parihaka: The Art of Passive Resistance'], *Art in New Zealand*, issue 97, Summer 2000-2001. Available online at: http://www.art-newzealand.com/Issue97/issue97htm

Sinclair, K. *The Māori Land League: An Examination Into the Source of a New Zealand Myth,* Auckland: Auckland University College, 1950.

Sinclair, K. *History of New Zealand,* Harmondsworth, Middlesex: Penguin, 1959.

Skinner, W.H. 'The Ancient Māori Dog', *Journal of the Polynesian Society*, vol. 23, 1914, 173-175.

Skinner, W.H. *Reminiscences of a Taranaki Surveyor,* New Plymouth: Thomas Avery and Sons, 1946.

Smith, L. T. *Decolonizing Methodologies: Research and Indigenous Peoples,* Otago, London and New York: Zed Books/Otago University Press, 1999.

Smith, L, McCalman, J, Anderson, I. et al. 'Fractional Identities: The Political Arithmetic of Aboriginal Victorians', *Journal of Interdisciplinary History*; vol. XXXVIII no. 4, Spring 2008, 533-551.

Sole, T, *Ngati Ruanui: A History,* Wellington: Huia, 2005.

Sontag, S. *On Photography,* New York: Penguin, 1979.

--- *Regarding the Pain of Others,* New York: Farrar, Straus and Giroux, 2003.

Sorrenson, M.P.K. 'Towards a Radical Reinterpretation of New Zealand History: The Role of the Waitangi Tribunal', *New Zealand Journal of History*, vol. 2, no. 1, 1987, 173-88.

Spillman, L. *Nation and Commemoration: Creating National Identity in the United States and Australia,* Cambridge: Cambridge University Press, 1997.

Spillman, L. 'When Do Collective Memories Last? Founding Moments in the United States and Australia' in Jeffrey Ollick, ed. *States of Memory,* Durham: Duke University Press, 2003.

Steedman, C. *Dust,* Manchester: Manchester University Press, 2001.

Stenson, M. 'History in New Zealand Schools', *New Zealand Journal of History,* vol. 24, no. 2, October 1990, 169-181.

Sutherland, K. and Ngata, A. eds. *The Māori People Today: A General Survey,* Christchurch: Whitcombe and Tombs, 1940.

Tau, Te Maire. 'The Death of Knowledge: Ghosts on the Plains', *New Zealand Journal of History,* vol. 35, no. 2, October 2000, 131-173.

Taylor, R. *Unearthed: The Aboriginal Tasmanians of Kangaroo Island,* Adelaide: Wakefield Press, 2002.

Thomas, N. *Possessions: Indigenous Art/Colonial Culture,* London: Thames & Hudson, 1999.

Thomas, N. (text) and Adams, M. (photographs). *Cook's Sites: Revisiting History,* Dunedin: University of Otago Press/Centre for Cross-Cultural Research, Australian National University, 1999.

Thomas, R. *The Imperial Archive: Knowledge and the Fantasy of Empire,* London: Verso, 1993.

Thompson, C. *Come on Shore and We Will Kill and Eat You All: An Unlikely Love Story,* London: Bloomsbury, 2008.

Thompson, J. *Taking Responsibility for the Past,* Cambridge: Polity Press, 2002.

Tonks, Gary H. *Tonks and the Bypass: 1847-2007 160 years,* Wellington: Wellington City Council, 2007.

Trouillot, M. *Silencing the Past: Power and the Production of History,* Boston: Beacon Press, 1995.

--- 'Abortive Rituals: Historical Apologies in the Global Era', *Interventions* (special issue), vol. 2, no. 2, 2000, 171-186.

Turner, S. '"Inclusive Exclusion": Managing Identity for the Nation's Sake', *Arena* no.28, 2007, 87-106.

Vaggioli, D.F. *History of New Zealand and Its Inhabitants, Vol. 2* [first published 1896] tr. John Crockett, Dunedin: Otago University Press, 2000.

Select Bibliography

Walker, P. *The Fox Boy,* London: Bloomsbury, 2001.

Walker, R. *Ka Whawhai Tonu Matou: Struggle Without End,* Auckland: Penguin, 1990.

Walker, R. *He Tipua: The Life and Times of Sir Apirana Ngata,* Auckland: Viking, 2001.

Ward, A. *A Show of Justice: Racial Amalgamation in Nineteenth Century New Zealand,* Auckland: Auckland University Press, 1973.

--- *An Unsettled History: Treaty Claims in New Zealand Today,* Wellington: Bridget Williams Books, 1999.

Ward, J. *Wanderings with the Māori Prophets Te Whiti and Tohu,* Nelson: Bond, Finney & Co, 1883.

Watters, F. *New Zealand Telegraph and Telephone Offices,* Auckland: Postal Historical Society of New Zealand, 1973.

Webber, M. *Walking the Space Between: Identity and Māori/Pākehā*, Wellington: NZCER Press, 2008.

Williams, H.M. *Dictionary of the Māori Language* [reprint of 1844 first edition], Wellington: Legislation Direct, 2002.

Williams, J. *Politics of the New Zealand Māori: Protest and Cooperation, 1891-1909,* Auckland: University of Auckland and Oxford University Press, 1969.

Yska, R. *Wellington: Biography of a City*, Auckland: Reed, 2006.

Zemon-Davis, N. *Slaves on Screen: Film and Historical Vision,* Cambridge, Mass: Harvard University Press, 2000.

Index

Italicised page numbers indicate photographs.

A

Adventure 82
Aitua, George Te Kahui Pokai 139
albatross feathers *see* raukura
Album, The Parihaka (booklet) 111–126
Alexander Turnbull Library 13, 237
Amelia Thompson 83, 244
apologies 186–188
Armed Constabulary 44, 47, *49*, 80, 84
Athletic Park 203–204, 211, 216
Atua, Tioko 148
Aurora 243
Australia 33, 37, 71, 174, 194, 257

B

bank (Nuku Te Whatewha) 77, *118*, 119, 127, 131, 134
Barrett, Richard (Dicky) 82, 248, 254
Bastion Point 170, 229
Baxter, Archibald 229
Benson, Marlene 182
biblical influences and references 24, 26, 30, 46, 73, 97, 157
'the Blue Book' 46
Boer War 67
Bolton Street Cemetery 235–243, *238*, 262
Bramley, Hannah 'Gar' (nee Wallace) 207–208, 212–216, 230, 243
Broughton, Agnes 217–218
Broughton, Raumahora 211, 217–218

Browne, Thomas 37, 87
Bryce, John 44–45, 47, 49–50, 74, 76, 81–82, 85, 127
    depiction in Sim Commission hearings 152–154, 156
    Rusden libel trial 98–107
Buchanan, Frank 216
Buchanan, Leo 203, 207, 211, 217–218, 243
Buchanan, Rawinia (Flossie) 203–208, 215–217, 230
Buck, Peter 18, 136–137, 145–147, 150
Butler, W.J. 48
Byrnes, Giselle 181

C

Cape Egmont Boat Club 197
Carroll, James 147
children of Parihaka 18, 24, 48–49, 90, 99–100, 148, 156
Christianity *see* biblical influences and references; missions
Chute, Major-General Trevor 38
City Gallery, Wellington 9, 11, 101, 171–172
Clark, Helen 222, 229
Coates, Joseph 150–151
Collis, William 118–126
comet photograph 114–118, *117*
comet Rauhoto Tapairu 193, 196
commissions of enquiry 43
    see also Sim Commission; Waitangi Tribunal; West coast Commission
Confiscated Lands Act 219

285

confiscation of land 38–43, 51, 138, 150–153, 160–161, 174, 254–256
Cooper, W. 151
Courtenay, William 42
Cowan, James 160
Croumbie-Brown, S. 48, 86

D

Daymond, Wiremu 150
decline of Parihaka 51, 138–139, 145–150
Dix, Emmanuel 132

E

Edwards, Moeahu 192
Egmont County Council 183
electricity 134
Ellison, Dr Pohau Erihana 159
Ellison, Raniera 127
Ellison, Tom 256
Epiha 86–87
Erihana, Raniera 256
Erihana, Tame Rangiwahia 256

F

feathers *see* raukura
film-making in New Zealand 63–64
food sources 40, 77–78, 85
Fromm, Anton 96

G

Gandhi, Mahatma 62, 171
Glenbervie 244
Gordon, Sir Arthur 45–46
Gorst, Sir John 104–105
Govett-Brewster gallery 4
Graham, Doug 186–188
Grey, Sir George 37, 40
grievance approach 151, 172, 174, 179–181, 188, 193–194
Guard, Elizabeth 82–83
Guard, John 82

H

Hall, John 42–43
Halswell, Edmund 252
Handley's woolshed 99–101, 103, 105, 107
Harriet 82–83
Hau, Mrs Wiki 193
Hauhau *see* Pai Mārire
Haumene, Te Ua 30
health 145–147, 253–254
Heaphy, Charles 254
Herewini, Akuhata 99
Hinemoa 84
Hiroki 41, 49
history, traditional 194–198
history-making 62–66, 70–71, 105, 107, 120–121, 168, 170–181, 189, 193–198
   forgetting ('the Dementia wing') 206,
      220–228, 257, 263–265
Hohaia, Te Miringa 6, 14, 34, 182, 184–185, 192–193, 196–197
Hunn, J.K. 208
Hursthouse, Charles 27, 48, 89, 97

I

Inia, Tom 197
invasion of Parihaka 24, 48–50, 61–62, 90–91, 156–161, 219
Iti, Tame 51, 101

J

Jackson, Sam 224
Jackson, Syd 169
James, Sir Henry 105, 107–108
Johnson, H. 262–264

K

Kaahui Maunga 52, 196
Kai Iwi Cavalry 99–101
Kapinga 156–158

Index

Kapo, Rangi 159
Karopihia, Tawhirikura 247
Keenan, Danny 195
Kemp, Major (Te Keepa) 136
Kenana, Rua 51
King family 70
Kīngitanga 37, 40
Kitts, Frank 240, 241
Kukapa, George 86–87
kūpapa ('loyal') Māori 16, 35–37, 38, 67, 86, 221
Kupe, Wi 150
Kura (wife of Te Rauparaha and William E. Wallace) 252

L

land *see* confiscation of land; leases; surveying
leases 138, 163, 176–177, 180
Ledger, James 77, 114
lighthouse at Cape Egmont 39, 57–62, *59*, 65–66, 80, 84–85, 182–185
Lord Worsley 83
Love, John 82, 248
Love, Ngatata 191
Love, Ralph 216
'loyal' Māori *see* kūpapa Māori
Lutheran mission, Warea 23
Lyttelton Times 48, 86, 98, 160

M

McCleverty, Lieut. Col. W.A. 211
McDonald, Donald Hugh 190–191
McDonnell, Thomas 38
McLean, Donald 40, 86, 218
McLean, John 41
MacLeod, Lindsay 4, 188–190
Manual of New Zealand History, The 248–249
Manukorihi 154–155
Māori Affairs Amendment Act 1974 207
Māori Affairs Department 263
Māori Land Court 180, 213–214

Māori Prisoners Act 1880 25, 43–44
Māori Prisoners Trials Act 1879 42–43, 46
Māori Reserve Land Amendment Act 1997 176–177
Marangi, Ahipane 256
Marine Department 183–184
Marsland Hill 66–68
Matakatea, Wiremu Kingi 83
Maxwell, George 99–100
Mellish, Liz 259–260
Messenger, Charles 129
missions 23, 30
Mita, Merata 4, 170
Miti Mai Te Arero 114–115, *118*, 119, 126, 127–128
modernity 16, 18, 74, 85
  adoption of 17, 51, *112*, 128–129, 134, 136–137
  see also utilities
Moeahu 192
Moeahu, Peter 192
Moke, Reverend Paahi 159
Motorua, Ropia 262
Motu (of Puneho) 86–87
Mullin, Hugh Joseph 213
Muru Raupatu marae 192
musket wars 33–35
Myhre, Steve 226

N

National Party 175–176, 223
National War Memorial 220–231
Native Department 212–213
Native Trust 162
New Plymouth 195
  as home town 64–66, 68–70
  settlement 32, 67, 82–83, 124–126, *125*
New Zealand Company 32–33, 209–211, 243–244, 252
New Zealand Times 50
Newall, Stuart 77–78
ngā mōrehu (the survivors) 167–168, 189

Ngā Puhi 95
Ngā Ruahine 41
Ngāi Tahu 33
Ngamotu 34, 195, 248
Ngaponga, Mohi 219, 252, 256, 262
Ngata, Apirana 150
Ngatata, Wi Tako 209, 219, 248, 254, 256, 259
Ngāti Maniapoto 34
Ngāti Moeahu 197
Ngāti Mutunga 25, 154–155, 188
Ngāti Tama 211
Ngāti Te Whiti 195
Ngāti Toa 34
Ngāti Tupaia 211
non-violence 23–24, 38, 49, 50, 73, 75–77, 104–105
    Parihaka's example 167, 169–171, 228–229
North Island Tenths 212
Northern War 37
Nuku Te Whatewha *see* bank
Nukumaru *see* Handley's woolshed

O

O'Connor, Doris Julia 212
Ohiro Block 212–214
Okeroa, James 196–197
Okeroa, Louie 183–184, 196
Okeroa, Ngahina 4
Opunake 40, 79, 212–213, 254
Otaka Pā 34, 248
O'Toole, Margaret 220, 230

P

Pai Mārire 30–31, 38
Pākehā *see* settlers
Parai, Arapera 230
Parai, Hemi 204, *205*, 210, 218–219, 230, 247–248, 252–256, 259
Parai, Mohi 219–220, 229–230
Parai, Te Awhi 219–220, 229–230, 262
Parata, Wi 102–103, 254
Pardy, J. 183
Parihaka *see* invasion; reconstruction; decline

Parininihi ki Waitotara (PKW) 162, 180
'parliament' at Parihaka 89, 119, 254–255
passive resistance 30, 62, 83, 171
    see also non-violence
Pereni, Ngaruaki 127
Perrin, Nick 235–236, 238, 262
petroglyphs (carved stones) 193, 196–197
Phillipson, Grant 181
photography 111–126
Pick, Seraphine *10*
Pigeon Park 256
Pipitea Pā 254
ploughing (as resistance) 29, 42, 51, 137–138
    re-enacted in 1978 171
Polhill Gully 212–214
Pomare, Maui 18, 145–148, 150–151, 155
Pomare, Miria 147
Port Nicholson Block Claim 216–217
Porutu, Rira 262
Pouwhareumu Toi 155
Preston, Tom 86–87
prisoners in South Island 44–46, 50–51, 76, 132, 189, 229, 231
proclamations issued to Parihaka 48, 87–88
Public Trustee 161–162
Pukaka Pā 66–67
Puke Te Whiti 196
Pukerangiora 34, 248
Pungarehu 45, 80, 123, 162
Purepo (Mt Rolleston) 24, 188–189

R

Rahotu 45, 123, 134, 162–163
Ramaha 86
Rangi Kapuia meeting house 132–133, *138*, 139, 148, *149*
Rangihatuake, Minarapa 23
Rata, Matiu 171
Rauhoto Tapairu 193, 196
Rau-Kupa, Matarena 4, 130–131
raukura (albatross feather) 24–25, 30, 132, 168, 192
Rawinia Buchanan Dementia wing

203–204
reconstruction of Parihaka 14, 17, 51, 113–115, 127–130, 177
Reed, V.H. 151
Reeves, William Pember 160
Regina 83
religious movements 30, 38
resistance 105, *106*, 137, 177
  continuity of 191
  see also non-violence; passive resistance
Revans, Samuel 250
Ringatū faith 38
Riseborough, Hazel 27, 40, 75, 116, 172
road-building 39, 44–45, 51, 61, 74–78, 87–88
  by Māori 134, 136, 137
Roberts, Lieut. Col. J.M. 134
Rolleston, William 78
Rongouaroa, Arapera 219, 246–247, 250, 252
Rongouaroa, Taare *see* Wallace, Charles
Royal Commission into Confiscated Lands, 1927 *see* Sim Commission
Rusden, G.W. (George) 98–108

S

schools forbidden by Te Whiti 136
Scott, Dick 3, 13, 105, 139, 167–169
Settlements Act 1863 39
settlers (Pākehā) 239, 249–251
  attitudes to Parihaka 27, 42, 73, 87–89, 95–98
  descendants' views 71, 170, 172, 184
  fear of Pai Mārire 31
  views on Māori 84–85, 184
shipwrecks 82–84
Short, Isaac George 213
Sim, William Alexander 151
Sim Commission 18, 151–161, 174, 180
Simeon, Ella 212, 214–215
Simeon, Frederick 214–215
Skinner, Thomas Kingwell 89
Smith, David 151–152, 155–158
Smith, James 251
songs 29, 90–91, 154, 188

Spain, William 211
stones, carved *see* petroglyphs
Sullivan, John 115–116
surveying 40–42, 47–48, 75, 77–78, 89, 96–97

T

Taikairaua (Ngāti Moeahu) 127
Taikatu Pā 41
Takatua, Kingi 99
Takiri te Raukura (poi) 25
Tamihana, Momona 148
Taranaki Herald 42, 89
Taranaki iwi 66, 174, 188
  defeat by Waikato invaders 34, 248
  at Wellington 210–211, 247–248
Taranaki Māori Trust Board 180
Taranaki Whānui ki Te Upoko o Te Ika 216
Te Ao Maarama 193
Te Aro 204, 210, 244–246, 253–256
  remnants of pā 258–260, *261*
Te Aroha marae 192
Te Āti Awa 34, 66, 211
Te Ika Roa 196
Te Kaahui Kararehe 27, 131, 134
Te Kaahui Maunga 52, 196
Te Kapinga Makarati 156–158
Te Keepa (Te Rangihiwinui/Major Kemp) 136
Te Kooti 38, 97, 133
Te Mahuki Manukura 96–97
Te Manuera (Emmanuel Dix) 132
Te Mapua 196
Te Maru 34
Te Niho o Te Āti Awa 8, 114, 128, 192
Te Opu Opu 197
Te Pae Pae meeting house 6
Te Puni 209–210, 219, 248
Te Puniho Pā 193
Te Rangi Hiroa (Peter Buck) 18, 136–137, 145–147
Te Rangihiwinui (Te Keepa) 136
Te Rangiwakarurua 189
Te Raukura meeting house 132–134, 139, 148–149

289

Te Rauparaha 34
Te Ua 38
Te Wharepouri 209–210, 248
Te Whetu Moeahu 78, 114, *130*, 183
Te Whiti, Ngaruaki Pereni 127, 149, 150
Te Whiti, Nohomairangi 148, 150, 156–160
Te Whiti o Rongomai 34, 114, 115, 127, 196
    arrest 49, 50–51, 76, 88, 157
    criticism by Māori 145–148
    death 145–148
    directing resistance 42, 45
    as independent leader 38–40
    knowledge of world affairs 136–137
    meeting with Rolleston 78
    modernisation and 128–129, 146–147
    monument 5, 132, 139
    non-violence 27, 49, 75, 83, 157, 169
    prophesies 18, 27, 152
    separation from Tohu 130–133, 136
    speeches, preaching and other teaching 26, 27, 48, 129, 190–191, 255
Teira, Miriam 262
telegraph lines 39, 61, 74–75, 78–81, 85
time 185–186
Tito, Parekaitu 4
Titokowaru 31, 38, 41, 49, 77, 104, 127, 192
Tohu Kakahi 23, 34, 83
    arrest in 1881 49, 50–51, 76, 88
    burial 132
    criticism by Māori 145–148
    leadership at Parihaka 38–39
    modernisation and 128–129, 146–147
    separation from Te Whiti 130–133, 136
    speeches and teaching 28, 129, 131, 191
    vision of future 27
tohunga 146–147
Tomb of the Unknown Warrior 220–231
Tomoana, Henare 43–44

Tonks Avenue 257–258
Treaty of Waitangi 31–32, 37, 73, 95, 104, 150, 187, 262
    see also Waitangi Tribunal
Tūhoe 51
Tuke, Captain 156
Tuuta, Dion 162

U

utilities 16, 73–76

V

Village at the Park 203, 218
Von Tempsky, Gustavus 149

W

Waikato, government invasion of 37–38, 75, 79
Waikato invasions of Taranaki 34, 248
Waikerepuru, Te Huirangi 6, 172–173, 230
Waimate Plains 40–41
Waipiro 235, 243
Waitangi Tribunal 63, 169, 186
    as history-maker 173–181, 193–198
    Taranaki Report 14, 116, 171, 174–181, 223
Waitara 37, 123
Waitara, Taare (Charlie) 51, 127, 131, 132, 134, 150, 190
Wakefield, Edward Gibbon 32, 85
Wakefield, William 209
Walker, Paul 211
Wallace, Arapera *see* Rongouaroa, Arapera
Wallace, Charles (Taare Warahi or Rongouaroa) 212, 219–220, 230, 250
Wallace, Cyril 212
Wallace, Hannah *see* Bramley, Hannah 'Gar'
Wallace, Harriet 252
Wallace, Isabel 212
Wallace, James 212
Wallace, John Howard 20, 237, 243–246,

248–253
Wallace, John senior 244–246, *245*
Wallace, John (son of John Howard) 252
Wallace, Robert 252
Wallace, Sarah Ann 237
Wallace, Turia Warahi 250
Wallace, William 212
Wallace, William Ellerslie 230, 243–247, 250, 252
war memorials 66–68, 220–231
Warahi, Taare *see* Wallace, Charles
Ward, John 76
Warea 23, 83
wars in New Zealand 36–37, 51
    see also musket wars; war memorials
Watene, Rangi Matatoro 155–159
water supply system 134
waterfront workers' strike 1951 167–168
Watson, Tahuaroa 189
Wellington
    early settlement 32–33
    land alienation 208–214
    see also City Gallery
Wellington City Council 238
Wellington Tenths Trust 203, 211–212, 218, 230–231, 256, 258
West coast Commission 44, 46, 74, 77, 119, 161, 174, 219
West coast Settlement (North Island) Acts 161, 168
Whanganui 32
Whanganui, Tamati 152–153, 160, 192
Wharepouri (elder) 197
Wi Tako Ngatata 209, 219, 248, 254, 256, 259
Winitana, Tom 186–187
World War I 150, 152
Wynyard, Colonel 159

Y

Young Māori Party 148